Juli Flintoff is an English artist from West Yorkshire. Initially studying drama she later obtained a bachelor of arts degree from Sunderland University. For several years Juli was a successful Community Arts Development Worker facilitating workshops throughout the Bradford, Calderdale, Leeds, Wakefield and Halifax areas. After exhibiting five large banners at the Bradfords International youth event attended by delegates from all over the world she became involved with projects for young offenders. This led her to train as a Prison Officer and later a Drugs Dog Handler. For the past 12 years she has dedicated her life to caring for her elderly parents. *The Secret Back Door* is Juli's first publication.

This book is dedicated to Emmeline the most unassuming, kind, gentle lady who has allowed me to share her journey of dementia to shine a light and to alleviate fear for others. Thank you for inviting me into your world and for giving me the permission to share your inner most thoughts and story.

Thank you to all the team at Austin Macauley Publishers for initially recognising the potential of 'The Secret Back Door' and for their continued support, guidance and expertise on the road to publication. Thank you to my sons Coban and Corai who provided much support and positive encouragement throughout the writing process and to my partner David who gave me the time and space to write at leisure. A massive thank you to Graham Brough for your professional direction and continued friendship.

I would also like to thank Carers Wakefield & the Alzheimer's Society for their years of support. The staff at St George's community centre Lupset for providing me with the training to understand the complexities of dementia. Also, Elaine Forrest for her continued support, advice and understanding during my darkest moments. And lastly Mary Dolan my lifelong friend who Emmeline always recognises & whose name she never forgets. Thank you, my friend, for walking alongside me, for proofreading my early manuscript and eagerly encouraging me to follow my heart.

Table of Contents

Part 1

That moment in life when time stands still, like a dragonfly in suspended
animation, hovering over stilled water.
And just as fragile as the mind, the silence is broken.

Chapter 1
The Carer
Present Day (March 2022)

Have you ever plummeted to the extent that you are crying from the inner depth of your soul? It's like an explosion of a million shards of glass piercing your inner most being. If you could end what could only be described as a living purgatory surely you would, wouldn't you?

Yet the only end for me is death and that really would be more unbearable. The fragility of my own mind as my heartbeat pulsates like a gigantic seagull flapping its wings within my chest, teeters on the brink of insanity. If I allow my thoughts to linger for even the briefest of moments, the bile begins to rise and the ever-familiar tingling sensation in my nostrils threatens the beginning of yet another surge of emotion just begging to be expunged.

I have become somewhat of an artist mastering the act of emotional detachment, normally it is my only form of resistance. And yet today somehow, I lost this battle. The thoughts didn't pass through my mind like wind blowing the sails of a boat, they created an eruption from a well sending tears steadily trickling one after another, like the steady flow of rush hour traffic.

I try to fathom why today is any different; am I just over exhausted? Am I trying to spread myself too thinly or is it just because I am overwhelmed again by my reality. I remind myself this will not stop; it cannot stop as there is only one alternative, death.

Emmeline, the most unassuming, kind-hearted, gentlest of souls is totally and utterly reliant on me for absolutely everything. I am her entire world, and my entire world revolves around her. I am her chauffeur, her hairdresser, cleaner, organiser, gardener, handywomen, decorator, house renovator, accountant, advocate, chef, entertainer, supervisor, financier, power of attorney for her health and wellbeing.

I schedule all her medical appointments: podiatrist; hearing specialists; opticians; doctors; vaccines; organise prescriptions; dentists; hospital/memory clinic; wheelchair services; aides and adaptations. I dispense her meds daily, aide her walking, plan her routines etc., etc., it is an exhaustive list. Is there any wonder I have no time or energy for anything or anyone else?

The next time you tell someone you are JUST a carer, please give your head a wobble and remember not only the service you provide but that without your expertise, dedication and pure love, your individual would not be able to lead the life they can. You are an amazing, selfless human being doing the very best you can under sometimes dire circumstances and situations. I know because I have worn that medal every single moment of every day that I have had the privilege of caring for Emmeline.

It is sometimes an unfair role thrown by a curve ball of life sending ricochets of bewilderment of what once was, is no more and can never be again. Maybe a freak accident or steady decline of a loved one's health? Either way, it can feel like your world has somersaulted out of control and suddenly everything you do is being inspected through some microscopic lens.

Each insignificant facet seems magnified, dissected and judged by an outside field who have no comprehension upon the mechanisms that keep your wheels somehow moving. Due to standing in the gap for Emmeline and refusing to allow her to be subjected to financial and verbal abuse, I had the displeasure of having false allegations made against me, possibly to gain control or to dishonour my reputation, but I am pleased to say it had neither affect.

It has, however, given me the insight to know the true core of others, so I take the time to not only cross the T's and to dot the I's but to reference everything, cross reference and tally everything multiple times over. To prove what? I am worthy? The reality is I have been nominated and entrusted to oversee all matters pertained to Emmeline's care because I have taken the time to develop a lifelong relationship that's been built on trust, openness and transparency.

If others have been excluded from this privilege, I would suggest there are grounds Emmeline chose to take this action and when the culprits then make false allegations, her reasons were totally justified. As far as my role is concerned, I take it very seriously and with the weight in which it has been placed upon me.

It is, therefore, my advice to anyone contemplating being a power of attorney to think very seriously about the implications, and to ensure they keep a log of all expenditures with proof of purchases and if possible, a diary of all actions taken. When in consultation with an Admiral Dementia Nurse, his vast experience had found that all too often only one member of the family supported the individual with Dementia, yet those who had offered no support were very good at dictating what should or should not be done and when anything happened to them, they 'soon came out of the woodwork.'

This is a saying I have heard on so many occasions and with that in mind, Emmeline made many decisions whilst still having capacity to do so based on the advice and experience from numerous professionals.

Being a carer can be the most unrewarding, exhausting, over exertive, poorly paid, time-consuming daily acts of kindness of a genuine unrecognised role that can result in an overall sense of worthlessness as a human being. Yet, we save the individual and at times the government thousands of pounds by devoting our time, money and dedication to enable the individual to stay within their own home at an immense expense to our own lives. WHY?

The only answer can be genuine unconditional LOVE. Why else would anyone choose such a role? Afterall no one cares if I am struggling, if I feel ill, if I would like a lie in or would like to socialise with friends or simply enjoy a walk or feel so bad today that all I want to do is shut myself deeper into my already miniscule world of nothingness.

As a carer, your friend base depletes unless you take the time to continue to manage it yourself. You soon begin to fall under the radar of invitations and if you're a single parent to begin with, then let's face it, it was probably already almost non-existent. For myself, I have worked tirelessly to ensure my world doesn't become so small I feel like I don't exist.

Don't get me wrong, I have been there on the outside looking in but that's why we all need help. For me, Carers Wakefield was my salvation, not only enabling me to access courses applicable to my role but for giving me the confidence to step back into a life for myself and to genuinely find a purpose.

At one point, I was feeling so low I didn't want to be here anymore. I couldn't face waking up each morning and having nothing to look forward to apart from 'groundhog' day. I seemed to have lost all motivation.

I no longer had the job I loved that I had spent years training for; my 3-bedroom detached house had gone, plus my holiday home (my only form of escapism). I had no time to do the things I once loved, and my life wasn't my own. My world revolved around Emmeline's needs, her meal preparations, cleaning, toileting, bills, shopping and appointments.

This just didn't feel fair; it wasn't what I had planned for my life, and I had two young children to take care of plus two dogs on my own. I wanted "to scream, to shout and let it all out" (as Will.i.am sang) but there was no one there to listen, to understand. I felt like I had not just given up my life but felt the heavy burden that my boy's childhoods were also being compromised, together with our hopes and dreams for the future.

Sometimes the pressure of caring can feel like your life has been possessed by someone else, squeezed into a snow globe and is rabidly agitated continuously. Hindsight may give wisdom after the fact, however despite those low moments when it felt like a living hell, I would make the same decisions every single time. To protect Emmeline, to care for her, to stand in the gap to safeguard her best interests was the single most important decision of my life.

At times, it feels like an onslaught of a spiritual attack to my emotional, mental and physical wellbeing but I rest in the knowledge that I have kept that one single most important vow and done you both proud, Dad. Until the day comes when the Lord releases Emmeline, I will hold my head up and know I am being a faithful servant despite what the accusers falsely state, and without either guilt, reproach or condemnation, I will wear the medals of being the best that I possibly can be.

Never a truer a sentence has been stated to best describe a carer than, 'Before you start to judge me, step into my shoes and walk the life I'm living, and if you get as far as I am, just maybe you will see how strong I really am.' (Author unknown)

Chapter 2
Emmeline
Where Would I Be Without You?

I don't think I could give you a date or time when I first noticed I was having memory issues because it seemed to creep up on me. At first, I thought it was just associated with my age. You will have all heard your parents/grandparents say, 'I can't find my glasses,' 'where did I put my keys?' or 'Now what did I come into here for?'

So, as you can imagine it was hard to establish the difference or say when it all began. Dr Doug Brown, Director of Research and Development at Alzheimer's Society said, 'Studies show that there may be subtle indications of Alzheimer's disease in thinking and memory as many as 18 years before a formal diagnosis could take place.'

At the beginning of February 2011, my husband had to go into a care home briefly until a care package could be implemented. At the time, I didn't realise I had any issues, but I couldn't grasp what the care providers were expecting of me as they were conveying his needs. Subsequently, they discussed their concerns at discharging him into my care with my daughter, Lois, and the real possibility of him having to stay in full time care as they felt I was incapable of retaining information, never mind looking after him.

Lois had already raised the fact she thought I was struggling but I didn't think I was. However, a couple of days later, when I was meeting Lois and her two boys in Wakefield, something occurred that changed that mindset. They had been to the cinema and invited me to join them at Pizza Hut afterwards. I set off at the allotted time but to my horror whilst I was on my way, I had a blank moment and had no idea where I was or where the Pizza Hut was located.

Luckily, I had my phone, so I pulled over and I rang Lois, albeit in quite a distressed state. She kept me calm and asked me to describe landmarks around me, so she was able to find me. I felt so lost, scared and utterly stupid as I sat there waiting for her to appear. Lois kindly played down the situation and encouraged me to get into her car, then we went on to the Pizza Hut and had our meal.

On our way home we collected my car, Lois taking the lead but observing me as I followed on behind her. We arrived at Dove Court in Horbury where my husband was temporarily staying, and I know Lois and he discussed the matter as she was undeniably concerned. On our return home, Lois made us a cuppa whilst the boys played outside.

She sat down with me and tentatively broached the subject of memory loss. I had a mixture of emotions; I was hurt, angry, upset and in denial but inside, I had to admit that something was wrong. When my husband came home, there were many more tell-tale signs, although I didn't care to admit them.

On one occasion, Lois arrived whilst I was having a bit of a meltdown regarding the carers not arriving on time and being inconsiderate at not letting us know. I was very angry and agitated, although looking back, it was misplaced because really it wasn't such a big deal. However, in the moment, I felt quite enraged. When I left the room, my husband told Lois he thought I had dementia.

He stated that he didn't know what I was on about as the carers had already been. He admitted I was getting worse and there had been several incidents to suggest I did have significant problems. This was April 2011. On further discussions, it was revealed I was making strange demands that he could only wear slippers in one room but not in the others, could eat in another but only have drinks in a third.

I hate to think now how awful I must have been to live with, but what neither Lois nor my husband knew was that I was keeping a grave family secret that was having a profound impact on my mental health and wellbeing. Here I was trying to protect them from the truth, and yet I couldn't disguise the truth at what was happening to me.

Lois began to shoulder more and more of the care responsibilities, often spending all school hours assisting us both. She provided for all our needs and really did go above and beyond every single day without anything being too much trouble for her. I marvelled at her skill set; her ability to negotiate with her dad when he must seek medical care because he wouldn't listen to me, but she simply took it all in her stride.

She displayed such a dedication to providing the best quality of care, along with effortlessly shouldering the responsibility of our everyday life that it made it easy for me to stop struggling.

In the August of 2011, my husband was given the 'all clear' on his final hospital appointment having suffered stomach cancer. The very next day, he had a massive heart attack and sadly passed away. I was bewildered, lost and in deep shock. I really do not know what I would have done if I hadn't got Lois to lean on.

I felt open to the elements and was emotionally battered with demands by those who should have been there to support me. Again, Lois was the beacon in the dark; a rock for me to lean on, unmoveable and impenetrable. When accusations started flying round, vultures came knocking and lies were being shed. Lois simply gave me impartial and unbiased advice signposting me to the professionals who could help and assist.

Lois would sit and simply take notes so I could mull them over at my leisure and then make an informed choice or decision that was right for me. A lot of the time she didn't agree with me but didn't try to talk me out of anything. She was always there if I needed her but respected my right to make my own informed choices and decisions.

From being young, Lois and I have always had a very close relationship. We used to go everywhere together shopping, days out, to church, for meals, trips abroad. When she had a family of her own, I worried this may stop but thankfully, I have had the pleasure of being included in everything they have done.

We have had holidays abroad to Tunisia, Spain, Portugal, ridden rollercoasters at Drayton Manor, Blackpool Pleasure Beach and Alton Towers several times over. I have been included in all their celebrations; gone bowling; done all the seaside resorts, and on one occasion, I even went down the dry ski slopes in Sunderland! And all this during my 70s and 80s. It's been a blast, and the phrase I have continually used is 'where would I be without you?'

In January of 2012, when probate had been sorted out over my husband's estate, the solicitor wanted to speak to me about appointing a power of attorney. Lois was in the waiting room so after discussing it at great length, he invited her in to join us and put forward my proposal to appoint her. She was exceptionally reluctant about taking on the responsibility, especially with having such young children and the inevitable objections my other children would raise.

However, I made it perfectly clear in my eyes there was only one choice as my feelings were, if at any time my life was in the balance, the others would simply turn the machine off and not give me a sideways glance. Having seen the dedication, she had bestowed on looking after her dad, I knew I would be in the best hands. Equally, she has always been 100% honest. She had always paid back any monies she borrowed and always gives me change down to the very last penny.

When I complained and told her not to be so silly, she would always say 'It's your brass not mine.' In the end, the solicitor made it clear that it was imperative for me to appoint someone whilst I still had the capacity to do so, and even then she would still only agree if I put a secondary person on the document, and given my understanding that any serious medical intervention would be discussed with the others and/or the medical team caring for me as she did not feel happy with such responsibility.

So, fast forward 18-month numerous tests, psychological assessments, community and home assessments, I am sitting in the waiting room of the memory clinic, and inevitably it was Lois that I wanted by my side.

I sat in the stuffy, overheated waiting room parched, even though I had just had a drink of coffee. I desperately tried to remember the date imprinted upon the newspaper as I knew it was a question I would be asked. I looked outside; we were on the ground level. It was August, so we were still in summer despite the overcast sky.

My hands were becoming clammy, and I knew my breathing was a little faster than usual, but I was trying so hard to keep calm. That was until Lois turned to me and asked if I was ok. The look of concern on her face brought tears to my eyes, wondering what on earth the diagnosis was going to mean for both of us. I caught my breath, swallowed and clasped her hand before saying, 'Whatever happens, please, just love me.'

She inhaled slowly and deeply before replying, 'Always.'

I wish I could have stopped time right there and then caught in a precious moment of deep love and gratitude for each other. My name was called and moments later, I was told I had Vascular Dementia with Alzheimer's, just like that. It wasn't so much that it was a shock but now that it had been said out loud by the consultant, there was no escape.

It would be on my records, and everyone would know. That was something I wasn't ready for.

And so, this was the start of our new journey together.

Chapter 3
The Carer
The Start of Our Journey Together

I felt like an overprotective parent waiting to go in and see the headmistress as we sat there in the bland, none descript yet clinical waiting room. I read and reread several posters adorning the many noticeboards containing information on where to get support, advice and information. My eyes flitted from one to the next and back again.

Was I nervous? Yes, but maybe not for the reasons you may think. I wasn't concerned by the consultant delivering a diagnosis of Dementia, in fact it was quite the opposite. I was nervous that he wouldn't. To some that may sound odd as some people receive the news with terror.

In our experience, going back and forth to the memory clinic with people skirting around the issue but never actually saying the words was frustrating beyond measure. My unease was coming from the fact I knew she had dementia. I just wanted to know what form it was, so I could educate myself in order to give her the best quality of care possible.

If we continued to be left dangling again, then it would be yet another 9 months of painstaking note taking, depicting the changes of Emmeline's behaviours and thought processing difficulties. It wasn't that I needed a label or proof that she had dementia, I just wanted the charade to stop so I could provide her with the help she required and get her on the correct medication to "mask" the decline.

I didn't want Emmeline to feed off my anxiety and knowing her so intricately, if she detected even the slightest of change her breathing would then start to become more rapid; her mouth would become dry and she would start involuntarily licking at her lips, creating a smacking noise with her tongue causing her to repetitively swallow. I had to act before this occurred and spied the tea trolley which was neatly stacked with those small white cups and saucers with a handle barely big enough to fit one finger in.

I casually reached for a newspaper left on the low-rise tables in front of us, gave it a cursory glance, then nonchalantly passed it to Emmeline to distract her whilst I made my way to the little tea trolley. I spooned in the coffee, added sugar for Emmeline and then holding the cup under its spout, depressed the top of the flask like cylinder holding the hot water. There was no milk.

I tried in vain to get the attention of the receptionist who seemed hell bent on continuing her conversation with some unknown recipient about her weekend away in Paris. As anyone who knows me well will tell you I do not do waiting well. So, my toe was soon tapping, leg started jerking, jaw line became clenched and if I had been Superman, my eyes would have been laser beaming that bloody telephone.

Finally, Felicity, as it said on her name badge, glanced up and reluctantly told the caller she would have to go. Damn right, Felicity, you're supposed to be working not using the NHS landline for private calls. She walked towards me and slid back the glass partition and just stared.

Wow, no apology of "Sorry for your wait", or "Can I help" or anything. Maybe I was supposed to be the one apologising, after all I had interrupted her private call. Anyway, she made me wait another five minutes before taking the time to fill the tiniest of porcelain jugs. Of course, I smiled sweetly and thanked her for her effort.

Maybe I was more nervous than I had realised. I poured the milk into the now lukewarm coffee and seated myself next to Emmeline, displaying a grin like the Cheshire cat despite how false it felt to me on the inside.

'Oh, that's lovely, thank you,' Emmeline said which suddenly made my waiting worthwhile. That is the one thing you can always say about Emmeline, she has a grateful heart. When I was young, I used to marvel about how resilient, strong and capable she was, which made sitting here right now ironic.

How could that person who boldly took on anything or anyone who crossed her path with such vigour and determination seem so small to me today? Alone with my thoughts, I could visualise her 30 years ago, playing hell with a guy in the old Hillard's supermarket, Wakefield because he dared to look down his nose at my punk attire. No way was someone going to get away with making an offensive, judgemental derogatory remark about me when she was about.

The image brought a smile to my face as I pictured this Barbara Windsor like character marching over to him, arms furiously pumping then squaring up to this bouncer of a man, screeching 'Get out of my pub!'

As I glanced up at the clock for the 100th millionth time, I noticed Emmeline was looking at the date on the paper and mouthing it over and over to herself.

'I know what you're doing,' I said.

'No, you don't,' she started defensively. Then seeing the knowing look on my face, continued, 'The date is always a question they ask, along with what level we are on, then I am supposed to remember Tap, Apple, Pen. You don't go in to war without being prepared.'

'Is that how you see this?' I asked, 'going in to war?'

'No, but they want to try and catch me out,' she said, a little hurt.

'It may seem that way, but they are not trying to catch you out. It's just a ridiculous test they do which probably works for people who are further advanced, but you are obviously too smart for them.' And then a thought struck me that she might think that I was trying to "catch her out" or in some way not on her side as we pressed forward with a diagnosis.

So I asked, 'You know I am here to support you, don't you? I promise you whatever happens along the way, I will always be honest with you and if things don't seem to be working, I will look for ways to make them better or at least easier for you,' I said.

She clasped my hand and said, 'Whatever happens, just love me.'

Her vulnerability at that moment overwhelmed me and my heart ached beyond all reasonable measure, so with tears in my eyes I responded in the only way I knew how, 'Always,' I said.

As if on cue, at that very point Emmeline's name was called and the spell and bond between mum and daughter was broken. We both inhaled simultaneously as if "getting ready for battle", then we dutifully followed our leader into an office for our turn to be seen. I sat listening intently to the young man as he talked about the results of the psychologist assessment in clinic and then went into depth about the assessment conducted at home and in the community.

All the time, I was staring at the printed sheets of paper that I had handed to the receptionist on booking mum in regarding the changes I had noted over the past few months. I never wanted to embarrass mum or make her feel as though she was being watched by openly discussing them in front of her. Not because I was trying to keep anything from her, I know she was only too aware of what she called her "misgivings" but it's not nice to have them listed in such a negative fashion.

Therefore, Emmeline and I would conduct the information beforehand so we could effectively communicate on the day and ensure we had given a full and precise appraisal. With such an enormous deluge of information, I could see he had soon lost Emmeline's attention so I asked for a printout of the report so that she could study it at leisure later. I then asked if she would need another brain scan.

'There is no point,' he stated.

A little put out at this phrase and his seemingly lack of interest in determining mum's decline along with my maybe taking it a little too personally. After all, Emmeline's health and welfare are my number one concern. I went on to explain, 'I mean to enable you to compare against the scan she had 2 years ago, just so you can identify more clearly the changes.'

His next statement knocked me for six. 'There is no need because it was quite clear from the previous scan that Emmeline has Vascular Dementia with Alzheimer's.'

From the confusion written on my face as I looked to Emmeline and back to him, it suddenly dawned on him that we had no knowledge of this diagnosis.

'If that is the case, can I ask you why we haven't been formally informed and why we have been going round in circles for the past 2 years trying to find out what was wrong with her?'

It was now his turn to look baffled as he quickly scanned through Emmeline's notes.

I went on. 'We were told at the time of the scan that it was "mild cognitive changes associated with old age". In fact it was played down to the extent as if it was nothing to worry about.' I knew from my own research and experience with Emmeline that it was more than "mild cognitive changes", which is why I had been meticulously keeping records and effectively communicating my experiences first-hand with regards to Emmeline's memory and processing abilities.

Also, with Dementia being a progressive disease, I was more than aware that studies stipulated that 'although some drugs may help lessen symptoms, such as memory loss and confusion, for a limited time. There are other drugs that change disease progression, with benefits to cognitive function.' (Alzheimers.org) So surely there are sound benefits in bringing about a quick diagnosis for the individual with dementia to empower them to live successful, coordinated, person centred lives despite the disease.

When he looked at me again, I couldn't help noticing how ashen his face had become. He explained that on each occasion since the first scan, our 6-month appointments had been continually changed but when rebooked, only a nurse had been available on that day. Therefore, no clinical diagnosis could have been delivered, which is why I felt everyone was skirting around the issue and not telling us directly.

The consultant apologised profusely for these errors not being picked up before now, then went on to tell me that due to the high levels Emmeline was scoring on the MMSE test, she wouldn't be considered eligible for medication at this time.

The **MMSE** (Mini Mental Status Exam) (dailycaring.com/-test-for-dementia-at-home) test has 30 questions that are scored with one point each.

The MMSE include questions that measure:

- The individual's sense of date and time.
- Sense of location.
- Ability to remember a short list of common objects and later repeat it back.
- Attention and ability to do basic math, like counting backwards from 100 in.
- Increments of 7.
- Ability to name a couple of basic objects.
- Complex cognitive function, like asking someone to draw a clock, or in mum's case, two interlocking shapes.

The grading scale is:

- 25 or more points=no problem
- 21–24 points=mild cognitive impairment
- 10–20 points=moderate cognitive impairment
- 0–9 points=severe cognitive impairment

The MMSE alone cannot be used singularly as a diagnosis for dementia as there are many other factors to be taken into consideration hence the fact mum had blood tests, brain scans and full psychological in-clinic tests along with full assessments both in her home and within her community.

These were far more in depth and gave a fuller insight into Emmeline's ability to function on a day-to-day basis within her usual environment whilst studying her processing of information, the retention of information, functioning ability, usage of money, personal safety, road safety, safety within the home and cooking abilities to name but a few.

I believe that because Emmeline was a high functioning individual who had been an accountant and businesswoman, she was able to find ways to score highly in these simple tests. There was no doubt in my mind that she had dementia, but her cognitive impairment hadn't declined to such a level that she would fall into the above categories.

The consultant then informed Emmeline and I that there were some representatives from the Alzheimer's society here today and offered us both the chance to speak to them before we left. The two ladies were very informative, and I was interested to hear of a pilot trial in Barnsley to make it a "dementia friendly" town. I decided right there and then that Ossett also needed to be a dementia friendly zone, so that mum and any other individuals could live independent, safe lives.

And so, our new journey together began!

Chapter 4
Emmeline
Present Day (March 2022)

They say that the eyes are the gateway to the soul, and at this stage of my life as dementia has ravished my thought processing abilities and robbed me of my precious memories, I have to say that for me it is true. I may not have the capability to absorb everything. I may look vacant at times, and it may seem like I have left and gone through the secret back door of my mind, but physically I am here.

Sometimes it feels as though I have strayed into the wilderness of the outback; do you remember the film Beetlejuice? When the occupants of the house tried to leave, they were in a desert like space with a humungous snakelike creature waiting to devour them. That is the place I become lost in.

The vast expanse of nothingness with neither shield nor shelter, just an overwhelming fear to envelope me, flood my senses and eventually course its way through my veins. To say I am overwhelmed would be like covering me in fish guts and dangling me over shark infested waters. Inside I am screaming to find my way back to you, to where safety consists of love, security and comfort wrapped in my blanket watching tv with you by my side.

You have this knack of noticing when I have gone through the secret back door of my mind, and somehow snap me out of it, like the magician on Little Britain, a click of the fingers and "Back in the room". It's what I love about you the most, you just know; you bring me back and I am safe once more. There are other times when a fog seems to ascend within me engulfing my ability to not just respond but to think actual thoughts.

I remember how we used to finish one another's sentences but when I first started to drift. You would ask, 'What are you thinking?' I worried that as time went by, we may lose this ability until in the end, it would be like an unused telephone number and the connection would be rendered dead completely.

That would have broken my heart, as much as your fear, that I would forget who you were completely. I thank God every day that you still pray for me; kiss me "goodnight"; tell me you love me and share your life with me. I am so sorry I no longer realise just how much you have had to sacrifice to allow me to continue to be Emmeline, but you must know in your heart how much I have loved you and cared.

In times of darkness, when the shadows creep ever nearer and our lost world swallows you whole, please know, I may not be able to communicate those things now, but this has always been the truth of my heart. If I could, I would harness those times you sob uncontrollably in the abyss of your own torment. Your dad used to say I was the love of his life and despite being ill, he still yearned to be the one to look after me.

I am your mother and looking after you should be my role, but unfortunately, I can only see from within, my ability to look outwardly has gone forever. It's not that I am being selfish but as we come into the world and our every need is taken care of by our parents, so as we are on our way out our every need requires that same level of care and assistance. It isn't that I don't care, I just don't know how to anymore. Please know there is a huge difference.

I have loved the life we have shared; I have loved our relationship and that you have made me an integral part of your family. The respect and honour you have given to me over the years have developed within me great strength and belief that I must have done something right.

Remember those little cards we used to give each other? They were credit card size that could easily be kept in your purse. Go back, look for those and reread them again and take in that I am still saying them to you today. Love like ours is unconditional whether in our youthfulness, at this later stage or in the afterlife.

Those words, our love, our connection is reality; it just gets stretched a little further away but can still be accessed in a different dimension of our minds and hearts. It will always exist because I exist in you, and you exist in me. We are not the same person nor as someone callously and bitterly tried to insinuate "joined at the hip".

But we have the same values, morals and ability to give abundantly without compromise and without strings. To give with a purse full is easy but to give when you have nothing left? Now, that IS true love.

I know you are exhausted, empty and running on fumes, to the point of being emotionally bankrupt but here you are refusing to give up and still finding reserve from somewhere. Others may use derogatory terms about me being "doolally-tap" that is the ignorance of their own mind. Don't use it against them, they know no better because they have no time for me. Don't be outraged, it is a negative emotion and doesn't deserve to take up space within you.

There are those who battle to be heard with their insults, outrageous claims, mocking taunts and lies just throw your head back and laugh then give them what they deserve, your silence. Sticks and stones and all that! Haven't you always found solace in the fact that just because people make allegations; it doesn't make them true, but it does reveal the hardness within their own black hearts. So instead focus your mind, then you will not be robbed of our precious time together, and allow the peace and knowledge that you have given me the best quality of life and happiness value I could ever have wished for.

Your dad would be so proud and when I go to meet with him again he will show me all that you have done, and I will also rejoice.

'Emmeline, come on, love,' Lois says tapping the red plate in front of me.

I turn to look in the direction the sound has come from. There is a cup in my hands that I suddenly become aware of, but it no longer feels warm. I glance down having to move the cup slightly to one side, so it is not obscuring my view as Lois taps the plate again. She wants something from me, but I am unsure what? I look up to search her face to try to understand.

'You were staring again, love. You need to eat your toast, look I put marmalade on like you wanted,' she says.

'Oh yes, I was, wasn't I?' I say, but we both know I have no idea what I was doing or what I were supposed to be doing. My mind is blank, so I continue to stare at the toast and marmalade on the plate. I do not know how long I have been here, what has just happened or what is going to come next.

Lois hands me a piece of the toast realising I am staring at it, wondering what on earth I am supposed to be doing with it. I eat the central area of the bread, leaving the crust part and then line it up with all the other ones in a row on my plate. A new habit I have formed.

Once Lois has removed the remnants of my breakfast and wiped the table down, she gets out some art therapy books but I have nothing within me today. She takes out my memory books and opens it to the first page; a photo of Jeff and I on our last anniversary together. He is in a hospital bed, and I am sat beside him. An involuntary 'Aww, just look at him,' escapes from my mouth.

Lois who had gone to the sink to do the dishes hears and returns. She points to the writing on the page above the photograph and tracing it with her finger reads, 'This was your anniversary.' Then below the photograph she continues "9 July 2010". A warm feeling radiates from within that generated a wantonness to be that woman so happy and close next to him. Lois feels it too.

'Who is it, Emmeline?' She asks, knowing full well I have the correct answer to give.

'Jeff, my husband,' I say proudly.

She turns the page to reveal six brightly coloured images of her two boys beaming out of the pages at me. She doesn't ask me their names because she knows I will get tongue tied at trying to find the answers. It's not that I am stupid, or that I don't recognise them, how could I not? They share every day with me.

I know who they are, just not what they are called. This is just one of the parts of having dementia, like not being able to remember special dates birthdays, anniversaries, Christmas, Lent, this is what Lois does for me. She remembers on my behalf and helps me to still celebrate in the way I always used to. It is what helps me to stay Emmeline for as long as possible.

We have a plaque in the lounge where I am sitting it says, 'To love a person is to know the song in their heart and to sing it to them when they have forgotten.' (Arne Garborg)

This is what Lois does for me through her creation of the memory books along with the "Little box of treasured memories" about our life together, or through each time she clears Jeff's grave and then takes me to visit when it is bursting with flowers to pay our respects or to acknowledge birthdays/anniversaries that are important to me. It allows me to still be Emmeline even when I have forgotten parts of her.

I sit for a while closely examining each aspect of the photos and maintain my concentration throughout the book which I can do repeatedly. I may have dementia which causes memory loss and processing issues, but I still find pleasure in the things that are important to me. It's like the cup that Lois has just brought my cup of tea in; it has a lovely photo on the side of a lady with me and the words, "R Lass. Happy 90th Birthday. Love you loads, Love Sammy xxx".

I don't know where I know the lady from but when I read her message and I see myself, I feel a warm glow and know she loves me. My emotions have not left me. I am able to know how someone makes me feel and the one thing Lois always asks people to share with me is their smile. It gives me the reassurance that you mean me no harm, and with it being infectious, I choose to share my smile in return.

It is lunchtime now and I am currently sat at the table in the middle room of our home, with a black and white checked tea towel around my front eating a rice pot with Lois sat in front of me typing away. She pauses, looks up and realises I have finished my chicken sandwich because all the crusts are neatly lined up, so she passes me another cup of tea.

'Thank you, love' I say.

'You know I told you I was writing a book about you?' She begins. 'I have called you Emmeline throughout it, is that ok?' She asks.

'Yes,' I say, waiting for more.

'I think Emmeline is such a beautiful name and one that you don't hear of anymore. I am sure that when people read my book they will think so too, and mothers will want to call their children Emmeline. Wouldn't it be lovely for people to call their children after you?' She finishes.

'Aww that would be lovely,' I say and genuinely feel delighted.

'Would you like me to read this chapter about how you are today?' She asks me.

'Yes,' I nod.

She begins to read, and I am immediately transfixed, it captures not only my interest, but I am astounded at her insight. I may not remember what was said afterwards but at the time each word touches me, and my heart is overflowing.

'That's lovely,' I say. 'Love you.' Suddenly blurts out.

'And I love you too. Did you like that?' She asks.

'Yes, it's brilliant.' At that moment, I feel so full of love and admiration. And, as she looks across the top of her laptop right back at me into the gateway to my soul, I know she feels it too.

'Would you like to sit here or go back and watch tv?' She asks.

'No, I would like to sit here with you I think,' I respond.

She smiles, pleased. She takes out my book of photos and I readily open it and become transfixed in a world of absolute pleasure. We sit for a while, Lois typing away; the Alexa gently playing some random music in the background and life is good. We are both absorbed in our own individual tasks, but we are here, in the middle room of "Grey Gables", my home of 50 years, together.

A song plays but unbeknown to me, it touches Lois, so she quickly searches for it via google not wanting it to be lost; it's called *Faith's song* by Amy Wadge. I don't realise it, but she plays it again and as I am giggling at the photos. I miss the tears that begin to fall down her face or the deluge that overflows.

When the music ends, I look up, but I don't recognise this expunged show of emotion and begin to leave the table, my attention has expired. I continue to the tv lounge, close the door, take my seat, put my feet up and pull my cosy, fluffy blanket around me. Lois is left in the silence, my presence no longer available; just her thoughts of yet another precious moment in time that I have already forgotten, but that she will hold in her heart and there it will remain, forever.

Part 2: 2016

The nightmares of our waking life are sometimes as real as a Freddie Kruger movie....they leave you both begging for sleep and dreading it.

Chapter 5
Emmeline
Chance Meeting (2016)

I felt the cool chill on my face as my eyes opened and adjusted to the shadows around the room. I wasn't sure if it was still the middle of the night or whether the day had broken; the thick, heavy duty blackout curtains blocked all trace of light from spilling across the room. One of Lois's ideas to help me get a restful sleep.

She was full of lots of ingenious proposals to maintain my independence and enable me to continue being Emmeline for as long as possible. Like the clock in the kitchen that displayed the day, date, year, and temperature as well as time or the wipeable, whiteboard with its days of the week for my appointments and important notes section at the bottom to assist me to keep a schedule.

I even had a twiddle blanket for when I felt agitated; memory books and brain training exercises she had downloaded on a Nintendo DS thing she had set up for me. I didn't have the heart to tell her I couldn't remember how to turn it on, never mind engage in the puzzles.

I gathered my thoughts as I contemplated what day it was and if there was anything to get up for. Nothing came to mind, so I lay there a while and just let random things wash through me like a slow tap dribbling. I yawned, stretched out my legs and rolled over on to my back.

As I stared at the white papered ceiling, I noticed the odd dust thread hanging down dancing, so I was right, there must be a draught coming from somewhere. I lifted my head up to scan the room, but it was no good. I would have to get out of bed. As I swung my feet over the edge of the bed, I caught them on the slippers I had haphazardly kicked off last night, so I slid my feet into them and with great effort pushed myself up and made my way over to the curtains.

The low, brightness of the winter sun immediately broke through and I had to momentarily screw my eyes shut before blinking rapidly to tune into its full affect. It was still a grey, overcast day despite the sting and although the bare trees along the bottom of the garden weren't moving as such, the leaves on the great big bush in the centre of the middle flower bed were dancing furiously. I bent my arms up behind my head, yawed again, and stretched my aching back then pulled back the curtains.

I gathered up the clothes that were strewn across my dresser and made my way along the corridors of the upstairs to the bathroom where I stripped and gave myself a full body wash. I made a mental decision not to glance into the huge inbuilt mirror at the side of the bath as I really did not want to witness the age-related demise of my sagging body. So, I devoted my attention to each crevice as I thoroughly soaped and enjoyed the gentle caress of the exfoliating sponge.

Once I had cleaned my teeth and dressed, I gave myself a cursory glance and instantly wished I hadn't. I looked old, but then again, I was old, 80 something.

Once downstairs, I busied myself by putting bread into the toaster and making a cup of tea. There was nothing like having a cuppa first thing in the morning, although this was a task and a half for me to achieve. Lois would be arriving soon, so I wanted to get it right otherwise I would feel a fool.

This may have been a task I have performed for years but do you know just how many steps there actually are when making a simple cup of tea? First you must remember where the cups are, fill the kettle (I have forgotten this a few times and just put it on to boil), put in the teabag, sugar, then locate a spoon, along with the milk. All these things are in different areas of the kitchen and these steps are before we even pour the water, add the milk, mash, and then stir it.

For someone with dementia, it is a complicated task, so it is easy to become muddled, forget where you are or simply leave out some of the sequences altogether. On several occasions, I have forgotten to put the teabag in so it can just end up being water and milk but at least I boiled the kettle, so it was hot!

Another task that seems to baffle me lately is the remote control for the tv. I know it is probably seen as a random insignificant household gadget to some people but with dementia to operate one is like trying to learn Japanese. I feel sorry for Lois; it must be really frustrating when I have asked her to drive all the way back from her house because I am unable to turn it on, again.

She always plays it down and says she doesn't mind but she must really because generally she has only just left me. Oh, I am such a nuisance. Not only is she studying in Leeds to assist her work with Home-Start helping families in distress, but she is studying on a dementia course too to help me, then she is working in a nursery and has her own two boys to look after.

Sometimes I feel like I must be a burden for her, but she always finds the time to visit, call me, spend time taking me out and collecting me after church on Sundays to spend the day with her. I feel so blessed and don't know what I would do without her input as the house feels so still and silent without Jeff. Do you know we were married for 56 years before he passed away?

I was shocked to find out it has been 4 and ½ years since he died. I don't know where the time has gone. Oh well never mind there is no use 'crying over spilt milk' as my old mum used to say.

'I miss you, love,' I say out loud to the wall of silence.

I glance at the clock to find out its Thurs the 18 February 2016, so I look at the whiteboard to find that today I need to call into the Building Society. I have my cuppa, put my shoes on (no socks, I forget these regularly) get my coat and make my way out remembering to lock the door, that is the important bit. I take the 'safe' route that Lois embedded within me.

I am happy to say I no longer have to think about this, I am on autopilot and quickly arrive at the bank. There is a queue and its cold outside, so I decide to go inside and take a seat whilst I wait. I glance at the poster with the family unit beaming out at me and the heading 'Need to change your Mortgage? We can help.'

I was beginning to get lost in negative thoughts around the word 'family' when I heard my name. Thinking it was my turn to be served I was beginning to get up when I suddenly realised there was a young woman stood in front of me.

'Hello, Emmeline, how are you?' It was Sarah, my ex-daughter in law.

'Hello love, oh its lovely to see you,' I responded appropriately.

'I was just passing,' she said. 'I thought it was you as I glimpsed in the window. You're looking well.'

'I don't know about that, love,' I gushed. 'I am feeling more my age with every passing day.'

'How is your Lois and the boys?' She asked.

'Oh, they are fine. She is very busy with this and that, but she still comes over every day and rings me each night before I go to bed,' I say.

I am then suddenly distracted as I notice that the man who had been in front of me in the queue is gathering his bank books and wishing the teller a 'Good weekend.' Sarah notices this quick shift of my attention and doesn't want to delay me further.

'Please, let her know I was asking after her, will you? Take care, it was lovely seeing you,' she offers.

'Yes, love, and you.' Then she is gone, and I am at the counter asking for my regular £100 weeklies. When "Caroline" as it says on her badge requests my bank book, I have for a moment a vacant stare on my face. She might as well have been asking me about the endangered two-humped Bactrian camel native to Mongolia and I wouldn't have looked any more confused.

'Your bank book, Mrs Rodgers, like this one,' she holds up an example and continues. 'We need it so we can log the transaction you are wanting today,' Caroline tells me.

A slight flicker registers as I realise, I had put it on the windowsill when I picked my keys up to lock the door and now I am stood here feeling somewhat of a fool.

'I am sorry, but we cannot serve you without it. Is Lois not able to assist you today? Maybe come back with her later and we will be able to conduct your transaction,' Caroline tells me.

I am furious; not only do I feel like a fool at making such a silly mistake but now she is talking to me like I am a child who shouldn't be out without their mother. I say nothing and turn away. I do not want to dignify her with an answer or embarrass myself any further. People seem to think that just because you have dementia you are some sort of idiot and make comments without putting their brains in to gear.

They seem to think that I don't have feelings, rational thoughts or are able to hold a conversation. Let me tell you my senses have been heightened and feelings are very much intact.

I walk back outside to the full force of the icy wind after being in the warmth and protective enclosure of the Building Society trying to gather my thoughts when I notice Sarah on her way out of Iceland. She sees me, pauses then cuts across the path of a man with a little brown dog and heads my way.

'Do you have time for a cuppa, Emmeline?' She asks.

A little confused, I say, 'Yes, love, but I haven't got my bankbook.'

She is kind, ignores my slight transgression and simply says, 'It's ok, I have mine. Shall we pop in here?'

We enter the little café and to my surprise there are no other guests, so we sit in a little window seat at a table for two. Sarah arranges her bags, takes out her purse, makes her way to the counter and is soon returning with steaming hot cups of lattes. There are two tiny packets of sugar along with a little biscuit on each saucer.

I empty one of the sugar packets into my cup and stir whilst Sarah uses both of hers. I smile thinking Lois would be surprised at my resistance to not use both.

Sarah glances to the unused one left on my saucer, 'If you're not using it, Emmeline, do you mind if I have that one too?' She asks pointing to my untouched sugar sachet.

'No, love, help yourself,' I chuckle.

She stirs the latte for what seems like an age as though she is stealing herself before glancing up and saying, 'I am sorry, Emmeline.'

'It's ok, love, it's only sugar,' I innocently reply.

'I don't mean about the sugar. I should have come and seen you before now.' I notice she appears nervous almost upset, there is a twitch at the corner of her mouth. I hope that she is not going to cry as I wouldn't know how to respond. I wait.

She gazes intently into her coffee cup like a fortune teller about to read the tea leaves. I noticed a slim vessel on the table with a single flower protruding out, I reach forward to touch it and to my amazement found it was artificial.

Sarah continued, 'I came to the funeral. I don't know if you saw me as I stayed at the back of the church and mingled in amongst the crowd. Lois did, she smiled in acknowledgement as you were all walking out. I appreciated that, it gave me confidence that my presence wasn't completely unwelcome.'

She lifted her cup in what felt like an exaggerated slow-motion movement like when you are trying to find a particular scene in a film. I noticed that her hand was shaking. I felt like I needed to be saying something, but I wasn't quite sure, what?

That is how Dementia affects me sometimes, when people express emotions, I am aware that I should respond but often I don't know how so I do nothing; it can make me appear uncaring, vacant, or inept. I am neither of these things; inside I am battling with myself and want to get it right but are so scared of getting it wrong. That was the problem with getting the diagnosis it's not just out there, but others have preconceived ideas about you being lesser of a person.

I am not, I am still me. I enjoy my life just doing things in a much simpler format. It helps when people look at me when they speak or say my name to get my attention, then speak slowly so it doesn't sound garbled. It doesn't help being a bit deaf, that's why Lois always emphasises key words, so I grasp the thread of the conversation. Sarah says something else, but I don't quite catch it as her head is low, and I can only just see her mouth moving. So, I ask her to repeat it.

She looks at me with tears threatening to break over the lip of her eyelashes, they are wet. I look sympathetic, this much I can do. Our eyes meet and she loses the battle as the puddle collection, bubbles over, literally dripping down her face. I feel overwhelmed so reach my hand across the table briefly touching hers before she begins to retreat then almost simultaneously decides against it and lets me comfort her.

Her hand is bony, she is freezing cold despite previously having had gloves on. I wait.

Finally unable to bear the tension of the prolonged silence any longer I ask, 'Whatever is the matter, Sarah, this isn't like you?' She takes a deep breath.

'I know you and Lois don't see the rest of the family and neither do I, not even Ruby anymore. I don't want to go into what happened but all I can say is when you take a step off the merry go round, the dizziness dissipates and what you're left with is a lot more clarity. There has been a lot of wool pulled over my eyes and lies told that I believed because there was no evidence to suggest otherwise.'

'Or should I say I didn't take the time to validate things. I believed the description she gave of you both. For that I am truly sorry.'

'You have nothing to be sorry for, Sarah. Ruby has severe problems, she makes things up and says them that many times she begins to believe it herself. She can be very convincing, so don't punish yourself too harshly. It doesn't matter how much you support her, she will always make herself believe she is the victim and then lash out like a viper to administer its venom.'

I felt guilty admitting this, but it was the truth. I had been on the receiving end on more occasions than I cared to remember, so I always trod on eggshells around her and treated her with kid gloves for fear of being on the receiving end.

'The thing is, Ruby has said some very disturbing things and I have battled about whether to come and see you but didn't know if I was still welcome at

Grey Gables after everything that has happened.' She shakes her head as if contemplating things. 'It feels like a lifetime ago,' she continued.

'You are always welcome anytime, you don't need an invitation. If you are in the area pop in, there will always be a cuppa for you. Although, you will probably be better making it yourself these days,' I chuckled.

My good humour soon disappeared when I saw the grave look on her face, now she had my undivided attention. 'Emmeline, the last few times I saw Ruby, she was saying some very disturbing things about both you and Lois. Ruby and Kelly are seeing a lot of each other these days and have been plotting to bring harm and devastation to Lois which in turn will affect you too. I have no idea *what* they are planning, only that it will come after his licence has expired which I believe is in June,' she stated.

I gazed at her in stunned silence.

'I am so sorry, Emmeline, I should have warned you earlier, but I didn't know how. I have been mulling it over for months then when I saw you through the window in the bank, I didn't want to miss the opportunity, but when we came face to face, I bottled it,' she admitted.

'Why on earth would they want to cause such pain? Surely to goodness they have better things to do with their lives. First, they abandoned me when I needed them the most and left Lois to pick up the pieces without being able to catch her own breath and grieve for her father. Then she is left shouldering all the responsibility of care when, if they both did a day a week each with a weekend thrown in once a month, they might appreciate the real difficulties of life without finding time to conspire, plot and scheme.'

'What has she done for them to be so evil?' I was beside myself.

'That is the thing, Emmeline, she hasn't DONE anything only protect you and stand up for you. According to Ruby, Lois was the child that nobody wanted and kept getting palmed off on to everybody else. You can tell from how she talks about her, she literally hates her. All they are interested in is money. They are greedy, jealous and think they have a right to swoop in and take all that's yours.'

'That's why Ruby said she couldn't "wait until anything happens to you" because she has been filling Kelly with all sorts of rubbish, putting words in her mouth like a puppeteer with her hand up her backside. She was laughing about the prospect of being able to "sit back and watch the fireworks, as Kelly is so enraged, she is, gunning for Lois". Apparently, Kelly is believing every word she says, then Ruby comes to my house laughing about her stupidity.'

'I know I don't have room to talk I was the same. It has given me a reality check seeing her for what she is, and has made me step back, assess stuff she has made me believe and so now I can question her motives,' she said.

I was furiously trying to scramble key words to remember so that I could relay our conversation to Lois when she came to see me next.

'I honestly don't know what to say, Sarah, my head is in a bit of a spin right now,' I confessed.

'I know it's a lot to take in and I am truly sorry for dumping this on you, but I had to tell you. Please just warn Lois to watch her back, they are sick and twisted. I should go.' And with that she stood, drank the last drips of her coffee, collated her bags in one hand and with her gloves in the other quickly scurried to the door and shot off.

I sat alone for a few moments; thoughts flying through my mind but couldn't manage to grasp anything specific to hold on to. I asked the young lady behind the counter for a pen and some paper which she tore off her order pad then handed it to me. I wrote down: *Warn Lois that 2 of her siblings are planning to hurt her and to watch her back, don't know what it is but it will be when HIS licence expires. June?*

I put the note into my pocket and thanked the lady behind the counter. I made my exit and absent-mindedly made my way across the precinct to the other side of town towards the Co-op. I perused the aisles up and down one after the other not really seeing any of the products on the shelves, they were just blurs of colours all mixed into one. The information was really pressing down on me and then I remembered I didn't have any money because I had forgotten my bankbook.

'Stupid woman,' I admonished myself and deftly took myself home, hoping it wouldn't be long before Lois arrived.

Chapter 6
The Carer 2016
The Attack

The year began pretty much as any other with high hopes and dreams for the future along with an array of New Year resolutions. I had committed myself to many things and was achieving my goals both through my studies, volunteering roles, as a carer, mother, and personally I felt I was accomplishing in all areas.

It had been 4 and ½ years since my beloved father had passed away and I had got into good routines of taking the children to school, walking the dog, and then arriving at "Grey Gables" for approximately 09.15 where Emmeline would be getting up for the day. I had not personally heard anything from 3 of my siblings during this time or the 4th for the last 2 years since she had been unable to extract funds from Emmeline for home improvements.

To my knowledge, Emmeline hadn't either, apart from the odd birthday or Christmas gift she had begrudgingly received from Kelly. So, as you can imagine, it came as an immense shock when one day in the middle of February I arrived at Emmeline's to find her quite distressed.

'Thank goodness you're finally here,' she said.

'Let me get through the door before you hit me with it,' I joked. 'Not to mention giving me the chance to get the kettle on so I can warm up and grab a seat first.'

It was quite clear from her body language and her agitated disposition that something had occurred to upset the equilibrium I had left her in the day before. My concern was further heightened when I noticed that her breakfast was still cradled in the toaster. So, once I had finished making us both a cuppa, I sank into the grey, corner settee that had once been mine engulfed by its numerous soft, plush cushions, in the middle room of Grey Gables.

Emmeline was like a cat on a hot tin roof as she spilled out the occurrences of a chance meeting, she'd had with a lady in the Yorkshire Building Society the day before.

Once she had finished, I said, 'Hold on a minute, so what you are telling me is, basically you have been forewarned that I am going to be under some form of an attack, but you have no idea what this may be?' I repeated back to her aghast.

'Exactly,' she said. 'Sarah said that you need to tell your Lois that two of her siblings are plotting against her and that they are planning their attack for when HIS licence has expired, and they are also going to try to get HIS sentence over-ruled and make out you lied. Then she told me that Ruby had stated she couldn't wait until anything happens to me because Kelly was gunning for you, and Ruby was looking forward to just sitting back and watching the fireworks.'

My brow furrowed as I breathed deeply and exhaled slowly through my mouth. 'That's incredulous,' I muttered flabbergasted and unable to quite take in what I was hearing. Firstly, I had to play this down as Emmeline was so upset and this type of worrying, I knew, could have quite an impact upon her mental health and well-being, and secondly, it was imperative that I contact Sarah myself and ascertain the facts before discussing it any further.

'So, what do you think they could be plotting against you, and why would they try to get him off when they KNOW exactly what he did and that he IS guilty. After all, Ruby was the one who pushed Sarah into going to the police in the first place and she is the one who made me keep it secret for nearly 18 months whilst the police built a case up against him,' she said, her voice shaking as her memory flooded with unwanted images engulfing her emotions.

'How do you think I felt? Being kept in the dark and only finding out the day HE was arrested. It's laughable really when you think of her ringing me bawling her eyes out down the phone at the fear of having to go in and give her statement. There I was feeling all sorry for her not realising she had orchestrated it all.'

'I had to sit there and listen to the whole sorry story unfold about how she wanted to sit in the gap for the children and she was going to tell the truth and not get impeded by misplaced family loyalties. Yes, she played us both like right kippers,' I admitted.

'The worst thing for me was having to keep it a secret all those months when I should have been concentrating on your dad, without all the stress of it on my mind and her repeatedly going into detail at every opportunity. I don't think I would have been like I am,' she stated.

'It wouldn't have caused the Dementia,' I reassured Emmeline. However, being sworn to secrecy about the details of such a sensitive case, knowing its effect on others, the trauma of the incidents surrounding it, not being able to talk it through with those you trusted and what followed could have had dire implications upon her mind and exacerbated it profoundly. I thought.

'Well, it's funny though, isn't it, how she was suddenly here all the time playing the victim and feigning the supportive role just to get the historical evidence of what he did to you, so it would help convict him in Elena and Danny's case. Then, as soon as it was all over, and he was convicted, she didn't need us anymore, so the real Ruby returned, and we don't see her for dust. Then like the bad penny she is, she only comes knocking when she wants money.'

Emmeline was getting a bit hot under the collar, so I needed to diffuse the situation and change the subject.

'Anyway,' I said, 'I will have a word with Sarah myself and find the underlying cause of it but in the meantime, it's market day so are we going to have a walk up into town, or what?' I asked.

Emmeline went off through the utility to use the toilet whilst I got her coat and shoes out ready, but there was no doubt in my mind, I needed to give myself time to think and to find a way of speaking to Sarah and figure out exactly what I was going to say. I chewed the phrase over again in my mind that she "couldn't wait until anything happened to Emmeline". It was quite incredulous to think that Ruby could be so devoid of humanity.

This was her mother she was referring to not some used carrier bag that had lost its purpose. How callous and sickening I thought.

When Emmeline had her coat and shoes on, we went through our usual checklist: purse; phone; shopping bag; bank books; glasses; keys; gloves; scarf; and lastly that she did have her teeth in, and we were finally set to head out. We did our usual route of crossing the road right outside the gate, down to the bottom of the hill; left along the lane and out towards the town along the main road.

We came to where the island was in the middle of the road making it possible to see the cars clearly from all angles and which afforded us plenty of time to cross safely. I had walked this route with Emmeline almost every day for years to enable her to stay safe whilst maintaining her independence, so it was now positively engrained.

We took one of the alleyways between the shops to the precinct, and suddenly ahead of us was an array of brightly coloured stalls selling everything from cleaning utensils, fresh produce, books, pet items, clothes, and electrical equipment.

As I meandered around from stall to stall, I let my mind wander along the intricate paths that Ruby had taken us through since dad had passed away. There was the time Emmeline stated Ruby had exploded into a rage whilst in the passageway at Grey Gables and that she had grabbed hold of her and shook her quite hard. Then there were several incidents of Emmeline being intercepted by Ruby whilst she went out going about her business in town.

At these times, Emmeline described being verbally abused in an aggressive manner because Ruby was unable to get her own way. The snide text sent when Emmeline had fallen over backwards whilst standing on the table hanging washing over the creel resulting in her banging her head on the freezer. Ruby didn't ask if she were ok having been taken to hospital but "shame there wasn't anyone else you could have contacted", referring to me.

Then there was the onslaught of the ins and outs of her divorce, several times a week going over the same stuff repeatedly. I remembered that at the time Emmeline thought Ruby had dementia too because she refused to believe she was constantly repeating the same story word for word or worried that the chemo treatment had affected her brain as she was irrational and obsessive. Ruby made numerous false allegations regarding her own husband too, accusing him of having affairs and unholy interest in young girls.

I also recalled her obsession doing research on Company's House records to see if she could find anything she could use to report her other brother to the Tax man for, so she could get him investigated for fraud.

All this time, effort and scheming just to cause distress, hurt and unrest to others, to prove what? I remember a very wise friend saying once that the only reason people are intentionally malicious is because deep down, they are hurting. However, left unchecked, these hurts turn to jealousy, which in turn creates a bitterness resulting in an unbearable thirst to interfere in other peoples' rights to live happy, fulfilling, peaceful lives.

For me, I couldn't comprehend wasting any of my precious time. Emmeline was too important and we had our own lives to live.

There had also been an incident when I had arrived to collect Emmeline for a weekend away at Alton Towers, where Ruby marched her way into the house and was so aggressively confrontational, along with being verbally abusive we were stunned; it had come from nowhere. Not only were some of the statements and allegations outrageous that she had spouted but one was that my son aged 2, (at the time of the alleged incident) had "stabbed her son" in the eye.

The actual circumstances had been a celebration party where her son had been behaving badly and jealous of the positive attention my son was getting (according to witnesses), he kept purposefully hurting him. When her son then spit in my son's face he reacted by poking him in the face with his finger. Whilst Ruby was screeching at us in the kitchen, she called my son an 'evil little shit'.

Yet despite keeping my cool, I did warn her not to overstep the boundary of abusing my child, a now very loving, responsible and caring 12-year-old. She also accused him of planting the seed in Emmeline's head that she had hit and shook her. Emmeline immediately rose to his defence, stating there was no seed to implant then looked her square in the eye and accused her directly of the said crime, 'You did hurt me, Ruby.'

It was at this point I reminded her of the warning I'd given her when dad had passed away that although I would forgive and forget these kinds of incidents up to that point; if she ever started this type of behaviour again, I would disown her. So, I advised her to get help and told her I wanted no more to do with her as I did not want this kind of behaviour having an impact on my children. She really was out of control.

In the end it lasted 1 and ½ hour before she dropped the bombshell of her real destination, she wanted money for structural repairs to her house. The moment she had marched in with a face like thunder, she had stressed that she wanted me present, so the penny began to drop, because I was Emmeline's Power of Attorney. We were then subjected to what Emmeline described as "crocodile tears".

It was nothing more than a charade. I had had enough so we made it known we were leaving, and without further ado we set off on our journey.

I don't remember Emmeline, the children or myself making much conversation on that 2-hour journey to Alton Towers. What should have been an exciting trip had been overshadowed and left us shell shocked at the dire display of disrespect we had been forced to witness. There were grey clouds over us and the mood sombre throughout the whole weekend. It was only on our return journey that we felt the need to discuss it further as we didn't know what we would be returning home to or what might be coming next.

'What you choose to do, Emmeline, is fine but from this moment on, I want nothing more to do with her. She makes things up as goes along; she takes bits of information from one story, adds it to another and then puts them together to make a string of nonsense and believes it,' I declared.

'What do I do about the money she says she needs for the house restoration?' She asked, confused.

'That is something for you to consider, it has nothing to do with me,' I said, 'As far as I am concerned, she is your daughter. It is your brass and you have the right to do what you want with it but I am not getting involved to have yet more unfounded accusations thrown at me,' I said.

'I know, love, but I value your input and advice,' she pleaded.

After pondering the thought for several moments, I said, 'OK, I will take the emotional element out and give you the advice that I would give anyone else in this situation and that would be to seek the guidance of your financial advisor. He is the person who can help you in this situation,' I said.

This had been 2 years ago in May 2014, now here we were again, faced with the possibility of further allegations, confrontations, and irrational behaviour. This was one resurrection I was not looking forward to.

I did not have to consider how to approach the situation for long, as the next day, 19 February 2016, I heard from Sarah via Facebooks messenger. All it said was, *Heads up, two of your siblings are looking to dig some dirt on you. Obviously, I have not told you this. Hope you're well x.*

Inevitably, I wanted to know more so asked for further information to be told:

You just need to watch your back, Lois; this is some serious shit. As you know Ruby and I were close, but I don't speak to her anymore and I have no intention of going into it. I have had the opportunity to sit back and look at the bigger picture, a kind of ariel shot where you see a whole host of different things and they are not as you first thought.

Kelly and Ruby are seeing a lot of each other and in some twisted parallel universe, Kelly now seems to think she can get access to Elena, not Danny just Elena! Over my dead body. She was the one who was allegedly going to 'sit on the fence' when he got arrested, but was then outspoken to Ruby stating, 'why do you care, it's not like it's your daughter!'

It doesn't matter whose child he abused she was a child, my child. I cannot believe that was her attitude and her supposed to have been a nursery schoolteacher. And then she put on such a display in the court room that even the judge asked if she was an actress?

Ruby told me they were plotting ways to get his conviction overturned for what he did to you and say you made it up. They are also saying that the reason you finished work was because you accused the priest of sexual assault or rape. Please just watch your back as they are two twisted pieces of shit.

They know what that sick bastard did, and I now know your truth and I am sorry I wasn't able to see it before. I didn't know you and although it's no excuse I just accepted what she said! I was told of their plans a few months ago and they were adamant they would prove that you lied, as according to Ruby you have cried rape a few times but never reported it to the police. I have no idea what they are up to now because I have not spoken to Ruby since December nor will I ever again.

I was beside myself at the extent Ruby was prepared to sink to, but for what reason to slander my reputation, cause unnecessary distress and havoc in my already difficult life? These allegations were totally and utterly outrageous and in the first instance Ruby was the driving force in securing his conviction quote 'I am going to get that bastard.'

She was calculated in the execution of her plan and had successfully manipulated both Emmeline and I for months because she needed our evidence to secure that conviction knowing full well, we wouldn't have voluntarily offered it. I had not wanted to get involved as I did not welcome standing up in court, having to tell everyone how that sick bastard ruined my life, or the years of therapy I have had to go through.

I was sickened to my stomach about her comments regarding the priest, not to mention the disgust at accusing me of crying rape but not reporting it. This kind of talk is not just damaging but can be soul destroying, especially when you live in a small village where fools will listen, some will believe it and idiots will continue to spread its malicious lies.

Initially, I looked inwardly not understanding why she hated me so much when I had never done her any harm. I had welcomed her into my home on several occasions for her to tell me she 'couldn't stand being in my company for more than 10 minutes'. I had included her into my circle of friends for her to cause division and unrest.

I was utterly bewildered. I gave myself 24 hours to contemplate the situation then made a conscious decision that it would not take up any more of my time.

The next day, I met with friends for a much-needed coffee morning where I spoke candidly about this latest saga. I have known these ladies since secondary school, so I trusted their opinion and required their much-needed guidance.

My friend Leanne wisely said that 'The problem is, Lois, you are trying to judge it by your yard stick of moral compass when they have absolutely no morals, and obviously have too much time on their hands. Both Ruby and Kelly have spent their lives trying to bring you down through their own deep-rooted bitterness and hatred. It's a shame they don't put their efforts in to building relationships instead of destroying them,' she wisely said.

Mia put it more simply. 'Maybe they ought to grow up and then they'd realise that their situations are a direct result of the consequences of their own actions. They blame you for not seeing their own mother, but the truth is no one would stop me from seeing my mother. It suits them to get on with their own lives and leave all the crap to you, but they will soon come round if they think there's ought to get.'

Laura, a true empath, said, 'My concern is for poor Emmeline and the effect their behaviour has had on her. She ended up losing her entire family when your dad passed away and that was the time they should have been at their most supportive. They have done nothing less than abandon her when she needed them the most.'

'In my eyes, they should be ashamed of themselves, not boasting about what despicable acts they intend to commit. As Leanne says, they have no moral compass.'

A single tear dribbled down my cheek, but I quickly wiped it away. 'I just don't understand it. How do you grow up in a house together and then them behave like animals stabbing me so furiously in the back? They have no idea who I really am and have never taken the time to get to know me.' I decided my tears were far too precious to waste any more of them on either Ruby or Kelly.

I could not go to see Emmeline as I did not want her to know just how much this had upset me and I knew I would not be able to hide my devastation. I decided to take the dog for a walk but did not feel much like bumping into other people either, so I plumped for a walk over the mountains to blow the cobwebs of lies, deceit and slander out of the corners of my mind. First though, I had to give it one last mulling over just to satisfy myself I was beyond reproach.

I thought over the venom we had endured in the kitchen and then her cheek to ask for money for repairs. I comforted myself in the knowledge that I had acted correctly by advising Emmeline to get financial advice. I thought about the continued abuse after this episode where she had again pressured Emmeline over the phone for the money, and Emmeline asking me to talk to her because Ruby was not listening to her and had resorted to abuse again.

Ruby was not interested that Emmeline was taking advice, her position was that she was outside the solicitor's office and was demanding a decision now. I also remembered the parting shot Ruby had given Emmeline the Christmas before when all this had started, stating, 'If you don't give me the money, me and your grandchildren will end up on the street, and it will be all your fault.'

This had had a massive impact on Emmeline because she believed she was responsible, and couldn't think through that Ruby was an adult and the situation was of her own creation and her responsibility to find a solution.

I remembered contacting her ex-husband at that time because Emmeline was so distraught. We'd had a lovely catch up and I explained the situation urging him to intervene as structural repairs to his home were not really Emmeline's concern plus, she had enough of her own expenses and responsibilities to take care of.

He was exceptionally apologetic; he knew he needed to deal with the situation but admitted he had put it off due to the level of aggression he was also being subjected to. He then went on to relay the various false allegations Ruby had made against him, and declared it had cost him over £40,000 extra in solicitors fees due to having to defend several malicious lies.

He stated that without this expense he would have been able to do the repairs, settle the divorce and have moved on but his torment had been going on for 4 years. He promised to deal with the situation and thankfully we heard no more until the kitchen episode.

As I walked, I then mused over the time Ruby declared she no longer needed the full amount because she was going to use her husband's secondary credit card, which he did not realise she still had with them being separated. I was blown away at her casual admittance of her intention to commit fraud.

The breakthrough for Ruby was finding out her father-in-law had passed away and the declaration she would no longer need Emmeline's money at all because she was entitled to more of her husband's assets with him owning his father's house too. Unscrupulous and devoid of any compassion came to mind!

As I walked and thought, I came to realise that I had not only worked in Emmeline's best interests but when Ruby was in dire straits, I had also worked in hers too, seeking the help from the person who she was too proud to ask, her husband. When I thought about the current situation with its slanderous, malicious intent, the threats to harm me in some form, the inaccurate, unlawful reasons of why I had left work (I was medically retired), and the wild, irrational consistencies of poor behaviour I had to deduct, there was no attack I could plan for.

Regardless of what I could perceive, my experience had taught me that Ruby could scrape beneath the bottom of the barrel and Kelly was no better than a puppet along for the ride. So, I would have to deal with it if the situation arose, but right now, I could not allow it to break through to disturb my inner peace as that would subsequently affect not only Emmeline but my two young children, and neither Ruby nor Kelly were worth that!

Chapter 7
The Carer 2016
Busy, Busy, Busy

So, I was the child that nobody wanted, the one that got palmed off on to everyone else? I was also the adult that Ruby couldn't stand being in the company of for more than five minutes, yet I was the one she rang bawling her eyes out to when she'd masterminded the allegations against her brother and was going to the police station to make a statement against him.

It isn't wasted upon me the fact she had known for two decades what had happened to me or that she needed my evidence to validate and bring weight to her case. There it is that word again, hindsight.

In life, we come across all kinds of people; some who we truly love, and they take this journey called life with us. There are others who may come in and out of our lives, but our bond is so strong that we are able to pick things up from exactly where we left them despite the length of time, we have been apart. There are also our children whose lives we enrich, we guide, support, teach, and most of all protect, then when the time is right, we step aside to give them the room to grow, to fly and yet we are always there ready to catch if necessary.

In turn there are our own parents who by the same measure have done the same for us, so surely it makes sense that when they are weak, vulnerable, alone, and afraid, we would give them the strength that they had once given us. But then there are the ones who hide in the shadows watching, waiting just looking for a chance to pounce to bring your world crashing down so they can mock, ridicule, and devour.

I ask myself why, and the only reason I can see is jealousy and a wantonness to possess all that you have either because they secretly wish they were you or they are consumed by their own inadequacies and black heart. I am by no means perfect, and no one can criticise me greater than the little voice knocking at the backdoor of my mind. I just thank God every day for His goodness, His Grace and mercy that I am relishing in taking the time to help, support, love and build others up not to destroy.

If there are any traits that live on in me from my parents these are them. People think the Bible is full of do's and don'ts and in a way it is, however if you take the time to do the do's, you don't have time or idle hands for the devil to engage you into doing the don'ts. Therefore, I am grateful that I can walk away from the hatred that consumes others, yet not without compassion.

I feel great sorrow for them despite being on the receiving end of their abnormal acts. So, for the time being, I made a concerted effort to drop this nonsense to the floor. After all, I had many other commitments and I couldn't afford to allow negative thoughts to overcome my every day.

During the early months of 2016, I was so busy, and looking back I am not sure how I manged to keep the wheels on, the balls juggling or change the many hats I was wearing. I had started a 24-week course in the Principles of Dementia September 2015, so was still committed to this every Monday afternoon at St Georges Community centre.

It was quite intense and covered many aspects of dementia; the differences between the main four types, the behavioural patterns, medications, case studies, experiments, research, how it affects the brain, the different stages the list was endless. Although, it is quite a cruel disease, I actually became quite fascinated by its trickery and in reality, found that Emmeline's Vascular element made you feel like you had it licked then there would but an almighty drop, and you were left like a headless chicken not knowing what to do.

(It wasn't until around April 2017 that I started to see traces of Alzheimer's introducing itself.)

As with any course to effectively understand, the topic it generated much home study to process the analysis of data, to take a closer look at the examination of studies, make comparisons between cases and the exploration of key facts were essential to complete weekly modules. I had to set specific time aside which was generally after I had collected the boys from school, done homework, reading, teas, walked the dog and put them to bed.

It was the only time I could truly focus and give it the attention it so richly deserved, and was regularly falling into bed drained. I am quite pragmatic in my approach to things. If I commit, I like to give myself fully; there are no half measures. I am self-motivated, driven until completion and will excel at whatever I put my mind to, because failing is simply not an option.

By the end of January 2016, I had completed a food preparation course, done a First Aid training course, and had just begun the Working with Parents (Complex Needs) Level 4 course, having completed the level 3 in 2015. So, my hands were a little full on the studying side, and although, I was supporting Emmeline, managing both our homes and a holiday home, I was also supporting a family via Home-start (I had volunteered for several years); was running a weekly playgroup for them and also assisting at another.

So, when I was sat in my Monday afternoon session and Sheena, the manager of St Georges, addressed the group wanting to recruit volunteers for a New Dementia café, there was no way I was going to raise my hand, right? I couldn't help myself; not only had St Georges given me the platform to absorb a wealth of information and knowledge to assist me in the care of Emmeline but this centre had enabled me to have the courage to keep going when I felt weary.

So, hell yeah, my hand shot up like Jack's beanstalk. I was only too grateful to give them something back in repayment.

The café was to occur on the first Wednesday of the month starting in February 2016, and initially my intention was to devote a year to them, however I became engrossed in the lives of our members, readily accepting anyone who wanted to join. We played bacca bowls, looked at memorabilia, played musical bingo, had singers in, enjoyed parties, visits form children in the creche, had weekly raffles and simply enjoyed a good old-fashioned natter.

I loved every single person who bravely shared their struggles with dementia, their achievements, funny anecdotes but equally felt as broken when sufferers lost their battles. After being there for only a short time, I was visited by a lady from Manygates Educational Centre, the body who had provided the Dementia Course. She was wanting to write an article about me.

For anyone who really knows me, I do not like the limelight. I am the person who works hard behind the scenes to elevate the achievements of others, recognising no matter how small it appears on the surface for that individual it could be massive. So, to say I was out of my comfort zone is a serious understatement.

Claire explained that my name kept being brought up in conversation regarding my dementia work, helping at the dementia cafe and the level of care and dedication I showed in my role as a carer to Emmeline. I was flabbergasted and didn't know what to say. She interviewed me, took lots of details then wrote a 'success' story for Educational exploits advertising the courses.

On another occasion, Sheena was producing new literature for St Georges and wanted to feature my story, but knowing how embarrassed I would be she didn't tell me what she was planning. I was in the kitchen of the crypt in the church next to St Georges, busy making drinks and preparations for the Dementia café when two young adults arrived to interview me.

'I am sorry, but I don't know what you mean,' I said. 'What interview?'

Sheena then bobbed her head around the door. 'Sorry, Lois, I knew if I told you they were coming, you probably wouldn't turn up today,' she said.

'Exactly what have I just been ambushed for?' I asked.

Sheena explained about the book that was being produced by St Georges to help promote the essential work they bring to the community. It was demonstrating the courses on offer, it's creche, café and drop-in centre facilities, the Dementia café, bereavement group, the masses of healthy initiatives that Sheena facilitated and so much more. What she wanted to do was feature our work at the café, my commitment to it and the courses that I had taken and why I chose to volunteer.

I gave them a totally unprepared, brief, yet to the point interview which was recorded and then came the worst part, photographs, so very embarrassing. Once finished, I shooed them out of my way so I could get back to making teas and coffees.

I was at a point in my life where I was making good progress. The boys were doing well at school; Joe was enjoying drumming lessons; Jack was a keen member of scouts. I was fulfilling my ambitions to restart my career. Emmeline was in a good place, and although, I was juggling so much, I was happy.

After Sarah had dropped her bombshells, I wouldn't say I was complacent or disbelieved her, I just chose to drench myself in the moments of my every day. There is absolutely nothing to be gained in worrying and besides all you are doing is giving someone else the key to your safe place. So I carried on regardless, however for Emmeline, this was not quite as easy.

At first, it was little things like; not being able to operate the remote control or I would find bread left in the toaster and observed her inability to construct a cup of tea. She also went through a phase of not knowing where her keys were, and she would ring in a highly distressed state when they were in her bag. Up until now, Emmeline was more than capable of navigating her way through the day.

She was safe enough to be left alone and despite her retention or processing decline, she was compos mentis. I had no real concerns. I was continuing to promote her independence and encouraging her continued integration within her local community. She was enjoying her daily stroll along the town, accessing the bank, chemist, shops and going for lunch at the café her neighbour owned.

I continued with my own activities planned around meeting all Emmeline's needs whatever I was doing, I checked in with her first ensured she had everything for that day, then like a boomerang went back and forth. However, since her warning of the proposed attack, she started to unravel and the first weekend in March seemed to push her further. I arrived on Friday, 4 March to find her quite distressed.

'Have you seen this?' She said handing me a small package. It was a box containing some biscuits.

Totally misunderstanding her point, I said, 'Yes, they are biscuits. Am I missing something?' I asked puzzled.

'It's what SHE has sent to me for Mother's Day. What a joke. Well, you can send them straight back,' she demanded.

'Hold on a minute,' I said. 'Who has sent them and why are you so angry?' I mused.

'They are a bloody insult. Does she think it will put us off the scent of what she is doing? Sly underneath bitch. You can send them back, I don't want them; they are probably poisoned anyway,' she shouted.

'Emmeline, I can understand why you are angry, but they are just a packet of biscuits. If it was me, I would enjoy them with a cuppa despite who sent them or what motives you feel are behind it,' I tried to reason with her.

'No, she spoilt my husband's funeral, then she lied in court to get HIM off, so I don't care what she says or does. I don't want her here or anything from her,' she stated furious.

There was no reasoning with her, in her eyes she had been wronged and although it was unlike her to hold a grudge, she was quite a feisty woman when she wanted to be. So, I let it go, unpacked the biscuits and placed them in her biscuit barrel in case she changed her mind, forgot or decided to eat them anyway.

The next day when I arrived, she was equally distressed saying my brother had turned up out of the blue complaining the bank had the deeds to his business and he was going to lose everything unless he could get some cash together.

'I kept him at the door. I wasn't having him coming in looking for assets to sell,' she said.

'Emmeline, I don't mean to be rude but there is nothing of value for him to gain enough money to help a failing business,' I tried to reason.

'He was wanting to know if your dad's car was still in the garage and if he could have a look and see if he could get anything for it,' she persisted.

'Really?' I said not quite comprehending the validity of this statement.

'Luckily, I didn't have a clue where the keys were, so he left.'

I tried to take in what she was saying but felt it more important to reassure her that she was not under any threat and diverted her to making a cup of tea.

Then she suddenly said, 'What if he comes back again when I am on my own and forces his way into the house? He might force me into signing everything over to him.'

'Why on earth would any one force their way in and even if they did, you call the police or ring me and I will call them whilst I am on my way over to you,' I tried unsuccessfully to bring calm.

'Remember he trapped both Ruby and me in when he came here before your dad's funeral. When everyone else was leaving, he hung back, waited then he shut the door, locked it and said he wasn't going anywhere demanding to know all the details of what had happened to your dad. And he cornered Ruby. I heard him in the back say, "it will be your word against mine",' she recounted.

It was clear I wasn't going to get anywhere but I was worried about her state of mind and the real impact this anxiety was having upon her, it wasn't good. The next day was Mother's Day, so I overcompensated the fact she would receive nothing else from her children and bought her lots of presents and a huge bouquet of flowers. We had a lovely meal out then bought cream cakes from Hampson's Garden centre on Denby Dale Road before eating them at home with a coffee.

The next day, as usual I arrived at Grey Gables after taking the children to school but was unable to gain access as she had attempted to barricade the door with a wheelchair, along with placing a key in the lock and having turned it, made it impossible to shimmer it out from the other side. When I finally gained access, I was shocked to see the overnight decline.

'What on earth has happened for you to feel a need to block the entrance?' I asked.

'I don't want him here, Lois, in fact I don't want any of them here. They haven't bothered about me for years and now they are making me feel unsafe to be in my own house,' she spilled out.

I could do no more than to take her in my arms where I held her tight until her sobs had subsided. I felt out of my depth. The events of the week had unbalanced her greatly and there was absolutely nothing I could do but be here as it was out of my control. Over the next few days, the same barricading technique was applied, so each morning I was unable to access the property.

She would be in floods of tears once she set eyes on me at the relief of being able to feel safe again, it was like having a small child and you were their comfort blanket. I tried reassuring her as she went from panic of them getting in, to anger at not wanting to be forced out of her own home; this was pure torment and not good for her mental health. Also, on the 18th March, we were planning on going to Hornsea for Easter and Emmeline was determined she wasn't coming, so I had to think of something and quickly.

I then remembered her financial advisor recommending a friend to her that installed CCTV, so unable to think of anything else after consulting with her, I rang him for the details and arranged for him to see Emmeline. This seemed to give her hope, but on the 12th March, when I went out with friends for a 50th birthday, an old neighbour of Emmeline's contacted me to say she had found her wandering over a mile away knocking on a door asking for Dorothy.

The CCTV, only a cheap monitor and camera, was installed just so Emmeline could have a little peace of mind to see who was at her door whilst alone and to give her the essence of being in control, so would hopefully make her feel less vulnerable or insecure. However, things went from bad to worse. Every day we were away, I kept in close contact with her sometimes several times a day, but for some reason, she'd had trouble accessing her accounts.

She was making little sense when we spoke and unable to depict the difference between reality and her dreamworld. It was no good, we could not relax knowing she was struggling and there was no way this was going to change unless we returned.

We arrived home Easter Monday, unpacked the car, put a wash on and were just about to leave for Emmeline's when my friend, Gillian, contacted me raising concerns for Emmeline's health. I had appointed Gillian as a cleaner for

Emmeline every Monday whilst I was doing my course. It was to free up some time rather than always doing tasks when I visited, so we had more quality time together and it gave Emmeline other adult stimulation through the week.

Gillian echoed my concerns; she was glad I had come home and suggested I observe Emmeline's legs as she felt they required medical attention. I was absolutely baffled.

As I arrived at Grey Gables, I gave the boys strict instructions to be their genuine loving, kind selves but to then go and watch tv whilst I assessed Emmeline, but it didn't quite go like that. They ran off ahead to find her as soon as we arrived. 'Emmeline, where are you?' They called.

'It's me and Jack,' called Joe, just in case there was any doubt she didn't know who they were.

The first thing I noticed was that the door through to the middle room was uncharacteristically closed which was odd. I told the boys to wait as I didn't know what we would find. As I opened the door, she was sat staring vacantly like she was watching some unseen speck on the horizon. There was no reaction, no emotion, no recognition.

She had temporarily left through the little backdoor of her mind again. I didn't know how long she had been in this state, and although, Jack didn't show it (probably protecting his brother), Joe was very frightened; he didn't understand. Jack took hold of Joe's hand redirecting him to the kitchen where he busied himself and distracted Joe making us both a cup of tea.

I sat beside Emmeline and took hold of one of her hands, gently rubbing the back of it, softly saying her name. I reminded her to breathe deeply in through her nose and out through her mouth repeatedly to the count of four. This went on for several minutes to the clatter of cups from the other side of the door.

As soon as I saw the slightest flicker of recognition and she started to respond to my commands to breathe in and out, I tried to give her the sound of the constant ticking of the clock to help ground her so she could take the passage back to us. She began to blink more rapidly and to make an exaggerated sigh noise on the release of her outward breath; it was working.

'Emmeline, can you hear me, it's Lois. I am sat here with you holding your hand,' I encouraged.

'Can you feel me rubbing the back of your right hand, Emmeline?' I continued. 'Focus on the back of your right hand until you can feel the sensation of my hand rubbing it,' I said. Slowly but surely to my relief, she began to return.

Then a tear escaped down her face until eventually she ever so slightly squeezed my hand. As I sat there holding her hand, I gave a little prayer of thanks.

Once she had enjoyed a cuppa with a couple of chocolate biscuits, she began to talk and make more sense than what could only have been described as babbling. I couldn't help noticing her scratching subconsciously at her arm which increased the more animated she became.

'I've barely had any sleep since you left,' she began. 'They have been having parties on the lawn making a right racket. And last night, some bloody carol singers came to the door, and they wouldn't go away.'

'Carol singers?' I questioned.

'Yes, carol singers; they were bloody nuisance,' she said.

'Emmeline, it's Easter weekend not Christmas,' I tried to reason.

'I know you think I am bloody stupid, but I am not!' She stated.

'Why didn't you just ignore them and go up to bed,' I bought into the conversation.

'I did, but they were here all night having a full service on the lawn. It was snowing like bill-io and there were children out in the snow without their coats on.' She said.

Thankfully, Jack cut in and began to tell Emmeline about the new friends he had met and how much he had missed her. Whilst she listened, I visually scanned down to her ankles and could see the edges of redness, so remembering what Gillian had said I took the opportunity to ask if I could look. I was mortified!

The skin on both legs looked like they had been scalded. I had never seen anything so raw, angry, or bright red. Her arms were not as bad but there was clear evidence, she had been scratching these too. The rest of her body was fine, but I instantly knew I couldn't wait for the doctors.

She needed medical attention now especially as the hallucinations could be an indication of a water infection. I packed her an overnight bag, put the children in the car, took them home so they could go to bed (they were far too tired to be sitting at the hospital); at 9 and 14 they were mature enough. I took Emmeline down to the A&E department at Dewsbury Hospital to find the waiting area was not overly crowded so we were quickly seen; unfortunately she had to be admitted which wasn't as straight forward.

Whilst she fell asleep and rested well, I sat at her bedside holding her hand distraught at the impact her situation was having upon her; a tear or two falling out of sheer frustration and anger. It was 3 am before she was finally transferred to the ward where inevitably I was unable to accompany her, so I made my way through the maze of corridors towards the exit.

Sleep beckoned me; I was beginning to feel the exhaustion of the drive home and the emotional turmoil I had experienced. As I reached the exit, the cold night air soon blew the call of sleep away. I arrived home but was unable to sleep. My worry for Emmeline magnified in the quiet and safety of my room.

Chapter 8
Emmeline 2016
Downward Spiral

Is this what it feels like to be in a coma? I was lost; stuck somewhere between reality and the abyss of my tormented mind. It was as if I had temporarily gone through the little back door of my mind, but then it had slammed shut, been padlocked, and become as heavy as steal. I could not shift it no matter how hard I tried, I just couldn't get through.

When I had Lois, she somehow signified the small speck of light at the end of the tunnel but right now, a train was careering down the tracks to slam me further into a world of nothingness. Lois was my safety blanket and without her, panic soon turned into terror and I was being exposed to an all-new dimension. Lois knew the secret keycode.

She could bring me back but how long would I be able to survive here without her to open it; be able to find me then guide me through the wilderness? Would I be lost down here forever? Forgotten? This is my one true fear that everything I have stood for and achieved would come to mean nothing. I would be rendered useless, pass my sell by date, in deactivation mode where I would be left to vegetate somewhere forgotten by the rest of humanity.

The brain is such a complex, powerful organ that controls our every being, thoughts, movements, touch, breathing, emotions, holds our memories, controls our sensory and motor skills, and basically everything that regulates the body so if it malfunctions in any way we implode. It is like the control room of a spaceship navigating us through the universe, only right now I felt like I was the astronaut attached to the outside and could not get back in.

As we go through life's experiences, the mind can compartmentalise traumas in a bid to anaesthetise itself against the pain. I am aware I can see through my eyes like two big headlights, but I had no recognition of my surroundings. I felt in the depth of some deep, dark well, alone, frightened, and unable to call out.

Where are you Lois, please come and find me. I did not know how long I had been there, but I was rigid with fear, unable to move. I felt as though I was floating vertically in water, my ears compressed by muffled sounds, I couldn't even tell if I was breathing. I suddenly felt panic; am I dying? Is this what it feels like when you pass over to the other side? I had to do something.

'Focus, Emmeline, focus,' I commanded myself.

I remembered a technique that Lois had installed in me for moments like this to concentrate on my breath. To breathe in through my nose and out through my mouth. I took slow deep breaths counting to four as the air went in through my nostrils, I held it for four then slowly released the air through my mouth.

I was alive. I continued to repeat this until the pounding in my chest had regulated itself to a steady ticking. Hold on a minute, that was not my heart it was the distant, rhythmic sound of the grandfather clock in the hallway; it must be close by, which means I am at Grey Gables. I am at home, so I am safe. This knowledge at least brought me some comfort.

It was only then that I thought I could hear Lois's voice; it seemed far off at first like a dream or was it my wishful thinking. Nevertheless, as I concentrated, it seemed to be coming nearer. Then her hand reached down breaking the surface of the water grasping my hand to pull me out.

Yes, I was surer now I was not dreaming. I could not only hear her, but I could feel her too. She has my hand in hers, and I am safe I know everything will be ok.

The most frightening part for me is my loss of control to stay present in the here, and now when my brain seems to go off in a pre-set trajectory without the ability to find my own way back. It is like when you cannot shut down after an active day and all you want to do is sleep but your brain plays a sequence of videos that you cannot pause or simply shut off.

It reminds me of an old saying "my head's a shed" which means it is on overload causing confusion and agitation to the point you cannot think straight. That is how I would describe one of the effects dementia has upon me, but I secretly like to think it is because I have many years of stored information that my brain sifts through what it no longer needs. It is a similar process with a mobile phone, when you run out of storage it deletes duplicate photos, unused apps, idle documents to raise up storage space.

Dementia affects everyone differently, no two journeys are the same. Some people may not recognise their loved ones, some may be catatonic; others aggressive, others speak repetitively, others babble with nonsense words. We all have problems receiving new information, processing it and then actioning.

A little like a computer with numerous tabs open all at the same time it causes it to run slow or even crash completely. When I exit the "little back door of my mind", it's my brain being on overload, and it crashes sometimes saving the important files; however a few may be lost forever.

The Alzheimer's Society calls it the bookcase affect to demonstrate our loss of memory regarding some of our files. If you picture the bookcase being full of files, so the bottom one contains your earliest memories of say your childhood with the next your early adult life followed by row containing your work, child-bearing years, midlife, becoming grandparents, your retirement and then the present time. This would take up several shelves of files all stacked on top of each other.

If that bookcase was shaken gently from side to side random files would fall off the shelves in no particular order, these are like the memories of the dementia sufferer. Once they have fallen from the bookcase, they have gone forever and trauma can cause the bookcase to become very unsteady indeed; and where at times the brain may step in and close down in order to anaesthetise the person.

Please do not think I am any less of a person because my brain takes over for me or I appear vacant. I am sure if someone started speaking to you in a foreign tongue you would look vacant too. The next time you are under immense stress, the kids are screaming and you're rushing for an appointment or work pressures are affecting your homelife and sleeping pattern, take a minute to assess how difficult it is to process information and make the right important decisions.

This is what it is like for me the whole time. I am so scared to make a mistake, to look foolish or to be criticised and judge that I often do not respond, you see I still have a choice. Be patient, be kind; do not put me under pressure and I will get there if you reassure me and love me enough to give me the space and time. And please, do not just take over because its quicker or easier for you, that would be taking away my right to be independent.

Lois has always promoted my rights to be Emmeline as she says I am not an NHS number, an address, date of birth or national security number; I am a person with thoughts and feelings and deserve to have them taken into consideration. I may have dementia, but it is not the one thing that defines me it is a fragment of my latter years, so please don't forget I have achieved a lifetime of accomplishments too.

I am still that person, and that person is still in me. So, if you are caring for someone look into person centred care as it promotes meeting the individual persons needs along with assisting to maintain a personal relationship rather than becoming task orientated, carer/cared for.

After enduring such a traumatic time, there was no wonder really that I ended up crashing. My mind was tormented, I was not sleeping, and I was living in fear therefore, when I came out of hospital, I made the decision to move. I could no longer stay at Grey Gables. I felt like a sitting duck waiting to be blasted out of the water.

At the time, I did not really think how it may affect Lois, I just wanted the torment to stop and that meant getting as far away as possible. So I told her I wanted her to investigate getting some estate agents in. She was horrified at the thought of another family living here and never being able to come here again but she had witnessed the affects upon me, and as my power of attorney she must take the steps to do what is in my best interests.

During the month of April, she came everyday so we could separate things for the tip, the charity shop and what I wanted to keep. I know I appeared emotionless at the start, but I had made a hard decision and needed to focus on moving forward not the memories we had built here. I had amassed a lot of stuff, buying unnecessary things; in fact 101 items of clothing went to the charity shop, along with bric-a-brac that had filled the cupboards.

The only problem was I did not have the concentration, so Lois had to enlist her friend, Laura, to help. She was lovely and very respectful to the situation, so I trusted her not to mention the times she popped in to check on me when Lois was away, take me for lunch or accompany me if I needed any support. They worked diligently together, taking up all the school hours over a 3-week period consulting with me about any decisions.

To be honest, I was at a point I had given up and wouldn't have cared less what we kept or got rid of. I needed to be safe, and the fact was blatantly clear I couldn't stay here on my own. I know Lois became concerned and would ask me to go for lunch, stay over for the company and encourage me to go to church but to be honest I did not want to go out.

One day after the massive clean-up, Lois sat me down and again approached the subject with regards to putting Grey Gables on the market. She wanted me to be absolutely certain this was the action I wanted to take as once it had gone it was lost forever. There was no doubt for me at the end of the day it was just bricks and mortar, but my sanity was everything.

It reminds me of a sign I have in my bedroom, "I have lost my marbles; I think my children took them". I was adamant this was not going to be a self-fulfilled prophecy! So, I reiterated I wanted her to take steps to get valuations and then we would sit and discuss it again.

On the 29 April, we went to Fieldhead Hospital in Wakefield to see Claire, the nurse, where it was discussed that now would be beneficial time to start medication due to my rapid decline. Lois asked her about the proposed selling of the property and whether a move would have a detrimental effect upon me. However, Claire backed my decision and told Lois that it seemed like the right decision for me as the house sounded enormous and was obviously too large for me to be rattling around in on my own.

I know I should not have, but a great big smug grin did appear across my face. I knew she was only looking out for me and concerned for my health, but it was my decision to make. We then went in to see Dr Musa who put me on Memantine to support the decline of the dementia. I knew I must have been a worry as this was the first time, I was having medication for dementia.

'Can I ask a question, Dr Musa,' Lois said.

'Yes, Ms Rodgers,' he said.

'Emmeline has decided to sell her property which is a massive decision to make; she has lived there for over 40 years,' she began. 'The thing is, I am worried that after this recent decline that it will exacerbate her condition further and I just want your professional opinion whether this would be in her best interests.'

Dr Musa turned to me and asked, 'Why do you want to make this move now, Mrs Rodgers?'

I was honest. I said, 'I feel tormented, and the house is playing tricks on my mind. I am wandering from room to room not knowing where I have put things, what I went in each room for, and I am scared to death being there on my own.'

'So where are you hoping to move to, Mrs Rodgers?' He asked.

'I want to live with Lois and her two boys,' I said.

He turned to Lois and asked, 'And where do you live, Ms Rodgers, in relation to Mrs Rodgers?'

'It is about 5 miles away,' she said.

'Oh, well I see no problem with that at all,' he said. 'In my experience it only becomes an issue when family move their loved one across the country to live near them but not with them. When you take someone out of their usual environment to live somewhere else alone and without support, this is when it has detrimental effects upon their dementia.'

'If Mrs Rodgers is happy to put her house on the market to live with you and your family, it's the perfect time to make that move especially where she can be supported and have company,' he stated.

A couple of days later, I had been to church and Lois picked me up as usual to have Sunday dinner with her and the boys. I decided I needed to talk to her and make her understand that I knew what I was doing and that I had given it enough thought, and it was time for me to move forward.

The following week, I had five different valuers in. After consideration, I decided on a young man who represented a company called Ewemove. He was dynamic, inspirational and I liked his energy though I didn't like the sign with the sheep on it, so I chose not to have one out front. Besides, I did not want Ruby, Kelly and the likes thinking they had a right to know my business or making life even more difficult than it already was.

This did not go to plan, over the next month I had a chance meeting with Kelly. Just the sight alone was enough to send shivers through me, unsettling my world. Then I thought I had seen her car parked outside my house and rushed too quickly across the road falling over the edge of the kerb.

Luckily, the post man had just pulled up in his van, so he picked me up and took me inside, bless him. On another occasion, I was walking towards Wellgate contemplating what I was going to order for lunch in the cafe when Ruby appeared from nowhere. She was angry about something and shouting at me, but I have no idea what I had done wrong or how I should respond, so I just looked at her, shellshocked.

When you have dementia, you do not always know how to respond, and your instinct says this person wants something from you, but you have no idea what? It is at times like this it magnifies my fear of looking foolish, so I appear 'vacant' because one minute your mind is on something you are doing and then there are expectations placed upon you from somewhere else.

It would be similar trying to play a board game without reading the rules, strategy or purpose or trying to build a Lego set without following the instructions. All these encounters reinforced my determination to leave Grey

Gables, as I had to protect not only my mental health and stability but to ensure I also had a future that I could enjoy.

On the 23 May 2016, Grey Gables went live. I did have nostalgic pangs of guilt but if I am honest, I was also relieved. Lois had a mixture of emotions but was realistic, recognising the impossibility of me being able to stay having seen the effects on my health, not to mention the condition of the property; it was very run down. As we discussed the future and the feasibility of us all living together at her house, we decided to explore all options and not have any preconceived ideas.

We looked at how we could structure the living accommodation to meet all our needs; the prospect of selling both properties to put together to have a newer one or putting Lois's house in part exchange with the sale of Grey Gables going towards the rest, just so I could stay in my location. At the end of it, we were just happy to work together for the best outcome collectively.

Little did we know that behind-the-scenes Kelly and Ruby were monitoring our every move, plotting against us and scheming like secret assassins, to not only destroy my inner peace but Lois's reputation too.

JUST LOVE ME

I look in the mirror but what do I see?
Who is this woman looking back at me?
At times there are glimmers, and I know I am here
But along comes a mist and along with it fear.
I stop and I think 'whatever was I doing?
Was it this? Or that? It's all so confusing!
I'm constantly searching for things near and far
My head is in turmoil, I don't know who you are.
I feel lost in a wilderness, empty, alone.
I then hear a noise and you shout, it's the phone'.
I stare and I watch as you belt down the stairs,
In suspended animation I just continue to stare.
I'm oblivious to what it is that you're doing
I haven't a clue, I can't make sense of what you're saying.
I do try my best to not let you down,
But then I look up and again see a frown.

I don't mean to upset you or say random things,
But with each new day I fear what it brings.
I stand at the sink, dirty cup in my hand,
I know it needs washing, but this, my brain won't command.
I look at my grandchild and call him my son,
Their names are so different but I'm sure it's the right one.
He's kind, he ignores it and just plays along
But then I hear him sobbing and I know I've done wrong.
I wish I could stop it, I will be better you'll see
But I won't, because Alzheimer's is robbing me of me!

Chapter 9
Emmeline 2016
The Breakdown

After Grey Gables had gone on the market, I felt I had a hope for a better future one with Lois, Jack and Joe that I felt happy and excited about. I am not sure if it was the new tablets I had started or the issues with Ruby and Kelly that were bubbling under the surface but the fog in my brain seemed to be getting thicker. At times I didn't know what I was supposed to be doing next or whether I was actually having any thoughts at all.

It was a horrible sensation that I couldn't control or explain. On one occasion, I was on my way back from town when I saw a car that I thought was Lois', so I tried getting into it only to find that it was locked, and she wasn't anywhere abouts. I became quite distressed as I suddenly didn't know where she was then a lady came from inside the shop having seen my distress.

I know she was trying to help me, but I just wanted Lois. Luckily, the one number I had memorised was Lois', so I gave it to the lady who rang her to find out where she was. I was shocked to find out that it wasn't Lois' car, that I hadn't been out with her today and she was in facts miles away. As Lois had suggested, the lady pointed me in the right direction as if I didn't know the way to my own house and went back inside the shop.

On another occasion, I went up to the bank and asked, 'Can I have cleap?'

'I am sorry, Mrs Rodgers, but I am not quite sure what you mean,' she said.

'I want cleap,' I said.

Looking rather confused she asked me, 'Is Lois in town with you?'

'No,' I snapped. 'I have banked here all my life and I come in here all the time, I just want cleap.'

The poor girl had no idea what on earth I was on about and suggested I come back with Lois so she could help me. This was the second time they had sent me away, so I rang Lois playing hell that it was my money, and I could do what the hell I wanted with it. Later when Lois arrived, and I had calmed down she asked me what I was hoping to receive when I had gone into the bank.

'I wanted to get £50 out,' I told her.

'Then why didn't you just ask her for £50?' She asked. 'Then she would have given it to you.'

'I suppose I could have,' I had no idea what the difference was I thought that was what I had asked for and the person at the bank was being snotty. I had been so angry, I was ready to shut all my accounts with them.

Later the same day, I became frantic again that I needed to go to the bank despite Lois having been with me earlier, and so went into town in the pouring rain at 5 pm, inevitably the bank was shut. I was confused and continued to walk through town looking like a drown rat until Debbie from Squires Deli kindly ushered me inside to take cover.

She was so concerned because I only had a thin coat without a hood on and was drenched to the bone. It probably made it worse because I was nonplussed about the situation. So she drove me home, made me a cup of tea and settled me back in. I had no perception of the possible dangers I was opening myself up to until I saw Lois.

She was shocked and decided to contact the memory clinic for advice fearing the Memantine dosage was maybe too much or that it wasn't compatible for me. Thankfully, she took the right course of action, and it was adjusted to a level that worked best for me. She also bought flowers and a card for Debbie to say thank you for her diligence and kindness.

Over the next week, as the drugs were being adjusted my behaviour worsened, and I was forgetting to take any of my medications. I kept setting the house alarm off, and at one point, rang Lois about having found £140 that I wanted to put in a bottle for the milkman. The worse experience was believing that there were funerals taking place in the garden and the big white flowers were skulls they had left behind.

It was really frightening for me, I genuinely thought it was happening but apparently, I had been dreaming. Although, having said that, the next day when Lois came, I still believed the white flowers were skulls.

Inevitably, Lois was really concerned about my deterioration so in consultation with me made a referral to Matthew Burns, the dementia nurse, along with another to Social Services as I was a vulnerable adult living alone.

She felt it important I had the support I required, and she had the advice and guidance from professionals that she needed to help me.

It was difficult for Lois as she was being asked to do talks for Carers Wakefield regarding being a carer of an individual with dementia along with supporting people at the Dementia café, that we attended together. Whenever she had commitments, she would phone me to let me know then call over before and after her appointments not to mention running the boys back and forth to school.

The day after the funeral episode was Tuesday, 28 June, and Lois arrived as usual to find me a bit subdued. 'Are you ok, Emmeline? You seem awfully quiet this morning,' she asked.

'I had a bit of a fall this morning, love,' I said.

'Are you ok? You didn't hurt yourself, did you?' She asked.

'No, I am ok,' I said.

'Why didn't you ring me? I would have come straight over, checked you out and if necessary, taken you to the hospital,' Lois offered really concerned.

'No, love, there was no need to worry, the carer was here so she helped me up,' I said innocently.

'Your carer?' she asked looking puzzled.

'Yes, the carer,' I stressed wondering why she was being so weird. 'She got me up, made sure I was alright and looked after me. So, don't get on at her. She was lovely to me, and she even got me a cup of tea, with 2 sugars,' I emphasised.

'Emmeline, you DON'T have carers,' she stressed.

I tried my best to camouflage my confusion, but I only made it worse. 'Oh well it must have been the nuns that were here; they have been baptising children up and down the landing all night!' I stated.

'Does that sound right to you? Nuns in your house baptising children along your landing all night?' She questioned.

'They were!' I snapped back convinced that it had happened.

Luckily, the gardener arrived so Lois was distracted but I was quite peeved that she didn't seem to believe what I was saying. Why would I lie? Anyway, Lois had to leave as she had a hairdresser appointment, so she put some money in an envelope for the gardener, placed it in my "purse drawer", we said our goodbyes and I went off to get washed and dressed for the day. When I came downstairs, I was thinking about having to pay the gardener and I wasn't sure if I had any money in the house.

I went from room to room searching, becoming more disorientated as I couldn't remember what I had entered a room for, so went back to the first to see if it would jog my memory. However, when I entered that room, again I had forgotten what I went in for so went back to the previous one to see if it would jog my memory. It was like a hamster wheel constantly rotating resulting in my becoming quite distressed until I saw the gardener at work outside, so I decided to go out to chat with him.

He immediately started going on about a dressing gown or something I had no idea what he was on about until he said he was going to ring Lois. Within a few minutes, Lois arrived and ushered me inside. I can honestly say I do not know what had happened or why she was here. Apparently, I had not finished getting washed and dressed so was only half clothed. Lois quickly assisted me then got me a cup of tea and a sandwich before going back to her appointment.

As I sat and ate my hot beef sandwich looking out on to the garden, I marvelled at the array of colours and watched the little birds flapping their wings in mid-air as they pecked at the suet balls hung from the gazebo when I noticed the gardener was here. I wasn't sure if I had any money in the house, so I thought I had better ring Lois to see if she knew.

'Lois, the gardener has arrived, and I don't think I have any money here to pay him,' I told her.

'Yes, you do, Emmeline. I have put it in an envelope it is in your purse drawer,' she recalled.

'My "purse" drawer?' I asked. 'I don't have a "purse" drawer.' I had absolutely no idea what on earth she was on about.

'Yes, you do, Emmeline, it's right at the end of the units in the kitchen,' she declared.

'Well, I don't know anything about a "purse" drawer. Can you show me?' I asked baffled.

'Emmeline, I am at the hairdressers. She has just put a colour on my hair so I can't come and show you right now,' she declined.

'But he is going to need paying and you say that you have put it somewhere. I don't know where you've put it,' I told her.

'Can you walk into the kitchen but stay on the phone?' She asked.

'Yes,' I said, leaving my half-eaten sandwich on the table. 'Right, I am in the kitchen now.'

'Can you walk over to where Poppy's dog basket is?' She said.

'It's right in front of me,' I told her.

'Good, the last drawer above the basket, can you open it and tell me what you see?' She asked me.

'Yes, there's my purse where it always is and an envelope for the gardener,' I then continue, 'in my purse drawer.'

'Brilliant,' she sighs. 'Can you give it to the gardener for me please?'

After her hair appointment, Lois came to see me which was lovely. I hadn't seen her all day and I had missed her. She made me a beef stew and dumplings for tea which was nice but for some reason there was a half-eaten sandwich on the table I wondered if it was the gardeners. When Lois left, I sat a while gazing at the newly cut grass, the turned soil of the flower beds and their blooms basking in the sun.

I decided to make a drink so went into the kitchen, however when I opened the fridge door there was an infestation of spiders, worms and bugs of all kinds spilling out of the drawer at the bottom of the fridge. I was screaming and shaking, not knowing what to do so tried hitting them with the broom and sweeping them to one side, but they kept multiplying.

I wanted to call Lois, but I was in such a distressed state I couldn't think of the right numbers, so I ran in to the room crying becoming increasingly anxious. To my relief, Lois dropped in to see me by which time I was in such a panic, I wasn't making much sense.

'There is nothing there, Emmeline,' she told me.

'There is,' I insisted. 'There are thousands of them and they are literally spewing out of the drawer at the back of the fridge,' I sobbed.

Lois took me to the door and asked, 'Can you see them now, Emmeline?'

'Yes, they are all there,' I pointed.

'You know I am terrified of spiders and bugs, don't you, Emmeline?' I nodded between sobs. 'Well, I wouldn't wave my hands through them if they were spewing out of here, would I?' She asks, demonstrating as she is saying it.

I felt bewildered and overwhelmed. I knew she wouldn't dare even walk through the kitchen if there was one spider, never mind place her hands in the wake of thousands. I slid down on to the settee and with my head in my hands and sobbed.

'It's me, isn't it,' I eventually said.

'I am afraid it is, Emmeline. There is nothing there. Why don't we pack you an overnight bag and you can come stay with us for a few days until we can figure out what to do next?'

Feeling rather foolish all I could do was nod. I didn't know it at the time, but this was the day we would begin living together as a three-generation family and I would never live alone again.

https://www.urbandictionary.com/define.php?term=cleap

(cleap: when you get bumps in your vagina for not cleaning a yeast infection)

Chapter 10
Emmeline 2016
Leaving Grey Gables

As Lois and Jack arranged a bag with some of my clothes and toiletries, Joe sat nestled into me on the settee. I was trying so hard to keep it together for his sake, the poor love must have wondered what on earth was going on. It was a different story on the inside. I was beside myself trying to scramble together what was happening to me.

How could I be seeing things that nobody else could see; it had appeared so real to me? I felt as though I had finally lost touch with reality, and my concern was this going to be the downward spiral to losing myself altogether? That was a very sobering thought. Surely if I was consciously wondering whether I was losing it, did that not mean I still had a grasp of things, so I wasn't going mad?

I once read that you were only going mad if you believed everyone else was wrong and you were right, although my behaviour of late had been erratic at best and there was only me who could see the bugs. If I wasn't mad, I was certainly going to send myself round the bend if I kept locking into this pattern of thought.

I looked down and saw Joe rubbing my hand. 'Grandma, mummy is talking to you,' he said.

I looked into his sad little face. 'Grandma, mummy is talking to you,' he repeated. He seemed so bewildered, then I realised it was my fault, it was because of me and my gut instantly tied into a thousand knots.

'Emmeline, we have packed enough for a few days I just need your tablets and then we can be off,' she said.

'Alright, love,' I managed to say, but stayed where I was just staring in to space, my head no longer containing any thoughts.

'Do you want to take granny into the kitchen, Joe, whilst Jack gets her coat?' She asked Joe.

Joe stood up but kept hold of my hand expecting me to stand with him, but I didn't. 'Come on, Grandma, we are going now you need to get your shoes on,' he urged me.

Lethargically, I obeyed my little grandson, feeling much safer with him than I did in myself and allowed him to guide me through into the kitchen. The next thing I remember was Lois on her hands and knees tying my shoelaces, the boys already in the car, seatbelts on with my bag secure in the boot. 'Are they comfortable, Emmeline?' She asked but all I could manage was a nod.

We soon arrived at Lois' home where my seatbelt was unbuckled for me and I was assisted out of the car and in through the front door. She sat me on her new highbacked light grey settee that had a Greek continuous meander pattern in the plush cushions and began undoing my shoes. All I could think of was I shouldn't have my shoes on in here it's a new carpet.

Funny how random things pop in that are not relevant to the situation. When I first started with dementia, I covered it up by either throwing my head back and laughing in agreement or smiling and nodding then saying 'I will have to go now.' No one seemed to notice but nowadays I cannot keep a thread to the conversation as there are too many blanks.

It feels a little like stacking a row of dominoes on their heads along the floor and when you push one down it tips to knock the next one over then the next. The purpose to knock the whole lot down, however there is always one that is just a little too far apart and so it stops short. With dementia, you are always trying to make that connection happen, but it just stops short and without the whole picture it doesn't make sense.

So, to cover it up, I try to put 2 and 2 together but it makes 17 and is way off. It reminds me of when the grandchildren were younger. We used to do dot-to-dots together trying to guess what the picture was going to become as it was forming. Nowadays it doesn't feel like there is any guidance, so I have no idea what the bigger picture is; it just feels like a lot of squiggly lines, and nothing seems to make any sense.

Lois must have already done the boys' bedtime routine because the next thing I remember was them both standing in front of me saying, 'Goodnight.' I gave them both a hug, each of them hanging on tight to me for dear life; perhaps they thought I was broken. Maybe I was.

The next day, Lois came in to check on me. I was sleeping in her bedroom whilst she slept in the top bunk of Jack's room, the boys popped their heads round the door. 'Hello, you two,' I said as cheerily as I could muster.

'Hi, Grandma,' said Joe.

'How are you feeling today, Grandma?' Jack asked.

'I feel good. Thank you, love,' I said. I then noticed they had their school uniforms on so it must be a weekday. 'Maybe when you have taken the boys to school, we could have a chat, Lois,' I said.

'Grandma, we've already been to school, we have just got home,' Jack informed me.

'What time is it?' I asked.

'It's 10 to 4,' Lois informed me.

I was aghast. 'In the afternoon?'

'Yes, you have slept all day, Emmeline,' she told me.

'Wish I could stay in bed all day instead of going to school,' Joe grumbled.

'Me too,' agreed Jack.

'Yes, but granny was worn out and needed the rest,' Lois chided them.

'Well, I feel worn out every morning when you wake me for school,' said Jack. 'I think maybe tomorrow I might need more rest.'

'Nice try, mate, but that's not happening.'

Lois set my clothes out for me then ran a bath so I could have a soak. By the time she called me through, I had fully woken up, so I gathered the towel she had got out for me and was greeted by a steamy, lavender filled bathroom. The tub was narrow and deep with the water taking up 2/3 of it and looked enormously inviting.

I pulled the toilet seat down, slid my things off and placed them on top of it. Swishing the fingertips of my hands into the surface it felt perfect, so I inched my way in so my body could adjust to the temperature. It's funny how it feels hot as you are getting in but within a minute or two you have acclimatised and can easily slide down.

The warmth engulfed me gently lapping around my shoulders as I rested my head over the edge at the end of the bath. It was lovely to finally relax, soothed by the hypnotic aromas daring me to surrender completely. The extractor fan hummed, drawing the steam to its evaporated exit.

I took in the assault on my senses with neither interest in time nor the events of the previous months. Here in this moment, I was simply enjoying being Emmeline when a light tap came to the door.

'Are you ok in there, Emmeline?' Lois asked.

'Yes, love, just enjoying the sensation of being,' I told her.

'It's not too cold, is it? You can put more hot water in if it is,' she told me.

'It's absolutely fine, love. I've only been in two minutes it hasn't had time to get cold,' I laughed.

'Emmeline, you have been in there for almost 40 minutes,' she informed me.

'Have I really? Oh, I am sorry,' I said.

'It's not a problem, Emmeline, I just wanted to make sure you were ok and hadn't fallen asleep,' she said.

'After sleeping until 4 pm!' I chuckled.

As I paid more attention, I realised that Lois was right, the water had become a little chilly, and then I also realised all the Radox bubbles had long since evaporated, the steam had disappeared and bath time was over. I eased myself to a sitting position then carefully stood up and climbed over the side of the bath. I pulled my towel off the radiator and swaddled myself in its soft, comforting warm embrace.

I felt so much better, yesterday felt like it was months ago. I quickly dried myself, got dressed, brushed my teeth and then appeared like a genie from its lamp, reborn after being cooped up for years. I found Lois in the kitchen stirring a pan of spaghetti Bolognese, the tomato rich and deep fighting with the garlic from the baguette in the oven.

Joe was sat at the dining table finishing his reading task whilst Jack was engaged in setting the table for tea. He had placed 4 glasses of water at each placing with spoons and forks for Lois, himself and I but at Joes there was a knife and fork, in the centre of the table was a dish of grated cheese.

'Hope everyone is hungry,' called Lois.

'Starving,' the three of us said in unison. We took our places as Joe returned his book to his schoolbag and Lois dished up huge platefuls of Bolognese with the baguette cut into segments on the side. It really was a lovely feast. I enjoyed listening to the mundane of everyday family life, the things they had done at school, their friends and Lois's studying tasks.

Today was a good day because I was sat here in the middle of this humdrum, I was alive. I was no longer alone, I belonged to them and they belonged to me. I was no longer afraid because I was safe.

That night I slept like a baby and didn't wake up until 1 pm the next day. Lois was busy on her laptop and the boys were at school. So, I went into the bathroom, got myself sorted then joined her downstairs.

'Hello, sleepyhead,' she said.

'I am up 3 hours earlier than yesterday, I call that improvement,' I said.

'The kettle has just boiled, I will make us both a cuppa when I finish this paragraph,' she told me. She was working on a talk she was giving for Carers Wakefield, so I pulled out a chair and eased into it mindful of not knocking the table whilst she worked.

Once she had made the tea and brought a small plate of biscuits through, she said, 'It's good you have been able to sleep so soundly, you needed it.'

'Yes, love, I think you're right. I feel so much better today and more like myself,' I told her.

'Glad to hear it. You will be pleased to know you have a hair appointment at 2.30 so I will drop you there, collect the boys from school then pick you up afterwards,' she told me.

'Oh lovely, that will be smashing, thank you,' I said chuffed to bits.

The simplicity of being amongst the throng of the busy little salon listening to the chatter between clients with their hairdressers warmed my heart as normality returned to what had been my tormented world. I loved the warm water cascading through my hair, after her fingertips had roughly massaged the shampoo suds to a lather, only to be repeated just as vigorously with conditioner and then soothed again with the warm water.

My scalp felt invigorated, pampered and yet the real transformation was still to come. She sectioned my hair into rows like tiny pigs in blankets as she neatly wound it around curlers then applied the perming solution ensuring the cotton wool was packed along the outline to catch any drips. The pungent chemical odour of the perming solution hit my nostrils, but I loved it a reminder that I was soon going to be restored and look like the old Emmeline.

As I sat under the freestanding hairdryer, its drone blocking out the world around me, I lost myself in a magazine about some woman who had escaped her abusive husband and was living a better life on some Spanish island. I wasn't contemplating a Spanish island but spending the summer away with Lois and the boys was something I decided I would love to do.

I needed to alleviate the strain and stresses of being at Grey Gables all alone and to have space and time to think, to be able to relax and to enjoy the bosom of the family who loved me. Yes, I decided I was going with Lois and the boys for the whole summer to Hornsea. My equilibrium was restored. For now.

Chapter 11
Emmeline
Moving in with Lois

After having my hair done, being able to relax whilst spending the weekend at Lois's and enjoying the safety of being with them I knew I would never go back to living on my own. Joe had been away on a trip to Robin Wood with his school and was to return Sunday teatime, so Lois took the opportunity earlier in the day to approach the subject.

'How are you feeling today, Emmeline?' She asked as she set down the cuppa on the bedside table in her room.

'I am fine, love,' I told her.

'Good,' she said. 'I will let you come round a bit and get yourself sorted then get some breakfast on. Maybe we can have a chat then on what you want to do next.'

'Ok, love,' I said. I could get used to this I thought a cup of tea to wake up to and my breakfast made, smashing. I sat myself up, laying a cushion behind me as the pine headboard wasn't as comfortable as my plush, velour one and reached for my cup. The liquid was soothing as it slid down my throat.

I held the cup to my chest warming my hands, it was comforting, and a smile spread across my mouth. Once I had enjoyed the last of the hot liquid, I replaced the cup on its porcelain coaster then took a moment to observe the room around me with its oversized wardrobe, king size bed, bedside cupboards and then I noticed the second door. 'I don't remember that being there,' I said out loud to myself and got up inquisitively to take a look.

'Lois,' I shouted, 'do you know someone has put a toilet in your bedroom?' I called down to her.

She came to the bottom of the wide staircase and quizzically asked, 'What?'

'Do you know someone has put a toilet in your bedroom?' I repeated and she started to laugh. 'I don't think it's funny someone must have been in here whilst I was sleeping,' I declared innocently.

Lois climbed the stairs and followed me back into the bedroom. 'Look,' I said pointing to the door and tentatively stepping back as though the boogey man was about to jump out.

'Oh, my goodness, Emmeline, you're right. What is this trickery that I see before me?' She asked.

'So, you didn't know either?' I asked as she carefully opened the door inch by inch.

'Emmeline, you will never guess what?' She said with a mock surprise, but I bought in to it.

'I don't think I want to know,' I said.

'Ok then,' she said and started to shut the door.

'No, what is it?' I ask.

'You're right, there is a toilet here but there is also a shower at this side,' she states.

'There can't be,' I begin in disbelief. 'A shower as well? I was only asleep for the night, wasn't I?' I asked totally unsure as I had been sleeping very late.

She then fell about laughing. 'Emmeline, this ensuite has been here since I bought the house 15 years ago,' she told me.

'Well, it wasn't there last night, and it hasn't been there all time I have been here,' I tried to reason. At that point, Jack had come upstairs to find out what all the commotion was about.

'Tell grandma how long this ensuite has been here, Jack,' she urged him.

'You have an ensuite in your bedroom, Mum, I never knew that,' he said with a twinkle in his eye and then we all started to laugh.

Once we had eaten breakfast, we decided to sit outside at the picnic table whilst Jack played pirates on the climbing frame that also had a high tower, periscope, climbing wall, ladders, and swings. His random 'aye, aye captain' said to no one in particular made us both laugh. This was the life; sitting chilled, no fear with the people you love and who love you.

'Have you decided what you want to do, Emmeline?' Lois asked.

'What do you mean, love?' I said.

'Well, we only packed enough clothes and things for a few days and Joe is coming home from his school trip today. I was ok on the top bunk the first night and it's been comfortable in Joe's bed for last two nights, but I cannot bedhop indefinity,' she told me.

'Are you wanting me to leave?' I asked feeling a little hurt.

'No, what I mean is, if you are staying longer, we need to get you some more clothes, if you are going home, I need to pack a few things so we can come stay with you for a few days until you feel comfortable being home alone,' she explained.

'No, Love, I am never going back,' I stated. 'Being here as made me realise I have been hiding away living in fear of what they are going to do next, but here, with you and the boys, I feel safe and alive, not just existing.' Lois was taken aback.

'So, what are you saying is you've made the decision and that's it? It's a big decision. Are you sure that you want to leave Grey Gables for good?' She questioned.

'I cannot live there on my own, they won't let me, and if I did, it doesn't bare thinking about what my mental health would be like by the time they have finished with their mind games. So yes I have made a decision, it's time to be free and to live a happy life with you and the boys,' I said.

'So are you saying you want me to clear out the playroom, drive to Grey Gables get your clothes and bring you a bed back here?' She asked me.

'Yes, love, that is exactly what I would like you to do, if that's ok with you and the boys,' I told her.

That afternoon, Jack and Lois cleared everything out of the playroom. Joe's drum kit went into the shed and much to the upset of Jack, all his Lego and toys. The room cleaned then the blue two-tone settee was placed in the bay window.

Jack and Lois then drove over to Grey Gables, dismantled the single bed in the spare room, brought that back and re-erected it then went back for clothes; a rail to put them on, a bedside drawer, bedding and some photos and personal belongings to dress the room. As they emptied the car for the second time, the school rang to say the children were back from Robin Wood, so off Lois went again to collect him.

While Joe told me about all the activities he had been doing, like crate building where they had to work in pairs one standing on a milk crate the other adding more on top of the previous one to see how high they could go, Lois and Jack busied themselves in the "playroom". It was just after 6.15 when Jack came running through as proud as punch.

'Grandma, come and see your new room,' he blurted out excitedly. He then came over, grabbed my hand trying to pull me up.

'Steady, Jack, let granny get up herself then we can all show her,' said Lois.

'I want to have a look too,' said Joe.

Jack led me through to the playroom door then stood aside so I could open the door and get the full effect myself. As I slowly opened the door, I couldn't believe the transformation; it was cosy, bright and homely. There were photos along the windowsill of my sister and I with our husbands at a family gathering, there was my wedding photo, photos of Jeff when he was young, the duvet was white with pink butterfly's and on the bedside table was a hardback book.

As I went closer, I could see that the cover had two toddlers on a miniature motorbike. I picked it up and sat down on the bed as I read the caption on it saying, *It's not WHAT I have in my life but WHO I have in my life that counts.*

I glanced up feasting my eyes on the bundles of love that stood in the doorway with tears in my eyes and was able to murmur, 'Thank you.'

The silence broken, Jack jumped to one side and not wanting to be left out, Joe to the other as Lois knelt in front of me and said, 'Welcome home, Mum.' And I cried tears of absolute joy.

'This is a book that I have been producing for you. It was going to be a present to mark your wedding anniversary, but as it was delivered yesterday, it seems more fitting you should have it now,' she told me.

'Look,' said Jack as he pointed to the bottom of the picture and tracing his finger across the writing as he read, 'A Little Book of Love Full of Treasured Memories.'

I wiped at my nose as he opened the book to the first page not quite ready for what my eyes were about to see. Staring out at me was a photo of my husband and I when he was in hospital. It was the last anniversary we were able to share together. I was overcome by the love they were showing me but also a new wave of grief began to wash over me.

'Come on, boys, let's leave Emmeline to have a look at her book in privacy and let her settle in,' Lois ushered the boys out.

'See you soon, Grandma,' said Joe.

'Let me know when you want a drink, Grandma, and I will get it for you,' said Jack.

As they were leaving the room, Lois turned to me again and repeated, 'Welcome home, Mum.'

'Thank you, darling,' I said. 'It's good to be here,' and she left me to gather my thoughts and to settle myself in.

As I looked through the pages of the book at the expressions of pure joy and wonderment at the world around them, I fell more deeply in love with my two precious grandsons, Jack and Joe. There were ones of them on holiday, in the swimming baths, Joe's first bike, in the park and a funny one with carrier bags knotted on their heads pretending to be me with my transparent plastic rain bonnet on.

There were ones with just me at some of the places we had visited together and on our traditional New Year's Day walk, and there were ones with Jeff and the boys, ones with me and the boys and then there were ones of just Lois and me. The most prominent thing we shared throughout was an intense love that manifested in smiles and generated from somewhere deep within. I then came upon a page with the following quote: *There is no friendship, no love like that of the parent for the child* (Henry Ward Beecher).

Lois had written inside a large red heart next to it, *My love for Jack and Joe. Your love for me x.* I really was truly blessed!

On the very last page was a photograph of Jeff sat in his garden, with his walking stick in front of him, his hands resting on top, his chin upon his hands staring straight into the camera. Underneath Lois had written the inscription she had carved on a bench for him: *In Loving memory of a Beloved Husband, Father and Cherished Grandad.*

I glanced across to my wedding photo on the window ledge and reminisced to a time when we were just starting out together full of promise and back to the book, to today, where I was starting out on another journey but this one was on my own without him.

Chapter 12
The Carer 2016
Happy Holidays

It was Monday, 18 July 2016, and I had driven over to Emmeline's to receive an NHS delivery on her behalf. Whilst there I did a quick clean round, ensured everything was in order and reset the alarm before returning home to pack the car. The boys were so excited at the prospect of spending our first full summer vacation with Emmeline that they had already cleaned the house and were eagerly waiting to set off.

Emmeline still wanted to maintain her independence, so I dropped her at the bank for her to get her holiday money whilst Joe, Jack and I bought sandwiches and refreshments for the journey. On the way, we were all in good spirits and chatting excitedly about the different experiences we hoped to have. We have always tried to respect one another's wishes, so I took the opportunity to remind the boys about having an equally good attitude and approach whether it was someone else's choice of activity or their own.

I have found that this positive approach ensures we continually have enjoyable experience regardless of what adventures we embark on. As always upon our arrival, Joe's responsibility was to take our beloved spaniel, Poppy, for a walk whilst Jack and I emptied the car. It was the essential food bits that went straight into the fridge first, then I put away the clothes that Jack had neatly laid onto each person's bed in turn.

Emmeline went into the bathroom to use the toilet then seated herself on the fawn ribbed fabric chairs at the dining table to enjoy the cup of tea Jack had made whilst I beavered away. Within an hour of arriving, we were linking arms and almost skipping down to the onsite pub "The Larkhams".

We absolutely loved being at Cowden Holiday Park. There was no pressure, we were welcomed with open arms and greeted with love. I got myself a pint,

Emmeline a Malibu with lemonade, Jack a diluted lime cordial and Joe a blackcurrant one.

Once everyone had their drinks and were comfortably seated, I left the boys checking the menu whilst I went through to see "Auntie" Helen to find out what gastronomical delights she had on the "specials" board today. Joe sat eagerly at Emmeline's side hoping to catch a glimpse of his favourite server, "little June", if she was working. Every time we arrived, the minute he clapped eyes on her his little face would light up and he wouldn't be able to stop himself from rushing over to give her a great big hug.

She was a petite lady in her 60s, wore a faded blue smock, and although, she sported a stern expression, once she saw Joe and received his embrace, she could not help herself but to be enveloped in the love he gave.

Joe was like that; he seemed to know instinctively that someone needed a hug, reassurance or a friend. He is a caring, kind and very compassionate young boy who flies a beacon for the lost, hurt and needy. Throughout his education, he has touched the heart of many teachers, particularly with his instinctive responses to the children with special educational needs.

He has a knack of being able to tune in to the tension released through their difficulty coping within the classroom. I have had numerous teachers praise him in his ability to calm a situation, create distracting solutions, devise coping techniques and if all else fails, accompany the individual on a few laps around the hall. He really does have a sixth sense whereas Jack has a sick sense of humour.

I walked into the corridor between the two bars to the little hatch where Auntie Helen and little June could be found chopping, stirring, and plating up food. 'Good evening, ladies, you two look snowed under in here tonight,' I started.

'Hello, love, well you are a welcome sight,' Auntie Helen said, then addressed June. 'Look who it is, June, young Joe will be pleased.'

She turned round from the pot she was serving from with a big smile on her face and said, 'Where is the little terror?'

I told her where we were seated so instead of going through the main door to where customers were seated and I had just come from, she quickly sneaked through the games room outside and then in through the French windows to make him jump for once. Both Auntie Helen and I conspiratorially watched through the glass of the fire door grinning at each other as we heard his shriek of surprise; Little June 1 v Joe 0.

It was heart-warming to witness the loving bond that had been uncharacteristically created by my 9-year-old child with this lady of such a generational gap. The only thing one could see that they had in common was their height.

On returning to the kitchen, I asked Helen what her specials were today.

'Your mother will have belly pork with apple stuffing and fresh veg,' she told me.

'How do you know that, has everything else sold out?' I asked.

'No,' she said confidently 'I just know.'

I memorised the dishes that were on the menu then went back to our table where I related them to Emmeline, 'Today she has veggie burger and chips, belly pork with apple stuffing and fresh veg, lasagne with Garlic bread, hot roast beef sandwich with fries and Mushroom stroganoff with wild rice. Which would you like?' I asked.

'The belly pork with apple stuffing,' she replied without hesitation.

I shook my head in disbelief as a moment later, Auntie Helen brought out her dinner. 'So, did I get it right then?' She asked with a knowing look on her face.

'I honestly don't know how you do it but every single time you know exactly what she will choose,' I said.

As we began eating, I couldn't help notice the other patrons around us nudging each other and nodding towards Emmeline. I was not in the least bit offended nor surprised because this happened every time, we sat down to eat at Larkham's. As I continued to eat, I was not disappointed when I heard the usual remark, 'That little old lady can't possibly eat all that.'

It was true, Auntie Helen was well known for packing rather large portions into her "basket" meals and today was no exception. The interest seemed to gain momentum as other people noticed the attention Emmeline's meal was getting and by the end of it, her little fan club may as well have been taking bets. As soon as she had finished the entire meal, a trickle of applause would emanate, probably out of disbelief and a malibu with lemonade would be sent by an unknown spectator.

At one point or another, I think it was this method that developed our strong friend base and integrated us into their community, Emmeline. She may have only been 8 stone wet through, but did she have an appetite. It became one of the only true measures to indicate when she was unwell.

Once she had finished, I would ask if she wanted anything else and her response was always, 'I don't,' she would emphatically declare.

'Not even ice-cream or Auntie Helen's homemade apple pie?' I would entice her.

'Oh well yes, I think I there's always room for apple pie and ice-cream,' she said. Not one or the other but both.

The next morning, we awoke to a bright sunny day with a sky of clear blue, there wasn't a cloud to be seen. After having showers and a bite to eat, we decided it was a beach day so jumped into the car with a very happy, excitable Poppy and made our way to Mappleton. It was only a short drive of approximately a mile, and although, the boys, Poppy and I had walked it several times, Emmeline was becoming less able, and the heat would also take it out of her.

Once we arrived it seemed that the whole population had the same idea, the small cliff top car park was full and the lane overflowing with cars. Nevertheless, we weaved our way through and only had to wait for a short time before being rewarded with a dog walker returning to their car. Once parked, we sauntered down the steep tarmac drive to the awaiting pleasure of soft, fine sand, the kind that trickles through your fingertips.

There are two parts to the beach, to our left where you walk all the way to Hornsea, or to our right where the beach is a little firmer under foot was where we liked to explore. With Poppy off the lead, the boys their buckets in hand and the warm breeze on our faces, we ambled along the water's edge enjoying the returning splashes of the waves rolling across our feet.

'This is the life,' said Emmeline.

'Yes, this is what makes all the planning, stress of co-ordinating everything and running around all worthwhile,' I agreed.

We walked for a while intermittently throwing pebbles for Poppy to retrieve and then took turns to see who could skim the most hits on the water's surface with flatter stones. We then spent hours collecting pebbles of all shapes and sizes along with searching for fossils that Mappleton is so famous for. It was a carefree, relaxed, enjoyable start to what we hoped was going to be the measure of our whole summer, filled to the brim with more memory making family days.

Three days later, we had a ride over to Danes Dyke with our friend, Pip, and her grandson, Kyle. A secluded area that one can easily miss from the main road. It has a wonderful approach through woodland which opens to a car park offering the use of toilets and a small café.

We parked side by side, Pip helping me to lift out Emmeline's wheelchair which I erected and then assisted her into before applying the safety belt. We began our slow walk through the woods which was terrifyingly much steeper than I had remembered from the previous year, especially with a wheelchair now but at least the tarmacked surface gave Emmeline a smooth ride. Before long, there emerged the most beautiful, enclosed cove of a fine sandy beach.

The area was almost deserted despite the glorious weather and time of year. The boys' outer garments dropped in a heap as a frenzied race ensued, who would be the first one to reach the sea. Their squeals of excitement and pure delight that only children exude in their own uninhibited style filled our ears.

I smiled and remembered what Emmeline had said a couple of days earlier, "This is the life", and to be honest, I couldn't have wished for anything else than sharing this time with her, Pip and the boys.

When the children had dug great trenches that interlocked by gullies, they spent an age fetching water back and forth only for it to be quickly absorbed. This tickled Emmeline immensely who was sat on the side lines with Pip and I literally belly laughing so much she started coughing.

'I think now would be a good time to have lunch, guys,' I shouted across to the exhausted crew of water fillers. 'And I think you could do with a drink, Emmeline,' I continued.

I handed her a bottle of water, but it was far too tight for her to open so Pip lent across and easily popped the top for her. 'Here you are, Mum,' Pip said.

'Show off,' declared Emmeline taking the bottle.

It's funny how Pip was the only one who called her 'mum' and Emmeline had so readily accepted it from the first time we had become friends. Pip may have been pushing six foot and covered in tattoos, but she had the heart of an angel and seemed to genuinely adore Emmeline, who reciprocated this in return. From the outside, it may have seemed an odd relationship but under the surface it consisted of great love, acceptance, and mutual respect.

As we began to unpack the bags of food, Joe suddenly shouted 'charge,' and the three of them darted towards us like bulls at the matador. This created an unexpected shriek from Emmeline much to everyone's amusement. Joe, Jack and Kyle fell softly on to the sand in heaps of laughter.

I dished out their chosen sandwiches, crisps, yogurts and fruit and we sat for a few minutes absorbed by our individual desire to quench our hunger. Then a call from the site came in that Pip was waiting for, to hear about her new lodge. We continued eating only half listening myself, gazing out to the dazzling ripples of sunlight reflecting off the sea when suddenly Pip screamed and pointed behind me.

As we tentatively turned around, we all erupted into a raucous circle of laughter; a little brown and white Jack Russell terrier had sneaked up behind us, pinched Pip's sandwich and was hot hoofing it back to its owner. Pip's mouth was wide open in sheer disbelief, her arms on her lap, the phone in her hand and with the caller still on the other end of the phone shouting, 'Hello are you still there?'

It was another lovely, satisfying day. The only problem we had now was trying to get Emmeline back up the hill in a wheelchair. It was the day I decided chivalry no longer existed as the two of us heaved, struggled and strained against the weight to negotiate our safe return to the car as several men walked past without offering any help at all.

Two days later, on Saturday, it was the Hornsea Carnival. A spectacular affair consisting of wagons dressed on particular themes ridden by local school children, old vehicles, bands playing, majorettes displaying their dazzling baton twisting and throwing, horses groomed with their tails and mains plaited with riders wearing their best attires.

The parade glided through the streets, five deep with supporting bystanders, the children at the front hoping to catch sweets thrown into the crowd or fortunate enough to be handed a lucky bag of pens, pencils, a keyring and pad advertising some new business venture. The excitement bubbled as the thunderous roar of the band stepped ever closer and then just as quickly, it had passed to fulfil the same eagerness of those waiting further along Newbegin and then on to Cliff Road.

We turned and made our way along Cinema Street and across the car park behind the Methodist Church to Hall Garth Park. This was one of Poppy's favourite parks where she loved to scent for squirrels and race after the swallows as they ducked and dived teasing her grounded paws. Today though, she had to stay on the lead as it was full of charity tombola stalls, food carts, beer tents, arts and crafts, an exhibition of old motor bikes, a stage where a band was playing, numerous fairground rides and an area cordoned off for displays of everything you could think of.

Throughout the day, the schedule advertised police dogs with their handlers, Coco, the clown, and his clan, dog obedience shows, horse jumping and of course the majorettes. As we meandered around, our senses exploding with a multitude of aromas, sights and sounds we giggled, played eye spy and feasted upon all that the experience had to offer.

Once we had finished taking in the sights, it was time to explore the rides and as always, we did our customary walk through first then I said, 'Right, guys, come on, which five rides would you like to go on most?' I asked. I usually found that they would choose the same ones so once they had enjoyed them, I would let them pick another one to either go on again or a different one, so they felt that they had got that little bit more.

The one thing I loved about Joe and Jack was that they were always grateful for what they were given they were never "can I have" children as they knew whatever I could give them or was appropriate was freely given. Nor were they ever competitive or ungrateful, like on Christmas morning they appreciated I would be working hard to give them a good day, so never came in to disturb me until 08.30.

They would give each other the chance to open their presents first then take it in turns to open another before we would go downstairs, open a couple from under the tree and have breakfast. They are well known for taking at least a week to open their presents not because they are inundated but because they truly treasure each gift and the person who has bought it for them.

Neither of them wants Christmas to be over in seconds by demolishing a mound of presents, so they choose to savour it and as Jack describes it, Christmas becomes every day of the holidays, where he enjoys the family time, the presents are a bonus.

Jack decided he wanted to go on the dodgems first, then the crazy frog and lastly the cyclone; whereas Joe wanted to go on the same, but he was also looking at the flying carpet, daring himself to have a go. I don't know where he gets his courage from as it was a ride I wouldn't have attempted.

Embroiled in the excitement, compounded by their impeding adrenalin rush, together with the fairground music, flashing lights and the obligatory 'scream if you want to go faster' announcement, they rushed to secure a blue dodgem car emblazoned with the number 12. On the side lines, Emmeline and I marvelled at the deft skill that Jack exhibited as he glided between cars narrowly missing a collision then accelerating as he left a carnage behind him.

It was just as exhilarating as a bystander. The crazy frog had us in fits of laughter as it shook them up and down, firstly going forwards then backwards. It was either going at speed or jerkily hopping both Jack and Joe hanging on to the handrail for dear life each time they went past.

When they came off, they both said in unison, 'We have got to go on that again, it was brilliant!'

Next was the cyclone, which I have to say, was a lot more aggressive than I remembered from my early days but having observed its performance, they were adamant they wanted to give it a go. I am not sure it was their best decision though as poor Jack had to sit on the outside being the older and more robust of the two, so every time the machine catapulted them from one side to the next, Joe was flung into Jack's side.

When the ride came to an end, poor Jack was in tears with Joe apologising profusely that he 'couldn't help it.' We softened the blow with a quick go on hook-a-duck then had to spend a good 10 minutes before being able to choose a prize to go home with. After hotdogs and a drink, the boys decided one last go on the crazy frog was a must before returning to the car.

The next day, we had the pleasure of surprise visitors when Karen and her wife, Shelli, arrived on their way home from a weekend away in Scarborough. We sat out on the decking with snacks and drinks listening to where they had been and then had a walk to show them around the site.

The following day was Monday, 1 August, Pip's birthday. So after taking her our gifts we spent it together at the beach then, in the evening we went out for a meal to Med Mex, along the high street in Hornsea before returning to Larkham's.

On the Tuesday morning, I decided to have a clean whilst the children played out with friends on their bikes and Emmeline flitted from sitting out in the sun, reading or watching tv. I was just about to put the kettle on when I received a call from my neighbour which was very unusual, so I tentatively answered, my heart racing worrying that something had happened at home.

'Hiya, Lois,' Glen began, 'I am sorry to ring you whilst you're on holiday, but a package came for you today and to be honest, love, it looked official,' he said.

I was a little perplexed not really understanding why this should be so urgent enough for him to contact me, so I asked, 'When you say official, Glen, what do you mean?'

'It was stamped with something across the front of it and they wanted me to sign for it,' he informed me.

'Do you have it in front of you or can you get it and read it to me please?' I asked.

'I am sorry, Lois, but I didn't like the look of it and didn't want to accept responsibility. As I said it looked official and from what I could see it contained some formal documents,' he said.

There was absolutely nothing I was expecting so I could not fathom what this unknown package either contained or ascertain its importance to interrupt our holiday.

'Lois, I really think you ought to come back and get it from the sorting office,' he went on.

'Seriously, you think it is something that important for me to do a 150 mile round trip?' I asked.

'Yes, it is, Lois. I honestly think you must,' he urged me.

I ended the call quite perplexed and a little unsure of what I should do. A part of me thought nothing was so important for me to interrupt our holidays that couldn't wait, and besides I didn't want to waste time on a return trip home. However, the concern in Glen's voice had unnerved me and I knew he wouldn't have contacted me unnecessarily.

I chewed it over briefly whilst I finished making Emmeline and I a drink. I placed the cups on a little side table along with an egg custard on a saucer for each of us before divulging to Emmeline my conversation with Glen. We were still contemplating the facts and surmising what the package could contain when the boys returned.

I took the opportunity to assess their feelings but didn't want to impede upon their enjoyment by making them sit unnecessarily in the car for 4 hours, on what was speculated as being yet another hot day. Inevitably, they wanted to stay with friends who had finally arrived today nor was Emmeline impressed with leaving so I called across to Jim and Lynn's, my neighbours, and arranged for them to manage things in my absence.

Emmeline was more than capable of getting a shower and making breakfast for herself and so were the boys, so to ensure I kept the disturbance to everyone at a minimum once they were in bed, I drove home that night so I could collect the package first thing and be home before lunch. Well, that was the plan, little did I know what horror was awaiting me.

Chapter 13
The Carer 2016
The Package

When I woke the next morning, I was a little confused and it took me a moment or two to get my bearings, firstly because I was in a different bedroom then also, I had to remind myself why the house was so quiet. Whilst here I decided to contact the doctor and get an appointment as I had been feeling ill for months and plagued with migraines.

I also rang Jack to make sure all was well in Hornsea, then spoke to Lynn whilst I busied myself rushing for my appointment. When I got there, my test results showed I had fibroids in my womb and because they were causing severe anaemia, she was referring me to a gynaecologist at Barnsley hospital for the earliest appointment 26 September. She then gave me a prescription to take 3 iron tablets per day, so I guess it was a good job I had taken the time to check in with her.

That is the problem when you are a carer, your individual becomes the centre of your universe and in ensuring their health, appointments and wellbeing are taken care of, you tend to undervalue your own health and needs.

I remember when I was dealing with an issue for Emmeline and I had to rush off apologising to the boys because they also needed my attention. It broke my heart when a young 12-year-old Jack said, "It's ok, Mum, I know grandma comes first". This is when things are grossly unfair, I have the youngest children of the "family"; I was the only single parent but not one person has ever offered to give the slightest ounce of help, ever.

And to add insult to injury, I then find out (from Sarah) Ruby has brainwashed herself into believing I have stopped her from seeing Emmeline. If it wasn't so serious it would be laughable. It never ceases to amaze me the excuses people give themselves for basically not caring. At least be honest with yourself.

If you are incapable of showing the care, love, and compassion that's required or you simply do not want to devote the time to engage with that person have the balls to say it. You can never make someone else your excuse for neglecting another human being. We all have choices and decisions to make there are no if's or but's you choose to deny yourself the pleasure of their company, full stop.

I remember having a conversation with Ruby after one of her tirades of abuse when she told me she wasn't jealous of mine and Emmeline's relationship. I thought it a weird statement to make at the time, one a psychologist would probably have a field day analysing the truth behind. Anyway, I specifically told Ruby that if she had a problem with me that was fine, all I asked is that she let me know when she was visiting Emmeline, and I would gladly leave her to it and take a well-earned day off.

Absolutely no problem. Needless to say, she never arranged anything then later took umbrage because Emmeline hadn't sent her son a birthday card. This wasn't because she was being mean or that she had forgotten, the year before Emmeline had sent one with a cheque in it, but Ruby had refused to cash it nor the one that I had sent either.

When I had collected the prescription, I checked I had definitely got the card the postman had left regarding my package and the suitable identification necessary, then set off to fetch it. When I arrived, I found a parking space then went into the tiny reception area where a young man with a fuzzy ginger beard carrying a hand-held device came out to attend to me.

He used the device to scan the card then went off on his merry way to retrieve it from a stack of shelves. As I stood there my heart racing, wondering if this was going to be a pinnacle moment in time he returned with a large thick brown envelope. So, this was the offensive package I had come all the way back from Hornsea for?

It suddenly felt like it had been a completely wasted journey. He handed it to me, I took it and then returned to the car. My curiosity got the better of me and I decided to open it and take a cursory look.

Wow; emotions can be such powerful responses to the occurrences or people around us but equally it depends upon our investment in those circumstances in which we are reacting. For instance, a child will have a temper tantrum because they cannot get their own way, having no understanding of the full implications of a situation. They simply react in the only way they know how or have been taught.

As an adult, we are called to behave in a more socially acceptable manner, to think things through, rationalise the situation then choose the most appropriate solution. Logically and rationally, we have more than the capability. However, when we fail to take the emotional element out, we tend to respond in the moment through feelings and not necessarily what we want long term.

It's a bit like a teenager slamming the door in her first love's face and screeching 'don't ever come back', then instantly regretting it. Words are equally as powerful and once said they cannot be retracted a little like a secret. It reminds me of the most prominent sign at Grey Gables. *Letting the CAT OUT of the bag is a LOT easier than PUTTING it BACK in again.*

One thing Emmeline has always wanted is for me to keep her counsel and to recognise that any information I have been party to is confidential and privileged which I have wholeheartedly accepted and always honoured. So, sitting there in a car park in the middle of Dewsbury being informed that allegations had been made against me regarding the misappropriation of funds along with concerns being raised surrounding her care, I was shellshocked.

This was the most heart wrenching, despicable, heinous crime for Ruby and Kelly to commit against me to make false allegations to the Office of Public Guardian. It did not make it any less palatable being aware that it had coincided with the expiration of HIS licence and that in 3 days it would have been dad's birthday. So, this is what the unknown attack had become that Sarah had warned me they had been planning, earlier in the year.

There are certain things I pride myself on and they are my honesty, integrity, openness, and selflessness. Although, I knew it was to disarm, to distress, emotionally cripple and harm me to the core of my being, I simply could not just set aside my feelings. I was absolutely devastated that not only could someone be vile enough to make such unfounded allegations, but that these were my siblings who could find nothing better to do with their time.

Judging by the extensive list served, they must have met on numerous occasions plotting, scheming, and colluding with one another, completely disregarding the full implications their acts would have on Emmeline, my young boys or myself. Their heartless exploits for me displayed a total disconnection from reality manifested through a misplaced revengeful, hatred and bitter contempt for the person whose only crime was to step into the gap to care full time for the needs of their mother. As Leanne had said:

"Both Ruby and Kelly have spent their lives trying to bring you down through their own deep-rooted bitterness and hatred. It's a shame they don't put their efforts in to building relationships instead of destroying them".

I could not comprehend why they did not endeavour to cohesively support Emmeline's everyday living, to demonstrate their love for her and simply enjoy the pleasure of their mother instead of trying to ruin her mental health. It then began to dawn on me, maybe Emmeline had been right in her observations over the past few months regarding being watched, followed and things being moved to create paranoia thus disturbing her mental health and wellbeing.

Afterall something had caused this rapid deterioration and perhaps this had been the prelude to the finale of attempting to gain control of Emmeline's estate and knowledge of her final wishes.

I sat there for some moments wondering how on earth their hatred had delved to such an all new low and felt sick at the thought of them feeling so proud of themselves at the devastation they had chosen to cause. Here I was devoting my every waking hour to meet the needs of Emmeline. I didn't moan about it, I didn't feel sorry for myself, I didn't get paid for it and nor did I expect anything from anyone else.

Now I had opened my home up to her that I was contemplating selling or putting in part exchange at great expense to myself simply to restore her mental health and wellbeing. Why? Because my love for her ran so deep, it was pure and unconditional. The question I couldn't find the answer to was WHY did they have so much hate in their souls to commit such an evil act against me?

As Emmeline had said so many times, "What have I done to make them hate me so much?" I could only ever reassure her that she had done nothing. As far as I was concerned, Emmeline had been there for each of us throughout our lives whether it was through ill health, paying off a mortgage, going to musicals that she had no interest in, looking after her grandchildren or just by being supportive in times of need.

She had played a part in everyone's lives and had always been selfless, honest, caring and loving the real issues was within themselves. It is another debate for nurture or nature?

I decided to get a coffee and to sit down and read the document, but it wasn't something I could do in a public place with such raw emotions, I didn't trust myself. I also didn't want to get a parking ticket for staying too long or walking across the road and leaving my car in the sorting office car park, so I drove across and parked in Asda. I collected myself together and walked through the automatic doors, my head down to conceal my red and now blotching face and made my way to the toilets.

After splashing some refreshing cold water on my face, I took a deep breath examined myself in the mirror and decided I would have to do, then made my way into the little cafe. I was relieved to see there was only one lady in front of me so hopefully I could be in, out and back to the safety of my car in no time. That was until her friend joined her from a seat in the corner and proceeded to bark orders to her child sat crying in a highchair, displeased at suddenly being left alone.

She took an age to order not knowing what she wanted, all the time having the superpower of being able to ignore the child's upset that had escalated to distressing screams. My head was throbbing, and I was just about to turn round and go when she finally received her change, picked her tray up and moved on. I got an americano then quickly made my way back out through the automatic doors to a welcoming summer breeze, found my car and breathed.

I decided to put some distance between the annoying mother and screaming child and started the engine, but on looking down realised I would need fuel if I was going to make it back to Hornsea. Calling at the self-service station on my way out of Asda, I decided I needed to have a place of safety so I drove to Grey Gables; at least I could check everything was ok whilst reading the document in private.

I glanced to the passenger seat to the unoffending looking package, but now knowing what it contained, I felt instant sickness, swallowing repeatedly just in case any bile rose. I arrived at Grey Gables a few moments later, not relishing what the whole contents of the package would reveal, yet knowing I was right; this was a pinnacle moment and there would be no going back once I had read it. I would soon become an only child.

Chapter 14
The Carer 2016
False Allegations

I locked my car and walked along the drive to the side door of Grey Gables, my feet crunching beneath the coarse, gravel drive. As I opened the door, the chill that greeted me was surprising, especially as the day was so hot and humid. It seemed dark and dingy and there was a faint smell of damp emanating from the kitchen; not the welcome I wanted under the circumstances.

Absentmindedly, I allowed the door to shut behind me and dropped the envelope I had clasped to my chest like it was the precious memoirs of a film star. As I approached the sink, I heard a dripping sound, at first believing it to be the tap I raised the blinds only then noticing a huge puddle of water had collected on the draining board and had overspilled to the floor. It was coming from upstairs; this was all I needed.

Feeling the pang of annoyance, I turned to make my way upstairs then heard the alarm signalling it was about to announce to the neighbourhood it had an unwelcome visitor. I quickly ran into the back to disarm its awakened attack, punching in the code without conscious thought nor feeling, I was numb and detached.

When I located the source of the water, I found that the tap had been dripping continually all the time we had been away (10 days), and for some reason Emmeline had left the plug in, so the sink was full, and it had gradually seeped its way through the roof to the kitchen below. As I removed the plug to let the excess water drain away, it reminded me of the film called Lost for Words with Thora Hird, where she blocked all the ends of the taps with toilet paper and applied the plugs to stop bugs coming through.

Tired and drained, I mopped up the remnants of the overspill then made my way back downstairs to concentrate upon the reason I had arrived here in the first place. Sat on the table looking all unassuming was the envelope exactly where I had left it. In reality, it represented a time bomb awaiting its audience and now here I was unable to ignore it any longer. I steeled myself as I carefully lifted it and took a seat to see what awaited my fate.

As I read, I couldn't help wondering who these people were for them to make such unfounded claims and to cast ridiculous aspersions; that was the real crime. It wasn't lost on me that the public office for the Power of Attorney is there to protect the vulnerable and ensure they stay in control to make important decisions about their health and finance for themselves.

I was appointed by Emmeline because she knew she could trust me unswervingly to maintain her complete independence, control and for her wishes to be heard and actioned for as long as possible. She knew I would put measures in place to promote her choices, hence I encouraged her to produce a "living will", so if she was unable to communicate effectively, there was no doubt what she wanted.

She had done this in advance of sound mind the year before because she knew that the vultures would circle to devour, and she was adamant she would stay in control. In effect it would also protect me because as her power of attorney, I had to follow her wishes and work in her best interest and they could not disregard it or take over.

Emmeline has had it on the money with each decision she has made because everything she had told me they would do have been worse than even she could ever have imagined. What kind of human being torments, bullies and plays mind games against a defenceless, elderly lady with dementia? Worse still, their own mother. I had never come across anything so despicable.

I was hurt about what they were saying about me but I was angry they were using the public office to vilify my reputation so they could disarm me and activate what they were accusing me of. Well, not on my watch!

When I left Grey Gables I decided to have a walk around the block just to gather myself so I could try to approach the staff at the bank in a less emotional state, however this fell by the wayside when I bumped into Leanne.

'Hey, stranger, what's wrong, you look like you have lost a fiver and found a penny,' she addressed me but I neither saw her nor heard.

'Lois, hey are you ok?' She asked now really concerned.

I glanced up but only managed a weak smile. She guided me to the nearest bench, and I willingly obeyed no fight left in me. Once seated, she took my hand and asked, 'It's not Emmeline, is it?'

'No,' I started, 'well, yes in a way.' I sighed, closing my eyes to stop them from filling, took a deep breath then exhaled slowly before letting the whole story spill out.

'Shit, what is wrong with these people?' She said.

'I know but now I have got to defend myself to prove my innocence, not them having to prove what lies they are saying are true. It seems anyone can say what they want, and it's taken as red without question regardless of the hell they put you through, as if I haven't got enough to cope with,' I said.

'You're right, of course you are but think of it from another angle. They have just shown you their hand not to mention how low they are prepared to sink. It would have been a whole lot worse if they had waited until something happened to Emmeline,' she said.

'How could it have been worse? Emmeline now knows how little they think of her and what they will do to hurt her,' I moaned.

'No, Lois, they are doing it to hurt you; to remove you as her power of attorney, then they can step in and get control,' she said.

'So, what is Emmeline; collateral damage?' I was getting angry.

'Yes, she is but they don't care. It's one thing to think something, another to put a plan together and a whole new ballgame to put it into action. It is done with malicious intent when you knowingly put those lies into writing and no doubt during the investigation they will be interviewed. Now that will take balls to have to sit face to face and lie,' she reasoned.

'Both you and I know Ruby will have already made herself believe it's true and Kelly, "the actress", will just put on her show like it's a role she is playing,' I said.

'Maybe, but let's face it, if she was any good, she would have got somewhere in the industry. The judge saw through her and so will the investigator,' she reassured me.

I sat for a minute thinking about what she had said, and I had to admit she did have a point. There was always a fake inauthenticity when she attempted to portray something she was not.

'Besides, Lois, they have just made their biggest mistake, and shown you their hand too early,' she said.

'I don't understand what you mean,' I admitted.

'If they had done this when something had happened to Emmeline, it would have floored you because you would have been grieving, so at your weakest,' she started.

'I guess,' I said.

'When you are angry, you are at your strongest, so use that anger and defeat them.'

'I know,' I said. 'But this is a government body that they are using to fight their battle, one that should be protecting us.'

'They are there to protect Emmeline's interests, Lois, regardless of your innocence; they have to do their job and investigate,' she wisely reminded me.

'In the meantime, it's at the expense of the public purse, maybe they should have to cover the costs of their handiwork using it to bully and vilify me?' I suggested.

'Either way, Lois, anyone who has encountered you knows you are honest to the core and this investigation will expose these lies and vindicate you completely,' she reassured me.

After we had said our goodbyes, I sat a moment longer to let her words sink in, then made my way to the bank to obtain the requested 4 years of statements concerning Emmeline's accounts. As I tried to explain the reason of why I needed these, I was suddenly overcome, perhaps saying it out loud here at the bank had somehow made it real and I completely broke down.

The lady behind the counter was shocked. 'Oh my goodness, Lois, I cannot believe out of all the people we have coming in here that someone has said that about you!' She was as upset as I was.

I could barely speak as I sobbed asking her for the documents. It felt like I was betraying Emmeline despite being named on her account, which had only taken place as a precaution in case she was ever unable to sort out her own finances. I had not been privy to her personal details in this way, nor did I want to be here having to gain access to them.

However, I only had 10 days to answer the allegations, provide the statements, to try a prove my innocence then return the documentation, so I had no choice as my family were still in Hornsea. There is nothing like being under pressure, but I had found when studying that this is when I give my best, and like Leanne had said, I am also at my best when I am angry. So I had a point to prove and I was going to make it, with bells on.

Chapter 15
The Carer 2016
Returning to Hornsea

As I left the bank, my mind a whirl of mixed thoughts and emotions. I felt as though I had just got off the waltzer and it had been spun violently by one of the fairground personnel. I was mentally and emotionally drained but still had to drive to Hornsea.

My family eagerly awaiting me to continue with our summer holidays but there was little chance of that now. I returned to my car and made my way towards the M1 motorway and once I had accessed the M62 at junction 42, I decided to phone Laura. She has always brought calm to my storm, being able to rationalise a situation along with being the voice of reason.

'Hi, Laura, it's me. Are you free to talk?' I asked.

'Yes, love, is everything ok you sound really upset?' Laura said.

'I am beyond upset,' I began. 'I am on the car phone on my way back to Hornsea.'

'On your way BACK to Hornsea?' She asked surprised.

'Yeah, it's a long story,' I said and then the events of the last 24 hours or so unfolded.

'Holy Shit! You must be joking me!' She exclaimed.

'I wish I was,' I said. 'I have my laptop in the car, and I am on my way back now to collate some supporting evidence to put together with the document they want me to fill out. I have to return the completed form so it arrives by next Friday. I don't feel like I have a lot of time to do it justice by any stretch of the imagination.' I told her.

'Oh, Lois, I am so sorry. This is appalling even by their standards. What kind of people take pleasure in maliciously bringing harm to others? I feel absolutely devastated for you. I make no wonder you are so upset,' she offered.

'I cannot help thinking what on earth has gone wrong in their make-up for them to think that this is normal, socially acceptable behaviour?'

'It's depraved to hide behind a government body that's supposed to help the vulnerable, and use it to cause devastation upon the very people they are there to protect is twisted,' she said.

'That is exactly what makes me so cross. I know they will have to go through their procedures but in the meantime, the stress and upset that they cause is immeasurable, both to Emmeline the boys and myself,' I stated.

'How are they? Have you told them what is happening yet?' She asked.

'No, unfortunately, I have that displeasure to come and let's face it, with this black cloud hanging over us, it will have a huge impact on us all. It is so frustrating as this is the first time Emmeline has agreed to come away with us for the whole summer, not to mention having just got her back on an even keel. Goodness knows what this is going to do to her,' I said disheartened.

'That would probably be my biggest concern. After the last hospitalisation, her complete breakdown and being unsafe to live alone, this is the last thing she needs. It could send her over the edge completely, Lois,' she said.

'In all honesty, Laura, you're right, that IS my biggest concern. It has been hard enough getting through the past 3 months with the extreme behaviours, barricading the door, hallucinations then trying to stabilise her again. My fear is that after another onslaught of this magnitude, I will not be able to get her back.'

'She has just started feeling good about life again, feeling safe and looking forward to a future with the boys and me. It doesn't bare thinking about,' I admitted to her.

'How can they be so cruel, and to their own mother? I would give my last breath to spend another hour with my mum but here they are wilfully trying to destroy their mother and more than likely put her in an early grave,' Laura said.

'Maybe that is their intentions, who knows. As Leanne said they are greedy and it's all about money for them. And, not forgetting what Sarah told me that Ruby "cannot wait until something happens to Emmeline as Kelly is gunning for me",' I reminded Laura.

'Heartless, they don't deserve your time or your tears, Lois,' Laura advised me.

'I know and when I think that we all grew up in the same household together, it just cripples me to think that they could do this to me, to my children and to Emmeline. What has happened to them that they would become so devoid of any ounce of humanity? It's such crazy, outlandish behaviour that it is scary,' I told her.

'I knew from the conversations I had with Ruby when she used to come out with us that she wasn't fully wired. Some of the things she would say about her ex-husband, the allegations she was making, and the constant talk of the divorce showed what a bitter and angry person she was under the surface. Then there was the way in which she tried to cause friction between us all and bring division so she could outcast you and take your place.'

'Did she think that we didn't know you well enough that we would believe her lies or that we couldn't see the mind games she was trying to play?' She spoke.

'Yes, but it worked with Darren. He listened to her lies and fell hook line and sinker,' I pointed out.

'You're right,' she said, 'and yes it was hurtful and yes, he was stupid, but he did see her for what she was in the end.'

'You say that, but did he really?' I asked.

'Yes, Lois, he did. I admit it took him a couple of years and yes, he was an absolute shit for not believing in you and knowing you well enough to dismiss her rubbish as soon as it started. But you know Darren, he wasn't thinking with his brain,' Laura reminded me.

'I know how manipulative she can be; she even had her own kid thinking they were going to move into his home after her divorce came through! Freaky,' I declared.

'She was so jealous of you, Lois, that she wanted to be you, to have your lifestyle because she had nothing else going for her,' Laura told me. 'Darren soon cut ties when she started asking him for money and then he didn't see her for dust.'

'But I included her in every aspect of my life; coming up to Darren's with me, socialising with you guys. I opened up my home to her just so she wouldn't feel like she was on the outside looking in. You don't then try to move your way in, take over and extract the person from their own life that's going out of their way to help you, that's plain crazy,' I was flabbergasted.

'They say that copying or mirroring a person is supposed to be a huge form of flattery,' she jokingly said.

'Flattery?' I screeched. 'Goodness me, Laura, it borders on the film *Single White Females*. It's an all-new level of crazy,' I said.

I was now just coming under the Humber bridge heading towards the town centre on the dual carriageway, so thanked Laura for her support and got off the phone so I could concentrate on the building traffic. Surprisingly, it was a swift passage along the ring road and I was able to move through, drive towards Preston and on to the country roads that I enjoyed so much.

By the time I had reached Aldborough, I had processed my conversation with Laura and was beginning to think about how I was going to convey our new predicament to Emmeline and the boys. Approximately 10 minutes later, I was pulling into the gateway of Cowden Holiday Park with its freshly cut, manicured gardens, sleek rows of mobile homes with a variety of cars set on their tarmacked drives and the glorious sunshine was still beaming down.

Boy, it was so good to be back. I loved the peace, tranquillity, and spatial aspect of my little haven of escapism.

As I drove along Eutopia drive, I could see Dave watering his brightly coloured flowerbeds, there was Jan pegging out her washing and Vanessa was sat reading her book laid back on her rattan sun lounger. They each glanced up at the sound of my car passing, giving a nod or wave of a welcoming acknowledgement. Yes, I loved my life here where everyone minded their own business and greeted you with fondness. It felt a world away from the harsh reality of home.

Chapter 16
Emmeline 2016
Happy Holidays (Part 2)

If I am honest, I had always expected that Lois and the boys would come and live with me; after all my house was so much larger and afforded the space for us to integrate more cohesively as a family unit. I had never contemplated ever leaving Grey Gables, but it had been impossible for me to stay, so moving in with Lois and the boys wasn't a hard decision, it had become my only option.

I realise for Lois it was probably a major shock as ultimately it was sprung upon her, however she graciously welcomed me with open arms. I settled in quickly although when I was left to my own devices even if she was only taking the boys to school, I did become quite anxious and would empty the drawers on to the settee looking for items I thought I had lost.

Even after the briefest of times Lois would return and the house looked like a bomb had hit it, so she would make me a cuppa, sit me at the table then systematically put everything back. Lois contacted the social worker to ensure any needs I had, like aides and adaptations, were provided.

She had a wooden handrail installed to assist me to get up and down the stairs, a bath seat that raised itself up then lowered me in and out of the bath, smoke alarms, carbon monoxide alarms, a medi-care monitor with a pendant in case I required assistance; an extra step into my bedroom as it was a little steep for me and a metal railing outside for my safety in and out of the house.

As if this wasn't enough, she then re-instated the downstairs toilet and sink so that I wouldn't have to keep going up and down the stairs. Yes, I was definitely being taken care of and nothing was too much trouble.

As the days and weeks rolled by, we neared the end of the school term and our impending summer vacation. I don't know who was the most excited, the boys, me, or Poppy, the dog. It was cute when Jack would ask her, 'Is Poppy going on her hodilays?' and she would cock her head to one side then run round in circles barking excitedly at the door as if it was time to set off immediately.

It's funny how words become part of your everyday vocabulary. As a little boy, Jack had said many words incorrectly like diveo for video, hodilays for holiday, pamshoo for shampoo or plocieman for policeman are just some examples and here we were, years later still saying the word "hodilays". On the last day of school, Lois dropped the boys off then returned to take me to Asda so we could buy the essentials for the first few days, things like milk, bread, vegetables, cheese, butter etc.

Luckily, not far from where we were staying, there is a large Tesco in one direction and Asda in the other so we only needed to get some bits as I knew as soon as we got there, we would be going down to see Auntie Helen at Larkhams. I loved going there. She did the most fantastic basket meals and packed so much in, you were always stuffed but I always made room for a bit of her delicious home-made apple pie and ice-cream!

When we returned to the house, Lois set about packing. It was quite a strategic operation; she would put her things into one bag, then place Jack's on top with Joe's next so that when we got to the other side Jack could place them on the appropriate beds.

'How are you feeling about being away for the whole summer, Emmeline?' Lois asked me.

'Do you know, love, I am right looking forward to it,' I told her. 'I feel like it's a whole new chapter: the experience of coming to live here, being part of everything you and the boys do and then having the summer by the sea. I cannot think of anything better than getting away and putting the last few months behind us,' I finished.

'I am glad, Emmeline, it was obvious things were getting too much for you and I told you right at the beginning of this journey together that I would be honest with you and always work in your best interests. Suggesting we pack a bag for a few nights was primarily to give you the space and time away from the situation so you could relax, sleep and be able to consider things in a different environment,' Lois told me.

'So, you didn't expect me to say I was never going back then?' I asked her.

'To be honest, no. It never entered my head I just thought you needed some respite and being at Grey Gables had affected you to such a degree. I was worried for your mental health and well-being. I couldn't sit back and do nothing. I had to do something and immediately,' Lois said.

'And now look at us, going on holiday for the whole summer,' I said really chuffed.

'You sound excited,' she declared.

'I am,' I told her. 'I can think of nothing better than breathing in the sea air, enjoying Auntie Helen's cooking, seeing Pip, taking walks along the beach, collecting pebbles, taking Poppy to the park and enjoying days out. And, I have the whole summer to do it in, no rush, no stress; just you, me and the boys. It's going to be smashing!' I gushed as I really was looking forward to every minute.

Once the bags were packed and in the car, Lois called over to Grey Gables to check everything was ok and to inform the neighbours that we were going to be away for the 6-week holidays; thankfully they kindly offered to keep an eye on the place. Whilst she was out, the boys arrived home from school having been collected by her friend, Sam. I had learnt that Lois took all the children to school, and Sam picked them up.

So as soon as they arrived back, they got changed and we set about doing a quick tidy up so we could set off as soon as Lois returned.

We were all about to set off when Lois said, 'Right, Jack, let's go through the checklist.'

'Keys for the caravan?' Jack asked.

'Check,' Lois said scrambling in the cup holder and dangling them in the air.

'Diesel?' He asked.

'Check,' she replied.

'Food?' Joe chimed in.

'Yes, we have food, love, you won't starve,' Lois said, everyone laughing.

'Trust you to think of your stomach,' I said.

'But do we have anything to eat for the journey?' Joe continued.

'Not yet, but I can pick something up enroute,' Lois told him.

'Phone…and charger?' Jack asked.

'Damn,' Lois said. 'It's still plugged in, in the hallway,' and she quickly jumped out of the car and raced inside.

'It's a good job she has you, Jack, or she would lose her head if it wasn't screwed on,' I laughed.

'And me,' said Joe.

'Yes, love, and you,' I reassured him.

When Lois got back in the car with the phone and charger, it was time to set off when jack suddenly said, 'Have you got your card, Mum?'

'Yes, love, it is in the back of my phone case so it's a good job you reminded me to get my phone!' Lois told him.

'Oh, speaking of money, Lois, I haven't got any,' I said quite dismayed.

'It doesn't matter, Emmeline,' Lois began. 'I can just use my card.'

'Oh no, love, that wouldn't be right. I am not living off you. Can we stop at the bank please?'

We drove over to Ossett and whilst I went in to get some money for my holidays, Jack and Joe happily rushed to the little bakery with Lois to get sandwiches, crisps and drinks and then it really was time to set off. I felt excited, like a child going off on an adventure with my best friends as in the books by Enid Blyton "The Famous Five", including Poppy, the dog.

I enjoyed the journey being happy to just sit and watch the world go by as we ate our sandwiches and I noted the landmarks along the way; Xscape was ¼ of the way then there was a huge bridge that marked ½ way, next the Humber bridge which was ¾ and another half hour later, we were turning into the gateway of Cowden Holiday Park. It's funny how a sense of calmness seems to wash over you every time you enter that gateway; it's a little piece of paradise.

The sun was shining, the birds were singing. Poppy was awoken as if her inbuilt satnav had registered "you have reached your destination" and so this marked the start of our hodilays.

I always loved the way Joe and Jack immediately went on to autopilot. They each had their own individual responsibilities so as soon as the car stopped, they were out and they just got on with them, there was never any grumbling. That was the thing about Lois, she had always been a single parent; something her dad and I worried terribly about but she never let it stop her and the boy's living life to the fullest.

She "cracked the whip" as her dad always said. She was fair, discussed with the boys where they were going wrong and put them on the right track; treating them as people rather than dismissing them as children. She was never heavy handed with them, she treated them equally and encouraged them to be self-sufficient, helpful, kind and caring. This style had obviously paid off because they were always respectful, were complimented constantly on their impeccable behaviour and were happy to be part of the team.

I felt really proud not only of them but also of Lois, I felt that I must have got something right. They all worked together whilst I used the bathroom and then I sat at the dining table and had a cuppa. As I sat there, I was secretly contemplating what delights Auntie Helen would have for me.

I might have had a sandwich on the drive here, but it was only to put me on until I could savour one of her meals. 'I hope she has pork with apple stuffing on tonight.'

Over the next few days, we had a ball going to Danes Dyke where a little dog pinched Pip's sandwich which was hilarious, but it wasn't so funny going back up the steep hill afterwards. I was terrified I was going to roll down backwards. We had walks along the beach, the freedom of the open expanse the waves lapping the shore, collecting pebbles and the shrieks of delight at Poppy jumping in and out of the water.

For the first time I was able to enjoy the electric atmosphere of the Hornsea Carnival, it was amazing there were so many people here. Then to my astonishment, I found Hall Garth Park, jam-packed with stalls and rides. It was a wonderful family filled day of love, laughter and an absolute pleasure.

It was so good to be here, I felt alive again and a million miles from the negative, mind-bending torment of back home. Then one day as the boys were out playing, Lois was busy making a cuppa so we could have the little custards we had got from Tesco's when she got an unexpected phone call from Glen, her neighbour.

When she came back into the lounge there was a sombre look on her face and she seemed quite puzzled from the snippets I had overheard. She set down the cups and the custards then proceeded to relay the conversation she had just had.

'That seems a bit weird, Lois,' I ventured. 'How on earth can Glen tell from the package that it is so important you need to travel all the way home for it?'

'I don't know, but it's got me a bit worried. I mean something must have registered with him for him to even ring me to tell me about it, never mind for him to think it requires my immediate attention,' Lois told me.

'So, what are you going to do?' I asked. 'It seems a shame for us to pack up and have to go all the way back,' I stated.

'I agree,' said Lois. 'the last thing I want to do is to spoil it for everyone else dragging you all home.'

'If you think it is imperative you go, maybe I could stay and look after the boys, after all their friends have only just arrived so they are not going to want to leave them,' I offered.

'You're right, they will not appreciate being stuck in the car for 4 hours just to go there and back, especially if it turns out to be something and nothing,' she looked pensive.

'What?' I asked. When she said nothing, it dawned on me that she didn't want to leave me in charge. 'You don't think I am up to looking after them, do you?' I continued.

'It is about my being responsible for all of you, Emmeline, and ensuring you are all taken care of and stay safe whilst I'm not here. Last thing I want to be doing is worrying about what's happening here or of being under pressure to get back as soon as possible and end up having an accident,' she admitted.

'That is fair enough, love,' I told her.

'I will have a chat with Lynn and Jim to see if she wouldn't mind coming over if I go and then I will make a decision,' Lois said and popped across to the beautiful lodge opposite that they owned. On her return, Lois told me they had decided the best option would be for Lois to go tonight once everyone was sleeping, then Lynn would come over first thing in the morning to keep me company until she came back. I was suited with that as I have always enjoyed a good chinwag and a cuppa with Lynn.

The next day when I awoke, I could hear the faint chatter of the boys who had already been showered and were sat out on the decking with Lynn enjoying their breakfast in the sun. It was a lovely outlook as our home was facing the opposite direction to the rest of the park. We were looking on to the greenery of the woodland with Mappleton Church spire protruding out of the tops of the trees.

In the distance I could see the huge wind turbines and became aware of the hum of a tractor harvesting in a nearby field competing with the rumbling of the odd vehicle along the country lane. I stood at the doorway marvelling on all that there was to enjoy, even the patches of midges in the humid air of what promised to be yet another hot sunny day.

'Hello, sleepyhead,' said Jack. I glanced in his direction and just smiled at his greeting.

'Good morning, Emmeline, would you like a cup of tea and maybe some toast and marmalade?' Lynn offered.

'That would be lovely, thank you, Lynn. Where is Lois?' I asked.

Realising I had forgotten, Lynn kindly said, 'She has just nipped out. I was just enjoying sitting here with the boys,' she said.

'Mind if I join you?' I asked.

'Of course not, here take my seat,' Lynn said as she got up and went in to make me a cup of tea and some toast.

The boys sat for a little while with us telling Lynn all about the days out we had enjoyed since arriving, and then they made their way inside to wash the breakfast dishes before collecting their bikes and peddling off as fast as they could to meet their friends. Lynn and I sat for a while simply enjoying the sun on our faces and then she handed me the morning newspaper she had brought over to peruse.

The one thing about being at Hornsea was I could completely relax, recharge my batteries and know that there was sufficient distance between home and here that I didn't have to worry about a thing. That was until Lois pulled up on the drive and disclosed the contents of her package.

Chapter 17
The Carer 2016
The Allegations

When I approached our plot and saw Lynn with Emmeline on the decking, my heart swelled with love, but my stomach knotted like an old man's hankie. I was about to blow her world apart. Why was this happening? In 3 days' time, we were supposed to be celebrating what would have been dad's birthday and going to Mr Moo's for an ice-cream; a place he loved where we could remember him and our time together.

Yet here I was with the weight of the world on my shoulders, wondering how the hell I was going to tell her what two of her children had done now. As soon as Lynn saw me, she instinctively knew it was bad so made an excuse to Emmeline about making us all a drink. I greeted Emmeline and followed Lynn into the kitchen.

'From the look on your face I gather it was a good job you went home, Lois!' Lynn quizzed.

'Basically two of my siblings have made the most outlandish allegations to the office of public guardian about my care and management of Emmeline's funds, and I have the nigh on impossible task of answering to them and posting it back in 7 days, to ensure to it arrives by next Friday,' I put it in a nutshell.

'Oh, my goodness what a shambolic state of affairs. So, where are these people who can sit in judgement. Where is their contribution to their mother's care?' She asked.

'It is like the dementia nurse said they don't want to have a hand in helping or trying to give her a happy fulfilling life. They sit back in judgement pointing out what, when and how things should be done. But lift a finger? You have got to be joking that might show they cared and let's face it, they don't give a damn about the poor woman,' I retaliated.

'You're right, this is not an act of love because they are concerned or care about her, if that was the case, they would have taken quick, effective action like going to the police, that would have an immediate effect. You would not go to the Office of Public Guardian as they will have procedures to follow and take months to investigate that is the act of someone wanting you all to suffer.'

'I have no idea what has motivated them to commit such a diabolical act, but my thoughts are jealousy because you have such a loving relationship with each other, greed, and a deep-rooted sense of hatred.' She was aghast.

'Seriously, Lynn, you don't know these people. I used to have to keep the peace with them for my dad's benefit but when he passed away and they lied in court trying to blacken my name, I was done. They are like a cancer that spreads with absolutely no value to offer.'

'It's funny, they cannot even stand each other, and Ruby just flits from one to the other spreading poison, befriending whichever will best suit her next plan.' I was getting seriously angry now.

'The only satisfaction they can hope to get is to bring hurt and devastation to your world but don't allow it,' she advised.

'That is easier said than done,' I admitted.

'Maybe, but you are good with words, Lois, and I am sure you can successfully communicate the high level of care you provide. You are a Christian, put your faith in place and tackle it head on,' Lynn stated.

'Thank you, Lynn, it just feels like a mammoth task where I am guilty until I prove I am innocent,' I moaned.

'Well, my love, take it in small bites but either way deal with it. I know you are innocent, and I also know you will be vindicated at the end of this. So, on that note, I am going to get off and let you tell Emmeline and make a start. If there is anything you need, I am only across the road. Good luck,' Lynn spoke.

I got myself and Emmeline a cup of tea and went out on to the decking to sit for a few minutes before letting her know that unfortunately, I wouldn't be able to do much for the next week as I had this paperwork to complete. She was clearly shaken despite the fact I had tried to play it down and quite sorrowful apologising for 'being such a nuisance to me,' not that it was her fault or responsibility.

I left her looking at the newspaper Lynn had brought for her, not believing for a minute that she was actually reading anything. I got her some sun cream and applied it to her exposed arms, face and neck before getting the form out to take a closer look.

The allegations were that:

- I was drugging her because of the time Ruby had jumped out of a doorway screeching in Emmeline's face when she was on her way to the café. Stunned not knowing what she had done wrong, Emmeline couldn't process what was happening and wasn't quick enough with a perceived, appropriate response so said nothing for fear of getting it wrong. Apparently, she was 'vacant' so I must be drugging her.

- Seemingly I had forced her into buying me a static caravan. The reality was that I had put a deposit down on an older one suitable for the boys and I in our choice of Cleethorpes. However, when out for Emmeline's birthday in 2012, we were passing Cayton Sands on our way from Scarborough to Bridlington, so decided to go in to have a look.

- Emmeline was so taken with how homey they were that she intimated if we got a newer one, she would actually love to share holidays with the boys and me. So, we found one to suit Emmeline's needs in her chosen area of Hornsea and on the site she preferred, and we had paid half each. The insurance, gas, electric, water etc I paid yet inevitably the site fees we shared together.

- I was also accused of making her pay for new doors and windows for my house. The year they were installed I had actually been Medically Retired NOT disgraced by making accusations of rape/sexual assault of the priest and my retirement money had paid for this.

- Apparently, they were afraid I was taking large sums of money off Emmeline, but I think this referred to the fact that for 2 consecutive years Emmeline and Jeff had given a tax relief of £1250 to each of their children. Dad wanted to see us all use the benefit of inheritance before either of them passed. I chose to lay a hall floor and benefit the children. They were now worried I may be receiving their perceived share.

- Less surprisingly was that they wanted to gain access to Emmeline's Will. However, she had instructed her solicitor independently and was unwilling to divulge the contents of this to anyone. So, all I could do was provide them with the solicitors details.

- It was also alleged I was selling Grey Gables purely for my own benefit, though goodness knows where Emmeline was supposed to reside then.
- I was also being accused of manipulating Emmeline and not allowing her to see her other children. Not being funny but like Laura had said, whilst ever I had breath in my body, no one would ever stop me from seeing my mum.

To all intents and purposes, Ruby and Kelly had tried to pluck things out of obscurity scraping the barrel to come up with nonconsequential rubbish. It wasn't lost on me that the thread throughout was all about money; perhaps they were concerned there wouldn't be any left for them, who knows. As far as I am concerned, I have earned the right to be Emmeline's power of attorney as I have managed her affairs diligently with honesty and integrity, thank goodness her solicitor advised her all those years ago.

Who knows what misdemeanours she would have been subjected to otherwise? Inevitably, the evidence displayed a complete lack of knowledge of dementia, no love or care for Emmeline, yet clearly in favour of greed and malicious intent.

Although, it wasn't any less intimidating than the first time I had looked at it, I proceeded to spend the next 3 hours making notes that I could work from the next day, Thursday.

After a really bad night's sleep, mixed with a variety of emotions and over thinking the situation, I got up and began making more notes. Once I had taken a shower, sorted out everyone's breakfast, I decided to look at it again. I did not feel that I had all the relevant information that they were requesting especially as I was unable to access all the statements for Emmeline's bank records and with only a week to respond, it wasn't adequate time.

I felt I required some assistance and guidance so decided to use the contact number at the top of the page. The representative was quite blasé as though it was just a run of the mill questionnaire and just advised me to answer what I could, then, to send the supporting evidence on, when it was available. For anyone who knows me they will tell you I never do things by small standards, if I am doing anything I am completing it to the best of my ability.

So, when I ended the call, I decided to get my laptop out and began to construct a directory of professional people I was in consultation with regarding Emmeline's care. I then added to that all the people who had been involved on a personal level and had witnessed the level of care she constantly received. By the end of it, I felt a lot more positive.

The list was immense and there were lots of people who could testify on my behalf to the deep love shown towards Emmeline, not to mention the tailor-made, person-centred care she was privy to on a daily basis. Her life consisted of going to a variety of dementia cafes, eating out, socialising in the pub, going to church, shopping, visiting her family (that she chose to see), having manicures, art therapy sessions, memory and nostalgic workshops or participating in 'singing for the brain' to name but a few.

I then went on to create a piece regarding dementia in general. How it had affected her then how we dealt with the daily challenges without the assistance of a family who had long since abandoned her.

On this day, I spent 7 ½ hours solid on the computer. The next day, I worked through until 4 pm but was becoming overwhelmed and tetchy every time anyone wanted me to deviate away from it. I was under pressure and feeling it. I was not being fair to my boys or Emmeline, but I had a tight deadline to meet.

However, it was Friday, so I gave my head a wobble, got a shower and assisted Emmeline to Larkham's, where we met the boys and Pip to let our hair down for a few hours and enjoy Auntie Helens thick cut chips and burgers.

The next day, it would have been dad's birthday and how I wished I could have chewed this situation over with him. With a very heavy heart, I decided to take Poppy for a walk along the beach before anyone else got up, just to blow the cobwebs away, to reset, realign and rebalance myself. As I walked, I closed my eyes and imagined him there walking at my side deflated.

I asked, 'What more can I do?' As soon as the words were out of my mouth, they were ripped away by the wind and overshadowed by the deafening roar of the waves crashing along the rocks. I knew instinctively how disgusted he would have been, that he would be ashamed and appalled because this behaviour would have been abhorrent to him.

He was a well-respected businessman, a man of honour who would lift people up not tear them down. He was honest, kind, private and he wouldn't want his dirty laundry washed so publicly, and so I knew he was not only by my side, but he was on my side like a warrior shielding my steps.

When I got back, Jack was at the door looking out for me and immediately came to the car to greet me.

'Mum,' he began, 'when we arrived here, it was for us all to have the best holiday together, but at the moment it's awful and no one is happy,' he began.

'I know, love, and I am really sorry. I don't want to have to spend my entire days on the laptop having to construct my defence for something I am not guilty of, but I have no choice.' I said.

'I am not blaming you, Mum, and I know you are really stressed with it, but you are taking it out on us and that's not fair,' he said so earnestly.

I looked at his little face and felt such remorse for being like a bear with a sore head. I hadn't taken into consideration how much this was affecting them too. To me, they were still able to go out, see their friends and play. I felt awful and teared up only able to say, 'Sorry.'

He took my hand, wrapped his arms around my waist and wept with me then said, 'I think the best thing we can do is go home.'

'Oh no, love, we cannot let this spoil our holiday. I won't let it,' I said, determined yet overwhelmed by his selflessness.

'I think we all need to go back so that you can focus on what you have to do. Then, once it is sorted, we can come back again next week,' he told me.

I looked at him and swelled with such pride. Here was my young son with a maturity and insight way beyond his years. I smiled, nodded and saw in him not only the image of my father but an acknowledgement that this was the advice he would be giving me.

I stripped our beds, took it to the laundrette then packed our things and cleaned our home. Before we left, I remade the beds explained our decision to Lynn, and we set off our holiday together well and truly ruined.

During the next couple of days, the boys barely came out of their rooms as I worked furiously 12 hours a day constructing a 7,000-word document regarding the reason Grey Gables was up for sale, what care I had given Emmeline, her levels of ability, her independence in making her will, reasons for my decisions and why they were in her best interests. I also received the bank statements we had ordered so I checked everything, photocopied it, downloaded my supporting evidence then read and reread it.

Despite being overwhelmed, I systematically worked through it all in "bite sizes" as Lynn had suggested and it soon gathered momentum that on Tuesday I was able to take Emmeline to a Dementia café at her church, and on Wednesday, I was able to take Jack to the cinema. Afterwards, I took the completed documents for Laura to check over for me as I needed another pair of eyes to ensure I hadn't missed anything.

As I patiently sat my heart in my throat wondering if I had done enough, but knowing I had no more time left. She looked up, smiled and simply said, 'WOW. You have certainly hit them and with bells on.'

'Do you think so?' I asked tentatively.

'Hell yeah, to say you have had less than a week that is one detailed document, and it's produced to the highest of levels. I really am speechless,' she said in admiration.

I breathed a sigh of relief, thanked her for her continued support, then with a sleepy Jack beckoning me towards the door, we left and reconvened in the car ready for our beds. As my head hit the pillow later that night, I delved into my thoughts recalling my walk on the beach and sent a silent prayer.

'Thank you, Dad, I promise to continue to look after the "love of your life", and despite what they do, I will walk in peace wearing the armour of God knowing that you are with me and that through you, my enemies have already been defeated,' I said. Then I had a fitful sleep knowing I had already been vindicated.

Chapter 18
Emmeline
A Spare Part

'I don't understand, love,' I told Lois.

'The package that I had to go home to collect is a legal document requesting me to explain my conduct regarding your financial affairs and my care of you,' Lois told me.

'But why would anyone want to question you about that? You haven't done anything wrong. Let them know I will tell them I am ok,' I told her.

'I wish it was that simple, Emmeline, but two of your children have made complaints to the Office of Public Guardian, so they have to check it out, and as your power of attorney whether I have done anything wrong or not. I am still answerable to them,' Lois explained to me.

'That is ridiculous, so anybody can accuse you of whatever they like, and you have to prove it's not true?' I asked.

'In a nutshell, yes,' Lois said. 'The day you made me your power of attorney, I became a legal guardian in the event that you couldn't manage things for yourself.'

'But you have helped me to stay Emmeline all these years. You've never taken away my right to make decisions you assist me, but only when I need it,' I reaffirmed.

'I know that, Emmeline, and you know that, but I have to show them that we are open and transparent. That is why I have had to request your statements from the bank so they can look for any inconsistencies. At the end of the day, there is nothing to see so we just have to walk the walk, as they say,' Lois told me.

'I am so sorry for being such a nuisance to you,' I told Lois again.

I stayed outside in the sun whilst Lois went back inside. A few moments later, she came back out and applied some sun cream for me to ensure I didn't burn.

'If you were not looking after me, you wouldn't be taking care that I don't burn, Lois,' I said ruefully.

Lois didn't reply but I could tell her mind was on overload, so as she went back inside, I sat with the newspaper in front of me but not particularly looking at it, feeling like I was a heavy burden. I could not understand what I had done to them that was so wrong for them to hate me so much. I sat and wracked my brain, but I had to admit I could not think of anything.

I had treated each one exactly the same, although when Lois came along, there was an intense jealousy from Ruby. Maybe she hated not being the youngest anymore but surely decades later, she should be over this sibling rivalry thing. I was perplexed. She had issues and there was no mistaking it.

However, I may be able to excuse a child's behaviour but as an adult, that was a different story and there are always consequences to our actions. For now, I decided to blend into the background and let Lois focus on what she had to do. I knew she hadn't done anything wrong and if truth be told, she danced to my tune not the other way round. So I would let her answer to the accusations and hope that we could move forward.

The next couple of days, Lois was transfixed by the documents like a possessed woman, furiously taking notes surrounded by papers. I really wanted to help, to lighten her load but I knew I would only be a hindrance; besides she was more than capable. So I just went for a walk, sat with Lynn or had a cuppa. The one thing I could do though and silently, was pray and I did a lot of that along with talking to Jeff about what had been happening and how the others had behaved.

How I wished my husband was still here. He wouldn't have stood for this nonsense but then again, they wouldn't have dared behave like this if he was still here. I couldn't have imagined as I had held them in my arms as babies with such dreams for their futures that they would have turned out so wicked.

I didn't care that they chose not to come and see me; I didn't care that they had lied to their children so that they didn't come either. I didn't even care now that they had banded together to lie in court forcing me to have to testify against them and tell the truth. They could lie to themselves as much as they wanted to if it made them feel better, but I did care what affect this had on Lois. The only one who had ever stood by my side and truly loved me no matter what.

My chest heaved as I tried in vain to keep the emotion to a minimum, remembering the times Kelly had looked down her nose at Lois. Like the time there was a family do and Lois was good enough to offer her brand-new house to Kelly, her husband and children, but it was beneath Kelly; it wasn't good enough. Or the time she got a new car and I overheard her on the drive, forcing her husband to not comment on it because it belonged to Lois.

It was always a matter of "How has she afforded that?" The fact that Lois was the only one who had worked hard, saved, bought her own home, had her own money, a good job and friends unlike either of them who had to rely on a partner to provide for them and put a roof over their heads, was beyond me. I guess it is a case of whilst they are pointing a finger and making remarks about Lois, they forget that in their accusing hands there are four more fingers pointing back at themselves.

I knew their behaviour over the years had hurt Lois. All she had ever wanted was for them to just be kind and act like sisters, not venomous serpents looking for an opportunity to strike. She had tried so hard to keep the peace with them for years, not retaliating or giving them an excuse to bully her, mainly for Jeff's sake, but that all changed when he died.

Not that his teachings, his morals or what he stood for had died with him, but that Lois did not have to accept the unacceptable anymore or excuse the inexcusable. It's quite outlandish when I think that Kelly actually wrote a letter to my dead husband and stuck it to my mother's grave stating that everything he had stood for had died with him.

In reality, she had never possessed any of the qualities that made him a great man, so for her it would have died but for Lois and me it lived on in us for we were one with him. Kelly, like Ruby had outcast themselves a long, long, time ago with their snide remarks, back biting, nastiness and selfishness unwilling to live peacefully.

As I sat here, the wind slightly nipping at my exposed ankles, my coffee dregs cold, I am struck by the sense of failure, not my own but in my children's lives as them as adults. In reality, Kelly's husband was married when she started having an affair with him. They later got married, but he has never really lived up to the expectations of her previous fiancé.

She aborted her first child a month prior to marriage, and later had an affair that only came to light because she caught a sexually transmitted disease. I still don't think she knows whether her third child is her husband's or not. It's hard to see if she has ever really committed to anything other than looking down her nose and thinking she knows better than everyone else.

So I am befuddled; what gives her a right to pick the bones out of other people's lives. She has always lied to make a situation fit her purpose and whenever we visited, Jeff and I felt very uncomfortable at the way she spoke to her husband, it was shameful. Jeff hated it when he was in hospital.

He would beg both Lois and I not to let Kelly know where he was, because she would embarrass him in front of the nurses; dominating them, telling them how to do their jobs. She showed no compassion for him. She talked at him, and he hated this brussen manner about her, so I know he would be up in arms if he was here today witnessing them bullying us in this way.

I glanced over again towards Lois and my heart ached for her. Why had I put her down as my power of attorney? I thought I was protecting myself from them forcing their way in and dictating what was and wasn't going to happen. Never did I contemplate I would be opening Lois up to such harm.

I felt so helpless and totally unable to protect her. I had thought I was doing the right thing, so that if I became unable to tell them what I wanted, it was already written down, no argument. Never did I think they would fight her to gain control. What have I spawned, and in turn, unleashed on to Lois.

The tension in her body that was emulated upon her face was palpable. I breathed deeply and faked a yawn as she glanced in my direction obviously sensing my prying eyes. 'Are you alright, Emmeline?' She asked me.

'I am more worried about you, love,' I told her.

'I am sorry, but I have to give this my undivided attention. It is too important to ignore,' Lois explained.

'I know, love, and I am sorry you are having to go through this because of me,' I told her as my lip started to quiver.

'Emmeline, this is NOT because of you. This is the hands of the devil masqueraded by the guise of "concerned family members",' Lois reassured me as she put the paperwork to one side, crossed the room to come over to me and put her arm comfortingly around my shoulders.

And I wept, hurt without measure by what they had done but also by her comfort because I didn't feel like I deserved it.

'I tell you what, why don't you give your face a quick wash and I will ring Pip, then we can meet her and the boys at Larkham's for some of Auntie Helen's thick cut chips. They are always a winner and to be honest, I have had enough for today,' Lois suggested.

'Oh, that would be lovely,' I said, instantly feeling a little brighter and readily made my way to the bathroom.

When I returned, Lois had already arranged to meet Pip and the boys, had replaced her laptop and was clearing the last of her papers away. We meandered down the short walk to the pub, happy to see a hive of people sat outside in the sunshine, dogs with water bowls at the ready and children playing tig in and out of the tables. It was lovely to have a bit of normality even if it was only for a while, it was exactly what we all needed.

We had burger and chips, interacted with our friends made new ones and left feeling fulfilled. At the time, I didn't realise it but the next day we would return home. I was incredibly disappointed at the decision, but young Jack was right. Lois did need to go back so she could concentrate and have access to information not readily available here.

So, we packed, cleaned, washed the bedding and came home. I must have been at ease, I already saw Lois' as my "home" now. As soon as we arrived, Lois wasted no time but got stuck in to challenging these horrendous accusations. I felt much better at home because I wasn't a spare part. I was able to help more like do the washing and peg it out, make cups of tea and chat with the boys or sit out in the garden at the picnic table.

On the Tuesday afternoon, Lois even found time to take me to the Dementia café at my church, where we played musical bingo, did a quiz, chatted with friends, did jigsaws and had tea and biscuits. It made a lovely change and I was thankful that despite the strain Lois was under, here she was still putting my needs first again. It was ironic that she was answerable to accusations regarding my welfare when the only needs she neglected were her own.

I went to my room that night feeling like an integral part of everything and could not have been happier. The next day, Lois completed all the work she was required to do and was able to take Jack to the cinema to see Suicide Squad. It was certified as too old for Joe, so Lois got us some snacks ordered us a pizza and blacked out the lounge so we could have our own home cinema experience. It was a lovely alternative and neither of us felt like we were missing, but by the time they arrived home, we were snuggled up fast asleep on the sofa.

The next morning to my relief, Lois was posting the paperwork back to the Office of Public Guardian, so thankfully we could breathe again and hopefully go back over to Hornsea to resume our holidays. Little did I know, this was only the start of the investigation, and worse was yet to come, for me.

Chapter 19
The Carer 2016
All for One, and One for All

Once I had dropped the envelope in to the post box and heard its soft landing amongst the other mail, I felt a rush of panic, because I could no longer reread it, edit it nor add any more supporting evidence. This was it, done, dusted and it was no longer in my hands. I knew I had done my best to accurately portray every ounce of my interaction with Emmeline, so whatever the outcome now, it was in God's hands.

Walking back to the car, controlling myself from looking back was like taking the boys for their first day at school. It was Thursday, the 11 August, and time for us to restore our equilibrium. So I had decided to take the boys to Barnsley Metrodome. Generally speaking, I would have gone in with them and enjoyed larking about on whatever equipment they wanted to try, however today Emmeline was with us, so I decided to keep her company with a cuppa at Calypso Cove.

The boys excitedly ran into the changing rooms, having already put their trunks on under their clothes so they could shoot out into the water as soon as possible. I steered Emmeline through the café to a heavyset table with benches along the water's edge; got her seated then made my way to the counter for our refreshments. There were large painted imitation rocks separating the spectators from the swimmers, which was a good job because every now and then someone would create a splash and it protected us from getting drenched.

Within minutes of making ourselves comfortable, two boys excitedly ran our way with enormous grins on their faces displaying their absolute pleasure to be able to let their hair down. The tension and strain of the past week having been drained away and now replaced by the uninhibited freedom that only children know. A warmth spread throughout my being mixed with the relief that we had managed to weather yet another storm, together.

Neither Emmeline nor I spoke of the experience we had endured during the last 7 days. I think we both just wanted to drop it to the floor and not give it any further attention along with simply being happy to shield the other as much as possible. Today we just wanted to forget, to enjoy our beautiful boys and reclaim the summer we had allocated to each other.

We took turns looking out for the boys, and every now and again, one of us would point and shout, 'There they are'; just like when we went to Blackpool and as children would shout "there it is" when we first saw the tower. The boys ran together up the steep steps of the wavy slide known as Splash Ahoy, sitting next to each other, then counting down as they propelled themselves off and hurled down towards the soft landing of the water.

They dared themselves to ride the Terror Torrent a fast, blacked out tubular slide that spit them out at speed plunging them into a well of deeper water. Then there was a volcanic rush where riders shot through the tube into a bright yellow spinning top that they circled before finally dropping through its bowels into the waiting sewers below.

Each time the boys dared themselves to join a queue to partake in the adrenalin rush delights awaiting them, their excitement would be expelled by furiously waving in our directions. I found the experience overwhelming and ever more pleasing having seen them grounded and withdrawn due to the outward force and effects the allegations had brought. I had to remind myself that I had dealt with it and needed to make a concerted effort to not allow it to rob us of even a second more of our time.

But I did feel that I was missing out. I yearned to be with the boys, interacting and enjoying the experience with them instead of looking on from the side lines; little did I realise but this would be my new position from now on. Here I would be staying watching them from a distance, no longer a part of things enjoying it with them. From now on I would not be able to participate as I would have to sit out to support Emmeline.

Once the boys had enjoyed a couple of hours, Emmeline was getting stiff and I'd had enough coffee to sink a ship so we beckoned the boys to make their way to the changing rooms and we cleaned away our dirty cups then went to find the toilets. When Joe and Jack came out looking fresh and fulfilled, they were awash with excited chatter of their exploits, which rides were the best what it had felt like, jumping off the various heights of the diving boards, the different people they had interacted with and how many times they had been on each one.

It was lovely to feel their excitement bubbling over and seeping into me, but I did feel jealous that I wasn't able to experience it for myself. I wasn't meaning to be selfish or anything. They were young children; I was their mother, and my place was by their side.

We bought drinks on our way out and once in the car, we decided to go for lunch to the Toby Carvery. So we made our way around the Barnsley ring road and towards the M1 as there is one at junction 37 known as Castle View, at Dodworth. All of us wanted the carvery so we found our seats, ordered our drinks then stood in line until it was our turn.

Jack went first as he is an old pro at piling his plate high, whilst Joe required me to hold the plate whilst I encouraged him to serve himself. Luckily, there wasn't anyone behind us, so he was able to take his time. Next I supported Emmeline but only in that I was there if she needed me and didn't struggle coordinating things.

Then I filled mine with veg poured on the onion gravy and joined my family. It was absolutely delicious and the boys had obviously built up an appetite as both of them went back for more vegetables, especially the creamy mashed potatoes which we all loved so much. Completely stuffed and totally fit to burst, we rolled out on to the carpark, got into the car, re-joined the motorway and headed for home.

'We never had pudding,' Emmeline suddenly said.

'Really, you could have managed a pudding too?' I asked her.

'Oh, my goodness, Grandma, I am stuffed,' Jack declared.

'Me too,' said Joe.

'You may be stuffed now but we could have got some and brought it home for later,' Emmeline said earnestly.

'Would you like me to stop and get you something, Emmeline?' I asked her.

'Well, I think it would be a fitting end to a lovely meal, and a good day out together,' Emmeline suggested.

'Ok then we will call at Hampsons Garden Centre and get some of their cakes,' I confirmed.

'Can I get the éclair, Mum?' Joe asked.

'Can I have the apple turnover?' Jack asked.

'Now see what you have caused, Emmeline; there will be a stampede when we get there,' I laughed.

Looking very satisfied with herself, Emmeline grinned and said, 'My treat.'

The next morning, my little pirates were ready for their next adventure so wasting no time I quickly got a picnic together and set off for Stockheld Park near Wetherby. Throughout the year, they have some amazing calendar themed events, like at Christmas the skating rink becomes an ice rink, the enchanted forest can be accessed on skis, and there is a Santa's grotto; whereas Halloween has a spooky based scare fest event.

We started off having a walk through the forest. Emmeline and I engrossed in conversation as we watched the boys climbing spider web rope nets, wiggling their way through tunnels, descending slides and swinging from thick ropes. Along the route were various story boards, little fairy doors in the base of trees, buttons to press revealing roaring bears, and characters giving clues to hidden extravagant exhibits.

The forest was captivating and propelled us gently from one charming area to the next. Our moods were light, our spirits were high and the atmosphere was energised once more. Despite the enclosure from the overhead trees, the heavily trod path with its partly exposed tree roots was damp and the coolness in places gave an eeriness, which its creators had used to their advantage with hidden motion sensors throwing sounds of twigs being trodden on, that gave the sense of being followed.

The atmosphere immediately changed as we froze alert to a new, perceived presence until the trance was severed when we located its origin. As we regained the heat of the day exiting the forest, Emmeline decided she needed a drink. So we found a café and seated her at a bench whilst the boys and I took instruction on the safe usage of the ingenious electric scooters.

We then propelled ourselves back through the forest along a path parallel to the one we had just walked and enjoyed our route from a different perspective. We giggled as we manoeuvred our new form of transport, becoming more confident the further we roamed. Then all too quickly we were back at the start to where Emmeline was sunning herself, relaxed and happy on the bench where we had left her.

This was the ideal time to take a break for lunch, so I returned to the car for our picnic whilst they hogged the bench awaiting my return.

'Mine's the ham sandwiches,' Joe said.

'Mine are the tuna one's, Mum,' Jack joined in as though somehow I may have forgotten.

'Yes, love, I know,' I responded.

'I don't remember what mine was,' said Emmeline.

'Yours was the egg mayonnaise, Emmeline,' I said, and carefully set each person's chosen food in front of them before unpacking a host of mini sausages, a tub of coleslaw, potato salad, crisps, yogurts, hard boiled eggs, then individual small Tupperware tubs with batons of carrots, cucumber sticks, black olives, pickled onions, a pot of cream cheese and humous.

'Wow,' said Emmeline, 'we are definitely not going to go hungry that is for sure.' Much to Joe and Jack's amusement.

'Where are we going next, Mum?' Joe asked.

'I think we should do the Maze,' said Jack. Both Jack and I had visited Stockheld Park during February half term and enjoyed the maze with its twists and turns. There were lots of hidden surprises, tricking you to go one way when really it was a totally different route altogether; like the street sign "wrong way alley" when it was the right direction.

At its core was a fountain, and in a couple of places you could climb on to a platform, so you were overlooking the entire maze, it was quite a spectacular sight. When Jack and I had last been here, it had started to snow heavily whilst we were in the middle trying to find our way out. We had then been ice-skating whilst it snowed which was magical, especially as a member of the Emmerdale cast was on the ice too.

'Are you up for getting lost in the maze, Emmeline?' I asked her.

'I don't know about that, love, maybe I should wait out here and then I can let someone know if you can't get out,' she said concerned.

'She is only joking, Grandma,' Joe started but then a little unsure he turned to Jack for reassurance. 'Isn't she, Jack?'

'No, it's really scary,' he joked. 'You are taking your life into your own hands and you may not get out alive.'

'It's fine, just an enjoyable stroll around and now we have refuelled, I think a toilet stop and then we can set off,' I said.

I gave Jack the responsibility to navigate our way through and to my surprise, he excelled himself having remembered some of the pitfalls we had previously fallen in to. We came out of the other end in record time so had enough time to take in a spot of roller skating. Joe wasn't so steady on his new, four wheeled feet so having hit the floor once or twice, decided it wasn't for him and chose to sit with Emmeline, giving me the opportunity to accompany Jack on a few laps around the rink.

That was the thing with the boys; I always promoted them giving everything a go. If something wasn't to their liking that was fine but at least they had experienced it so were able to make informed choices and decisions for themselves. A skill that would be an essential assistant to them in later life.

I also made an effort to spend quality time with each of them independently, so they were never jealous of the other. They were the best of mates, equal in everything and never felt they were in competition with each other, so there was never any vying for attention.

Once we had returned the skates, we decided on a hot, comforting drink to warm ourselves up and to bring our day to a satisfying end. Jack and Joe chose hot chocolate with whipped cream and marshmallows for themselves and Emmeline, whereas I stuck to my regular white americano.

'Today has been great, Mum, thank you,' said Jack.

'Yes, I am glad we can enjoy our holiday again,' said Joe. 'It made me sad when we had to come home.'

'I know it did, love. I think we were all disappointed, but Jack made the right call, it was the best thing we could do,' I reassured them.

'I'm sorry I spoilt your holiday,' ventured Emmeline.

'It wasn't your fault, Emmeline,' I said quite taken aback.

'But it wouldn't have happened if it wasn't for me,' she said.

'It might have been about you, Grandma, but you didn't make it happen,' Jack wisely said.

'He is right, Emmeline. You are not responsible for the actions of others. They will be held accountable for what they have done but right now, all we need to think about is enjoying the rest of our holidays together,' I told her.

'Does that mean we will be able to go back over to Hornsea?' Joe asked.

'I don't see why not, love. What do you think Jack?' I asked.

'I think we should. Grandma was looking forward to her holiday with us and we were looking forward to her being with us,' Jack replied.

To our surprise, Emmeline suddenly thrusted her arm into the air as though she had a sword in it and declared, 'All for one and one for all.'

Chapter 20
Emmeline
Meeting Mr Jacobs

I think I was being a little naïve expecting that once Lois had posted the documents back, that would be the end of it. I hadn't realised quite how much the experience had affected me. I mean, ok, when I was in Hornsea it had troubled me to the point that I had got lost on several occasions.

Lois had played it down probably because she had more important things to worry about, but I am sure she must have been concerned that I might be having another relapse. I had only gone for a walk to the onsite shop for a newspaper; a stroll I had taken on several occasions but somehow had gotten completely lost. Danny, a man that lived on the site, and who always had a laugh and joke with me ended up bringing me back in his car.

I got him to drop me at the end of Utopia Drive but the next time we were in the pub, he mentioned it to Lois. There was another time that Graham had found me wandering aimlessly so he made an excuse to walk me back, and then also a time the boys had been cycling round the site looking for me. When we arrived back home, it was still impacting me; maybe the separation it created from Lois and feeling so helpless that inside I was still in turmoil.

Once the documents had been posted, I thought this may settle down and to some degree being able to reinstate our family experiences with a trip to Barnsley Metrodome and then to Stockheld Park, it did to a degree. Or maybe it just meant that I was being distracted. I don't know, but I felt off my food; I wasn't sleeping so well and then I started with pain in my lower back.

Lois could always tell when I wasn't right, like she had some sixth sense, so on Monday, 15 August, she called the doctor and took me straight over to the surgery where he examined me and referred me to the A&E department at Dewsbury. We arrived about 6 pm and after much consultation, I was admitted on to Ward 14 at around 10 pm. Lois came up on to the ward with me to make sure I was settled before she left.

It was a scary experience and despite the staff doing their utmost to reassure me, I really did feel so sad, alone and very low. It didn't help that the next day was the anniversary of Jeff's passing, yet here I was, separated from the people who loved me and so I became thoroughly miserable. Lois arrived the next morning with a bag of clothes for me including some toiletries, underwear and nighties.

She stayed until after lunch ensuring that I had eaten so that it wasn't just left on the bedside table, then taken away because it had gone cold. I slept most of the day because there was nothing to occupy me and the bright lights, continuous humdrum of the nurses back and forth, together with the monotonous chat of other visitors were draining, mentally.

Before I knew it, Lois was back again for the evening visit. I wasn't much company and felt awful she was having to tend to me again instead of being on holiday with the boys. She told me she had been busy washing and drying my bedding and that she had done some painting in my room to brighten it up for me. I don't know how she found the time.

I could see how tired she was. There were dark circles forming under her eyes and her complexion was greying. She had been plagued with horrendous migraines all over the weekend, probably due to the excessive screen time on the computer and the stress she had endured. Looking at her now, it appeared she was close to having yet another migraine, despite this she stayed for another two hours.

This was the pattern over the next few days, although I was put on "nil by mouth" whilst tests were conducted, just in case they showed anything and the doctors wanted to do some emergency surgery. I had x-rays, a MRI, an ultrasound, blood tests; they really did give me a full M.O.T. and the only conclusion that surfaced was kidney stones. I was asked if I wanted to have them out, but why would I want to put myself at risk going under an anaesthetic, so I said no.

The doctor was going to keep me in until the following Wednesday but suddenly decided on the Sunday (21) I could go home, probably a shortage of beds. Lois arrived at 11.15 to find out I could go home but we had to wait until 3.30 to receive a discharge note and to obtain some antibiotics. It was during this wait, she dropped a bombshell on me.

'Emmeline, you know the paperwork that I was busy with for the Office of Public Guardian?' She asked me.

'Yes, love, have you heard back already?' I asked.

'Not about the information I have sent them, but you have had a letter regarding it,' she informed me.

'Oh,' I said a bit bewildered. 'Do they need me to tell them how well you look after me?'

'Kind of. I called at Grey Gables to check everything was ok and to pull back the curtains on Wednesday and the letter was there. I had to open it in case it required a quick response, but I didn't want to bother you with it whilst you were poorly,' Lois told me.

'Thank you, love,' I said. 'What do I need to do?'

'Well, they have appointed an investigator who wants to come out to see you,' Lois began. 'The doctor had initially said you would be in the hospital until Wednesday, so I rang him last night because he was travelling up from Birmingham. I tried to explain you were in hospital, but I don't think he believed me.'

'He was cold, dismissive and I felt like he had already decided I was guilty as charged. When I came off the phone, I was in tears. He was horrible and told me he would come to the hospital and interview you if need be. I thought that was uncaring and uncompassionate a statement,' Lois said to me.

'Oh dear, is he going to be horrible to me too?' I asked Lois.

'I hope not, but my concern is how you will cope with this because I won't be able to support you when he interviews you,' Lois said.

'But, Lois, I don't want to see him on my own. What if he brings Ruby or Kelly with him. I don't want them anywhere near me,' I told her.

Lois could see I was becoming agitated, so asked a nurse who was seated at a desk in our little six bed ward for a jug of water for me. When she came back, I wasn't just upset, I was sobbing my heart out.

'Why can't they just leave me alone, Lois?' I almost shouted out.

The nurse looked our way as Lois did her best to comfort me and when I didn't calm down, she approached us to see if everything was alright. I think she thought it was Lois that was distressing me but that couldn't have been further from the truth.

'Are you alright, Mrs Rodgers?' The nurse asked me giving Lois a sideways glance.

'No, love, I am not,' I answered frankly.

'I have just had to give her some bad news,' Lois informed her. 'I have had some false allegation made against me and the investigator wants to interview Emmeline. Personally, I don't think she is in a fit state, but the investigator has stated he will come to the hospital if he has to. The thing is, Emmeline is frightened to be on her own with him and I cannot sit in the interview with her, so she feels exposed.'

'Why don't you contact Age UK? There was a similar case like this a couple of months ago and I heard that they sent a representative to advocate on behalf of the elderly lady as she was a vulnerable adult too,' she informed us.

'I never thought of that,' Lois said.

The nurse said, 'It's worth a try,' and proceeded to return to her desk.

'What do you think, Lois? Can we get someone who can sit with me?' I asked her.

'I guess it's a possibility. Let's face it, if you have disciplinary or medical meetings you can have a representative in as an ally, so why not?' She said. 'I would feel better knowing you had some form of support, as otherwise I would feel useless like I have let you down.'

'Lois, you have never let me down. So don't ever think that I don't know what I would do without you,' I said.

That night I don't think either of us got much sleep. I tossed and turned yet again wondering what the heck I had done to make them hate me so much; to put this much strain upon me. I could hear Lois up and down to the toilet too, so it didn't surprise when she was sat in the living room at 07.30 when I ventured out of my room.

'I take it you cannot sleep either?' Lois asked me.

'No, love, I am mithered about what this fella is going to ask me, and I don't want to mess it up or make things worse for you,' I told her earnestly.

'You cannot mess it up, Emmeline. All you can do is tell the truth and answer any questions he asks to the best of your ability,' Lois told me.

She got up and made me a cuppa with two slices of toast and jam, then left me to eat it whilst she went for a shower. On her return I asked, 'Are you going to try and get in touch with Age UK?'

'No,' she started. 'I have had a better idea. I think it would be hard to organise someone to come from Age UK at such short notice, besides you need someone who knows you.'

'Like whom?' I wondered.

'I am going to contact the Alzheimer's society to see if someone can support you. At least they would be understanding of your condition, and therefore, able to give you the best support possible,' Lois told me.

She then made a phone call and spoke to Becki Dodds who was the lovely young lady that had supported us in many ways before. Becki spoke with her boss who gladly released her to support me. I felt so much better, at least she was a friendly face and would have my best interests at heart.

Lois then contacted the investigator to ascertain a time he would be arriving so she could coordinate our arrival with Becki's at Grey Gables. The investigator was quite off hand with Lois again and told her she couldn't be there. She explained that she needed to know a time because she would have to drive me to Grey Gables. He soon softened his tone when he realised that I no longer lived there and that we all lived together at Lois'.

At 1.30 pm, Lois and I arrived at Grey Gables just as Becki was pulling up in her silver BMW saloon car. We said our hellos, then went inside together.

'My goodness, Emmeline, what a beautiful house you have,' Becki exclaimed.

'Thank you, love. We have been here over 40 years but it's getting a bit too much for me now,' I told her.

When we went inside, I decided to show Becki round just to distract myself whilst we were waiting for the investigator.

'I cannot believe how large each of the rooms are, Emmeline. It's absolutely massive!' Becki exclaimed.

'You're telling me, Becki. I was having to clean it and search every day for Emmeline's glasses or her keys, or some other item she had put down and couldn't locate,' Lois laughed.

'Is this where you grew up, Lois?' Becki asked.

'Yes,' Lois said. 'I don't think I appreciated it until I went away to college and would come back for the summers.'

'I bet you have loads of wonderful memories,' Becki stated.

'Some but there are a lot of bad ones too,' said Lois.

'It must have got too much for you, Emmeline. It's far too big a place for someone with dementia to function properly. Going to Lois' was definitely the best decision in the long-term, Emmeline,' Becki told me.

'Yes, but here we are again being dragged back to the crime scene, so to speak,' I said as we all heard someone downstairs.

'Hello, Mrs Rodger?' A man's voice called out.

Lois was the first to retrace her steps back to the kitchen where a man stood at the open door. He wore a black overcoat with a crumpled suit underneath, wore glasses at the tip of his nose and was holding a battered black briefcase in his left hand.

Addressing Lois and extending his right hand, he said, 'I am Mr Jacobs from the Office of Public Guardian, and you are?'

'I am Lois Rodgers, Emmeline's carer; we spoke on the phone,' Lois reminded him.

'Ah yes, yes,' he acknowledged.

'I am only here because I have had to bring Emmeline over from my home where she lives now,' she told him.

'Yes, Netherton Brow I believe, I have just been over to have a look. It seems a lovely property,' he told Lois.

'I appreciate I cannot be present whilst you are interviewing Emmeline but due to the fact she has dementia and may require support, she has elected to have a representative from the Alzheimer's Society to advocate on her behalf,' Lois informed Mr Jacobs.

'That won't be necessary,' he began.

At this point, both Becki and I entered the kitchen so I told him, 'If you want to ask me questions that is fine, but it will be in the presence of Becki.'

Mr Jacobs was outnumbered so waved his hand as if to say "whatever", then Lois left so that the interview could begin. We sat in the middle room and had to wait a few minutes whilst Mr Jacobs arranged his paperwork, so he had everything to hand and could go through his list of questions methodically.

'Can I ask you, Mrs Rodgers, how long you have lived at Grey Gables?' He started.

'Yes, since 1971, so we have been here 45 years,' I said. I glanced at Becki who smiled and gave me a nod of reassurance.

'If you went to the bank to take £20 out then bought something for £4.35, how much money would you have left?' He asked.

'£15.65,' I said.

'Do you know what season we are in at the moment?' He asked.

'Of course,' I said wondering what on earth these questions had to do with anything. 'It is summer, and we are in August.' I answered before he asked me what month it was too.

He smiled. 'Mrs Rodgers, we are here today because two of your children have raised concerns about your power of attorney,' he verified.

'Yes, I am aware they have made false allegations,' I told him.

'Well, this is what I am here to investigate. It has been alleged that Lois has stopped you from having access to the rest of your children,' he stated.

'That is absolute rubbish. I don't want anything to do with any of them,' I told him.

'Why is that, Mrs Rodgers?' He probed.

'One abused Lois and my grandchildren. Kelly ruined my husband's funeral with her snide remarks, then got together with my other son to lie in court. Ruby verbally abuses me in the street and tries to manipulate me into giving her money. I don't want them here!' I said getting flustered.

'What would you do if any of them turned up at your door?' Mr Jacobs persisted.

'I would slam the bloody door in their face! I do not wish to see them nor do I want any of them on my property,' I reiterated.

'So, are you saying that Lois is not preventing you from seeing your children?' He asked.

'No, she isn't, it is my decision. Lois has encouraged me to keep contact by letting me know when birthdays are, but I don't want anything to do with them,' I told him.

'Speaking of birthdays, it was recently your granddaughter's 18th birthday. I believe, you sent her some money,' Mr Jacobs said.

'It was not a recent event, it was 2 years ago,' I told him.

'Do you remember how much money you sent for her birthday, Mrs Rodgers?' He asked.

'Yes, it was £50 but apparently, Kelly didn't think that I had sent sufficient. Well, I did,' I told him.

'Yes, I think she was expecting more like a sum of £500 because wasn't that the amount you sent to her other children on their 18th birthday,' he said.

'I have dementia so I couldn't remember how much I had sent them all those years before, however under the circumstances, I felt she was lucky to even receive that,' I told him.

'Under the circumstances, Mrs Rodgers?' He asked.

'Yes, they have not been to visit me or contacted me in any way since my husband died, so £50 was more than enough as far as I was concerned,' I told him.

'Fair enough, Mrs Rodgers. Talking about money, there was an allegation made that Lois had forced you into purchasing her a caravan. What can you tell me about this,' Mr Jacobs continued.

'When I decided not to go abroad anymore, Lois made the decision to buy a caravan for a base for her and the boys in this country so she could be here if I needed her. We were out one day and came upon some for sale, so went in to have a look. I was enthralled that they were just like a proper home and told Lois if they looked like this I would go with them,' I told him.

'So, you're saying that it was you who put the idea to Lois?' Mr Jacobs enquired.

'Exactly,' I told him.

'So, when you decided upon the one you bought who purchased it?' He asked.

'We both did; we went halves on it,' I told him.

'But how could Lois have paid half towards it? She isn't working is she and she hasn't a husband to support her.' He tried to trick me.

'No, she hasn't now but Lois had a very well-paid job and saved for a number of years, then when she was medically retired, she also got a decent pay out. She paid half and I paid half,' I told him.

'So is the caravan in both your names then?' Mr Jacobs persisted.

'No, due to my age I wanted Lois to put it solely into her name in case anything happened to me. She may be down as my power of attorney but firstly she is my daughter, and her children are my grandsons, who do everything for me,' I hit back.

'So, there will be paperwork available to verify this?' He asked.

'Yes, ask Lois, she will show you,' I told him. I was getting tired, and Becki could see my battery beginning to drain.

'You say you wanted Lois and your grandsons to benefit in case anything happened to you. What provisions have you made for your other children and grandchildren,' he asked impertinently.

'Sorry?' I asked in disbelief.

'I believe you have recently changed your Will?' He asked.

'Have I, who says I have?' I was getting mad.

'The allegation made is that Lois has forced you to update your Will making her the sole beneficiary, is that true?' He continued.

'What I have or have not left in my Will is between my solicitor and myself!' I stated.

'So, no one is aware of the contents of you Will?'

'No, I made my Will in the presence of my solicitor and only my solicitor and the contents will only be verified when something happens to me,' I told him.

'Will you consent to the Office of Public Guardian gaining a copy of your Will, Mrs Rodgers?' He persisted.

'I most certainly will not; it is my private business and that's the end of the matter.'

'There are a couple of other pressing matters raised, and that is the sale of Grey Gables. Who put the house on the market?' Mr Jacobs asked.

At this point, Becki tried to intervene to ask Mr Jacobs to rephrase his question as it was too leading, she recognised that he was obviously wanting me to say Lois, but he shot her down and told her not to speak.

'I am sorry, Mr Jacobs, but I will speak,' said Becki and then she turned to me and continued, 'Emmeline, what Mr Jacobs wants to know is, why Grey Gables was put on the market, and did you give your permission?' Becki rephrased for me.

'My children made it impossible for me to live here on my own. They were terrifying me until I felt unsafe, so I told Lois to put it up for sale as it is too big for me on my own,' I replied.

'So, Lois isn't selling your property for her own gain?' He asked directly.

'Absolutely not. We want to buy somewhere where we can all be happy. Grey Gables is very run down and too much for me to maintain on my own,' I told him.

'But didn't you say you had been here for 45 years, surely that would be a very difficult decision to make on your own?' He asked.

'Not really. My husband and I had decided to put it up for sale the year before he passed away but then he became ill, so we put it off. Now is the right time. I cannot stay here anymore on my own, that's why I moved in with Lois,' I explained.

'You said that the house needs improvements. Did you ever give Lois money to renovate her house at any time,' he changed the subject.

'For Lois, no,' I said puzzled.

'For new windows and doors?' He clarified.

'No,' I said simply.

'But you are aware that she has had new windows and doors fitted to her house,' he persisted.

'Yes, she did about 10 years ago and she paid for it from her own savings; it was nothing to do with me,' I stated.

'Have you ever given Lois a large sum of money?' He asked.

'No, she wouldn't take anything even if I tried. She even gives me my change to the last penny,' I said.

'Ok, Mrs Rodgers, I think I have got all the information that I need. Can I thank you for your time, and once I have completed my investigation, I will be in touch,' he said and gathered together his things and replaced them in his briefcase.

As he went off through the kitchen, Lois arrived and I could overhear him asking her a couple of questions regarding the caravan and how we had paid for it. Luckily, Lois pre-empted his interest in the payment for the caravan and had brought her bank book, so was able to prove we had paid half each. He thanked us all again and made his way across the drive to his car and left.

Lois, Becki and I reconvened in the kitchen, and Lois asked, 'How did it go?'

'It was awful. I cannot believe I have just been subjected to that,' I said.

'Was it that bad?' Lois asked looking really worried.

'He certainly put her though it,' Becki confirmed.

'Emmeline, I think you need to go to the toilet,' Lois said noticing a large wet patch on my trousers. I was so embarrassed and quickly made my way to the toilet whilst Lois got me some more clothes to put on. This was the first time I had wet myself but I guess it was hardly surprising with the stress I had just been placed under.

'How did she do, Becki?' Lois asked Becki once I was out of earshot.

'She did really well. He started by testing her mental capacity and was obviously satisfied she was able to answer for herself as he proceeded with a long line of questioning. Each question she was clear, and it was obvious they were her words and her decisions and that she had not been coerced. She really

146

did make her point about not wanting her children here; in fact she has just told me she never wants to see them again,' Becki said.

I came out of the toilet and left my dirty soiled clothes on the floor which Lois put into a carrier bag to bring back with us to wash. As we said our goodbyes to Becki, I was relieved it was over and couldn't thank her enough for being with me today. It had been quite an ordeal. On the way home, my head was spinning like an old washing machine with all the things the investigator had been asking and insinuating.

'Do you know what, Lois, after today, I never want to see them again,' I told her.

'Never is a long time, Emmeline. I know you are angry now so don't make a decision in this emotional state,' she urged me.

'No, they have not just crossed the line, but they have chosen to put me through hell today,' I told her.

'I know, I feel the same, but anger eats you up if you let it and we cannot allow them to have such control over us,' Lois said.

'They have accused you of some horrible things to get your name off as my POA, pretending they care for my welfare but it's only so they can get their hands on my money,' I said alarmed.

'Yes, they are accusing me out of their own black hearts. They could never reach my standards because they don't have the capacity for such understanding. They are to be pitied, Emmeline. Time to move on and forget all about them,' Lois said.

'That is easier said than done. I will move on, but I won't forget or forgive them for what they have done,' I said angrily.

Lois was right, I was angry, and I had every right to be. Who the hell did they think they were interfering in my life, making up outrageous lies and forcing me to prove I had the right to make my own decisions. They may have become adults but that didn't suddenly render me the child or give them the right to treat me like an imbecile.

I was raging that Kelly had the audacity to look down her nose because I had sent her daughter a £50 birthday gift; wasn't how much I sent my choice. Maybe she ought to examine her attitude. Most people would be thankful for £50, not making a complaint to a governing body about the fact.

And as far as wanting access to my Will, what I do with my brass is up to me. I wouldn't dream of telling them what they should or shouldn't spend their money on, so why would they assume my money is any of their concerns. It's none of their business and I didn't mind telling Mr Jacobs so either, and as for Lois stopping them coming, I don't want anything to do with either one of them again.

After today, I would wipe them out without a sideways glance but thankfully it was over with now, so I don't need to have anything to do with them again.

Little did I know that the sly little bitches were still monitoring everything we were doing. They were calling in to my neighbours and trying to access any information they could, to continue with their mind games. It wasn't over yet by a long shot!

Chapter 21
The Carer
A Whole New Level of Crazy

To say I was concerned about Emmeline's mental health was an understatement. So far this year, she had endured an onslaught of incidents, one straight after the other that had only sought to exacerbate her condition further. Anyone that knows anything about dementia will know their minds are fragile in cases of trauma, and each time I was fighting hard to bring her back.

The Vascular part meant she would experience a sudden drop but if supported I had been able to tease her back. However, it was never to the same level; skills would be lost, and I felt I was fighting against an unknown enemy. After her interview, she became withdrawn.

She wasn't just angry, she was hurting too. So we made the decision to try to salvage some of our summer together and went back over to Hornsea. It made no difference. She was just going through the motions. The light we had seen in her eyes the last time we had been here had well and truly been extinguished.

So, we didn't go off on any day trips together, we just took things easy. The children played out on their bikes with friends until the streetlights came on and I pottered about keeping an eye on Emmeline. Before long, it was time to return for the new school term and I had an interview with Social Services as I had been asked to do the training to become a foster carer.

This was my last interview before my board was being sat the following month, however when I returned the social worker cancelled that morning having found a placement with another borough. As I called over to Grey Gables to do a check on things, the neighbour beckoned me over as he had taken in the mail on Emmeline's behalf; only taking a cursory look over it I brought it back.

'There is some mail for you there, Emmeline,' I said placing it on the coffee table and walking into the kitchen to put some shopping away.

I was just stacking the tins in the cupboard when I heard her say, 'You have got to be bloody joking!'

Leaving the cupboard door open and an array of tins on the surface, I popped my head around the door to enquire. 'Is everything ok?'

'Have you seen this?' She said handing me a postcard.

I could see from the front that it had been sent from Spain. A shiver went through me as I turned it over, and to my astonishment, it was from Kelly.

'What a bloody smack in the face. Is she really stupid enough to think this will cover her tracks and distract us from what she has done?' Emmeline asked.

'I really do not know what to say.' I was dumbfounded so simply handed the postcard back.

Emmeline read aloud. 'Hi, hope all is well. Just to let you know that we are all away on our summer vacation. Charlotte has come this time. Well, it is a free holiday (lol) and it's the last one before Haley goes away to college. We are having a lovely time and of course going to our favourite Karaoke bar. Lots of love, "The Fletcher" Family,' Emmeline read in a sarcastic singsong tone.

'So, she ruins our "family" holiday then sends you a postcard to let you know she is sunning herself in Spain with her family without a care in the world. Twisted!' I said and slid down on to the settee absolutely sluffened.

'There is nothing like sticking the knife in,' Emmeline said dejectedly.

'Do you really think this is her way of trying to cover her tracks, like we suddenly won't suspect she has anything to do with the allegations because she has sent you a postcard?' I asked incredulous.

'Maybe it's her way of normalising the situation or fooling herself into thinking she can paper over the cracks, and it will all go away,' Emmeline suggested.

'What in a "I was only looking out for your best interests", let's forgive and forget type of manner?' I verified.

'She needn't think this is going to be smoothed over and as for having my best interests at heart, she is 5 years too late,' Emmeline said referring to her abandonment since dad's passing. 'Besides, it's obvious she made the allegations. Who else would complain that Haley didn't receive enough money for their birthday?'

I went back into the kitchen astounded at her audacity and angry as I thought about the summer we had planned. It had started out exactly as we had hoped; carefree, sunny fun filled family days out surrounded by love and laughter in our little haven of tranquillity. We had believed the summer was stretched out before us and we eagerly awaited each adventure hoping to have many tales to tell by the end of it. Not to mention memories to hold and cherish having Emmeline with us.

But both Kelly and Ruby had put paid to that. They had made sure we had a summer to remember but it wasn't of the kind we had hoped for; it was filled with stress, hurt, anger and worry. It was awful because when I didn't think they could sink any lower, they surpassed themselves. This was beyond being two-faced; it was sick and yet another mind-bending hit on an elderly lady with dementia.

It didn't stop there. A week later, I went over to Grey Gables to open up for a viewing to find an unassuming box, approximately a foot long but only 10" square, sat on the table. It was addressed to Emmeline, bore a Yorkshire postmark but there was nothing else remarkable about it. The only person who had a key to the house was the neighbour so he must have brought it in.

When the viewing was over, I took it back to give to Emmeline thinking it might have been a birthday gift from someone and again placed it on the coffee table for her.

'This has got to stop! Why won't she just leave me alone?' Emmeline screeched.

'What is it, Emmeline?' I enquired.

In front of her on the coffee table was the box, now open and revealing a few straggly, long-stemmed flowers. Emmeline pointed at them. 'She has sent these now.'

'Are you sure they are from her? I mean, is there a note with them,' I asked.

'Is there a note?' Emmeline screeched. 'Just look at it!' She demanded.

I took the note and read, '*Heard you had been in hospital. I've had kidney stone issues too; they are very painful. Hope you are feeling better now.* What the heck?'

'Emmeline, this is mind-bending,' I told her.

'She just wants to let me know that she is still watching me and that someone is keeping tabs on me and letting them know everything that happens. This is enough to send anyone around the twist. What is wrong with them? Don't they have anything better to do?' She yelled.

'Maybe you should try and calm down, Emmeline. If they want to waste their lives keeping up a surveillance on what happens here, let them get on with it.

The best thing you can do is ignore it and just carry on as though it doesn't bother you,' I tried to reason.

'Doesn't bother me? But it does. I am sick of them thinking they can control me, dictate what I can and cannot spend my money on and bully us all in this way. No, it has to stop,' Emmeline stated.

'What do you want to do?' I asked.

'First of all, get me a pen and paper. I am going to tell her exactly what I think of her and then you can send this back to her,' she said pointing at the box.

I got her the pen and paper she had requested and left her to it, in the hope she would calm down once she had got it out of her system. She didn't. About half an hour later she said, 'Right there you go,' and handed me the full A4 piece of paper. It wasn't pretty; she had clearly had enough and was taking back some control.

She told Kelly in no uncertain terms exactly what she thought of her, her antics and that she had washed her hands of her. She wanted no more to do with her and to not contact her ever again.

Once I had read it, I simply said, 'Wow, you really are fired up.'

'Yes, it needs saying and now I want you to put it in with these flowers and to send them back. If anything else comes from either of them, I do not want to know. Just send anything and everything back no matter what it is until they get the message.' She stated.

'Are you sure about this, Emmeline? I would be gutted to get a letter like this never mind from my mum,' I tried to reason.

'But you wouldn't play mind games for months on end and try to force me into an early grave, nor force me to testify in court, abandon me or put me through the stresses these two have. No, I am telling you, I want you to send this back to her. Enough!' She had decided and so I had no alternative but to abide by her wishes.

Less than a week later, I was waiting outside Jack's school at the end of the day to collect him when I saw Sarah. She tentatively approached and asked how things were and if anything had transpired now it was the end of his licence. So I told her about the false allegations, Emmeline's interview, her hospitalisation, the postcard and now the flowers.

'Lois, this will not be the end of it. Ruby told me they would make allegations prior to Emmeline passing away just so it gave them foundations afterwards, to say that they had already raised concerns,' she told me.

'So, what you are telling me is this is all just a prequel to the grand finale? Wow, that is some long term premeditated well planned freaky shit! Seriously?' I gasped my mouth open wide in utter disbelief.

'I am telling you, Lois; you won't believe the levels Ruby sank to when I decided to marry Shaun. He never liked her from the start and she did everything to split us up to get rid of him. When she realised I was going to marry him, meaning our friendship was coming to an end, she made us both pay,' Sarah told me.

'What do you mean, made you pay? Surely to goodness it's a case of you become man and wife, she makes herself scarce so you can settle into married life together,' I said.

'That would be the "normal" way, but it wasn't Ruby's. She had to make me pay for taking my friendship away and make him pay, because he had taken her place.'

'So, what happened?' I asked.

'She was supposed to be my maid of honour but went haywire the night before the wedding. Shaun had paid for her and the children to stay at the hotel for the night so she could help set up and then come to the house to assist me. Shaun was in a right state not knowing what had happened.'

'He couldn't get her on the phone, and he didn't want to ring me and stress me out, so he was left freaking out. She turned up at the last minute with the wedding cake that she had made. I say "made" but she had deliberately undercooked it, so it wasn't edible.'

'She spent the entire day making jibes at Shaun, winding him up and his sister who he doesn't get on with until he blew up. Ruby then rang the police and accused him of being threatening and aggressive, so they turned up and when he wouldn't leave the premises, they arrested him.'

'On your wedding day? The heartless bitch,' I said shocked.

'Yes, on my wedding day. Then she came the next day with the cake and (she made inverted commas in mid-air with her right and left index and middle fingers) "accidentally on purpose" brought the boot door down onto it!'

'Holy crap, Sarah, that is someone with severe psychological issues, bit like Harley Quinn; a whole new level of crazy,' I commented.

'What I am trying to demonstrate, Lois, is she plots, plans and executes it with precision. It doesn't matter how much time it takes, the end will always justify the means with Ruby. Kelly doesn't know it, but she is just a pawn to fire the bullets whilst Ruby will be salivating on the side-lines.

I told you before, she cannot wait until something happens to Emmeline so she can see her plan come to fruition. So, keep watching your back, Lois, as this is not the end of it,' Sarah warned me.

I decided not to worry Emmeline with this new information, but I did however, feel I needed to protect her as much as possible. The next day after I had dropped the boys off at school, I went to Grey Gables and was intercepted by the next-door neighbour informing me that Ruby had contacted her out of the blue. Apparently, she had tried to sound all casual asking how she was etc but inevitably the neighbour realised there was a purpose, so asked outright what she wanted.

Ruby then enquired about Grey Gables, wanting to know if it was on the market to which the neighbour had told her she had no idea, and maybe it was a question she should be asking Emmeline. She noted that Ruby never made any enquiry with regards to Emmeline, her health or where she was, just about the house itself.

She also said she felt as though the line had been put on loudspeaker, as she hadn't been able to hear her properly at first, like it wasn't fully up to her mouth. It seemed Sarah was right, the spies were still deeply engrained in the woodwork.

At the end of the week, it was Emmeline's birthday, so I decide to take her over to Leeds to see her sister whom we then ended up bringing back to St Georges with us to enjoy an afternoon tea of singing and bingo. After I had taken her home, we settled with a cup of tea with the boys to open her presents. Inevitably, she has not received anything for years from my siblings, so I always overcompensated to ensure she didn't feel like she was missing out.

This year we got her a long black cardigan, a dark blue sparkly top, a turquoise and white t-shirt, a black, green, blue tunic, The Green Mile DVD, The Lady in a Campervan DVD, flowers, a tub of Celebrations, Toffifee, a notebook to write her thoughts in and some After 8's. In the evening, I took her to our favourite Cantonese restaurant, The Royale, on Leeds Road, Lofthouse. It's an unassuming building at the end of a row of terraced houses with parking down a little hill to the back.

Inside it has the customary deep red décor with tables laid for four around the edges and larger ones set down the middle of the restaurant. The staff are always helpful, courteous and attentive, and the food is to die, for especially the lettuce wrap, my all-time favourite starter, much to the amusement of my meat devouring pal, Selina. We left stuffed to the brim.

'Happy Birthday, Emmeline,' I said for the umpteenth time today.

'Thank you, love, it really has been a wonderful day,' she told me.

'I hope so, you deserve it and I have tried to make it special for you,' I said.

'You have definitely made it special, love. Nothing is too much trouble for you. I cannot thank you enough,' Emmeline gushed.

'Don't forget, tomorrow we are going to Hornsea too, to make a weekend of it,' I reminded her and smiled to myself as she had no idea of the surprise party that was awaiting her.

Chapter 22
Emmeline
Clearing Out Grey Gables

Lois gave me the most wonderful birthday. Not only did we visit my sister but she went back and forth to Leeds so she could come over and enjoy the afternoon with me at the Dementia café. I had lots of presents to open and then we went out for a lovely meal too! As if that wasn't enough, the day after she organised everything so we could collect the boys from school and go straight over to Hornsea.

Once we were unpacked, it was down for an Auntie Helen's special where we were met by a whole host of people. We spent the evening chatting amongst friends before going into the best room for an evening of Karaoke. John that we were sat with, and his brother, Mike, sang my favourite song *The Wonder of You* by Elvis Presley, especially for me as it was my birthday.

It was lovely that people here just accepted your warts and all. It didn't matter that we hadn't known them for long or that it may be weeks before we saw them again. This was why I loved it here so much. I was a part of things; I felt safe, respected and I knew I was cared about.

They say you cannot choose your family, that you can only choose your friends but at Larkham's, they chose me and that made me feel very special indeed.

The next morning, Lois took me to have a wander around the old market town of Beverley. There were plenty of stalls to browse, second-hand shops and fascinating olde-worlde shops. We stopped at Subway where I had a 6" sub, a cuppa and a packet of crisps then we had a ride back to Cowden.

For some reason, Lois wanted to go out early so she assisted me to shower, blow dried and styled my hair for me, then put some new clothes out for me to get dressed in. Once I was ready, we had a stroll down to Larkham's where I was greeted with 20 of our friends singing 'Happy Birthday' as soon as I walked in the door. They had come with cards and presents just for me, for my surprise birthday party.

I was absolutely over the moon! It seemed a million miles away from the stress and terror induced by my children, where here, I was overwhelmed by the warmth and readiness of the love, they encapsulated me in.

An area had been cordoned off to the left of the French windows, with brightly coloured balloons and banners wishing me a "Happy Birthday" and everyone was smiling and cheering. I really felt the belle of the ball, and there is no mistaking it. Pip moved up and with a massive grin on her face said, 'Come on, Mum, sit here next to me,' and I was ushered in whilst Lois went to the bar and got me a malibu and lemonade.

I had a wonderful time, especially when Auntie Helen came out with the food that Lois had organised for everyone; hot pulled pork sandwiches with apple sauce, stuffing, chips and salad. Is there any wonder that I look at Lois with such fondness or why I feel so safe when I'm with her. When she goes above and beyond for me continuously making sure I am living the best life possible?

There are so many elderly people who live alone, abandoned and forgotten yet I am so blessed to have this amazing woman who pulls out all the stops for me and often at the expense of her own health. Sometimes, I look at her in awe not just the amount she does but how she seems to take everything in her stride and juggles it all simultaneously.

I stayed out until 10 pm, having had the best birthday surprise and the next day, we took pleasure with a walk along the beach then enjoyed fish and chips before packing up. Once she had cleaned the van, packed the car, drove us home, unpacked the car at the other end, there were 3 loads of washing to do, ironing of the boy's uniform, tea to make and then it was bedtime routines and back up to start all over again.

Over the next few weeks, we eased into a routine of school runs and appointments where Lois took me for my eyes testing, a trip to the podiatrist, the dentist and to the nurse for my ears syringing. She organised my yearly house insurance only this time as an unoccupied building, ensured my wheelchair was serviced then she broached the subject of "Grey Gables".

'Emmeline, I just want to check with you whether everything is alright?' Lois asked.

'Yes, love, why wouldn't it be?' I responded.

'It isn't that I think there is anything wrong, it's just you have been with us for 3 months now, so I wanted to check in with you that you are still happy to be here with us, that's all,' she explained.

'I am more than happy, love, as I keep telling you I feel safe with you and I love being a part of everything. I couldn't ever go back to living on my own again,' I stated.

'I am just thinking about Grey Gables and the prospect of it being sold. The cupboards are full to capacity, and it is going take a lot of time and effort to go through all your things, I just don't want to be under pressure when that time comes,' Lois said.

'What do you suggest, love?' I queried.

'Well, I am not particularly looking forward to it, but I think we need to make a start and tackle a room a day until we have cleared it,' she said.

'I am happy for you to get rid of anything and everything. The furniture isn't up to much and unless you think there is something we need take it to the tip or a charity shop,' I told her.

'I am not comfortable making those decisions without you being there as I might get rid of something that's really important to you,' she explained.

'Lois, all I want is here. Grey Gables is my past and there is nothing that I need or want to keep. I trust you to make any decisions you feel are appropriate,' I reassured her.

She took a deep breath as though totally overwhelmed, 'I knew this wasn't going to be easy but that puts an awful lot of responsibility upon my shoulders, Emmeline. I am really not comfortable making such decisions especially in light of the allegations that have just been made about me,' she stated.

'I understand that, love, but I am telling you this is what I want you to do, as I am not up to going through things myself,' I told her.

Lois was very despondent and quite dejected at the prospect of taking on such a mammoth task. I guess it was something Jeff and I should have paid more attention to instead of spreading ourselves out and neglecting our responsibilities. Now poor Lois had this to do alone on top of all her other responsibilities, and she was right, it wasn't her place to have to go through everything, it was mine, but I did not have the capability or concentration required.

On the first day, Lois tackled the kitchen removing out of date tinned things and bringing back what could still be used at home. She sorted through ten of the cupboards and drawers, stacking things in boxes and then dropping them at the local Sue Ryder shop in Dewsbury before being present at a viewing. She then collected the boys from school, packed the car, bought us all food and took us to Hornsea for another weekend.

Inevitably, we had a packed weekend then she cleaned the van, drove us back to several loads of washing and school uniforms before getting up the next day to school runs, then back to Grey Gables for another day sorting through things. This day, she did two large spare bedrooms along with the bookcase I had on the landing before loading the car up and donating things to Flutterby's, a charity shop that supported individuals with dementia and the Alzheimer's society.

Then it was a race to collect the boys from school, cook tea, take Poppy out and then she took Joe to Cubs before the bedtime routine and falling into bed exhausted. I was beginning to wonder if I was becoming a burden for Lois because she never seemed to stop or have any real time for herself. She was always on the go providing for all our needs, tending to Grey Gables, Hornsea, her own home and Poppy, the dog.

I noticed she rarely sat down and she was beginning to look really tired, was having dizzy spells again and persistent migraines which worried me, but I didn't say anything.

It was now the beginning of October and on the Monday after returning from Hornsea, Lois took the boys to school then returned to Grey Gables to continue with the big clear out; this time concentrating on the large walk-in pantry that held numerous things. She took a car full to Sue Ryder, collected the boys from school then took Jack back over to Grey Gables, where they struggled to put the bench she had bought in Jeff's memory into the car and brought it home.

She didn't even let me know she had done this because she wanted it to be a surprise, but then spent the evening sanding it down, her intention to completely restore it for me.

The next day, Lois worked hard going through the bathroom, laundry, she finished the kitchen and then did the morning room and drawing room, bringing several files home for me to go through at leisure. To be honest, they meant absolutely nothing to me. I looked but I didn't really know what to do with them, they had lost any importance or meaning so Lois suggested we keep them in storage for now.

The next day, Laura came over to Grey Gables to check on us and to see if we needed a hand. It brought Lois a much-needed break and also a good diversion for me as Laura took me into town for lunch whilst Lois continued, but she still found time to take me to the Dementia café in the afternoon, although we had to rush for the boys from school.

This is what I mean about her constantly rushing from one thing to the next, with no time for herself as nothing she did was of any value for herself. It was mainly for me or managing the boys' timetables too. This excruciating schedule continued for another 2 weeks until Leanne invited her to go out for an evening. Inevitably, we all encouraged her to have the time for herself. Unfortunately, she ended up with food poisoning and was bed ridden for 2 days with sickness, diarrhoea, fatigue and vertigo, feeling ill for the full week.

She must have felt absolutely wretched because I think she was at the point of giving up. She had lost her spark and I had gone well within myself too, unable to stimulate any conversation and the boys were staying in their rooms. We were no longer a band of merry men but never one to be beaten, Lois sat me down one day to have a chat.

'Emmeline, I have to admit that I am completely whacked. I have aches in places I didn't even know were possible and I feel that no matter how hard I try nothing is working,' she told me.

'I know what you mean, love, everyone seems to have lost their sparkle,' I admitted.

'I don't know what more I can do. I am just one person, but something somewhere has got to give otherwise I think I will end up having a breakdown myself trying to keep everything together,' her heart unfolded.

'What can we do, love?' I asked perplexed.

'I don't know. I feel we have run out of options, and my energies have depleted no matter what I try to do. It seems like I am flogging a dead horse,' Lois said.

'Do you need me to move back to Grey Gables?' I asked not really wanting to hear the answer.

'No, absolutely not. That is not what I am suggesting at all. It's just I feel pushed beyond my limits with everything and I am not getting any quality time with the boys, and they are becoming withdrawn,' Lois explained.

'Yes, love, I know you used to always be out and about with them but other than Hornsea, they haven't had you to spend any time with them,' I acknowledge.

'The reality is that as you were isolated at Grey Gables, they have now become isolated in their bedrooms. It's like we are all living independent lives behind closed doors. We have no space here to stretch, socialise or grow we seem to have stagnated and are treading water, trying to catch our breaths without affecting each other,' Lois said.

'What can we do, love?' I asked earnestly.

'I don't know, Emmeline. I just feel if we don't do something soon, my boys' mental health is going to start being affected, and that then feels like I am not protecting them,' Lois told me.

'If I am honest, love, I have noticed they have pulled away. Maybe because all your attention is on my needs and not theirs,' I told her.

'Remember last night when you shouted me to help you out of the bath, Jack had wanted me to help him with his homework and it broke my heart when he said, "it's ok, Mum, I know grandma's needs come first",' Lois confessed.

'That's not right, Lois. They are children; they should be your first priority,' I told her.

'I know but I am split in so many ways I don't know what to do next. This house hasn't sold, the part exchange rate was £30k under the valuation and the last viewing at Grey Gables was a builder who offered £100k under the asking price. I cannot make things move forward but I feel we are on a downward spiral that I have no control over,' she said.

'What if we moved over to Grey Gables? We would have all the space we needed there,' I put to her.

'But, Emmeline, it needs a total refurbishment; new bathrooms, a kitchen and windows to bring it up to today's habitable standards. I cannot take my children there in its present state,' she sighed.

'If I sold it to the builder, I would get £100k less than it's worth. Then he would do the work and make a packet on it, that doesn't seem fair,' I reasoned.

'It isn't fair, but a builder would be able to turn it around in no time and bring it back to its former glory,' Lois ventured.

'Why can't we make it our home again? After all, we are looking for properties in Ossett, yet we already have one there waiting for us?' I asked.

'I suppose when you take into consideration the costs of moving, the stamp duty, estate agent and solicitors fees for both our properties this could be put into the cost of renovations. But what about the allegations? I don't want to be accused of making you spend your money because you know they will say it's only to benefit me,' she said.

'Buggar them, it's my brass and I will use it in whatever way I decide. In fact I will write a statement giving you permission if that will make you feel better,' I told her.

'It is ok you joking but God forbid something does happen to you, as we have already been warned they are gunning for me, so yes I would feel more comfortable you putting something in writing to protect me from future allegations,' Lois insisted.

'At the end of the day, Lois, it is my property and my responsibility to maintain but it's your position to work within my best interests and no one can argue that being in my own home with you and the boys is not fulfilling that role,' I pointed out.

'I wouldn't know where to start, there is that much that needs doing, not to mention the money it will cost,' she pondered.

'Well, to be honest, Lois, I have been thinking about it since the investigator said Kelly and Ruby had accused me of giving you money for your doors and windows. Then there was Ruby wanting me to pay for her house improvements and the other one wanting me out of Grey Gables because he wanted to make a packet on it himself,' I said.

'I suppose I am damned if I do and I am damned if I don't, but I do know for all our mental health and well-being we have to make a decision and soon,' Lois said defeatedly.

'Let's sleep on it and have another chat tomorrow,' I said.

'Just to be clear, you are saying this is what you would like me to do, Emmeline; renovate Grey Gables and move everyone there?' Lois asked.

'Yes please, love,' I admitted.

'It is not an easy fate and before I agree to anything, we will have to sit down with the boys as this will affect them immensely, so they have to be on board with it,' she reasoned.

'That's fair enough, love. All I ask is that you give it consideration because as you say we are knocking at all the doors, but nothing is opening for us maybe that's because this is the way we should be going.' I said.

Lois raised her eyes to the ceiling, shook her head, swallowed and exhaled sharply, probably overwhelmed at the prospect at having even more pressure and weight applied to her already heavy load. As I went into my room that night and glanced at the photos of Jeff, I picked up the memory book and flicked through it, feeling such warmth from the pages of happy smiling faces.

I lay down feeling certain we could bring back the sparkle to everyone's eyes by securing our forever home, and that Grey Gables was where we needed to be to make new memories to replace the old bad ones.

Chapter 23
The Carer
Be Ready to Go

I sometimes wonder how on earth I get myself into situations. Here I was, thoroughly drained emotionally, mentally and physically having my elderly mother living with us and been dragged through the mill with a ridiculous investigation. Yet, I was now agreeing to clear out Grey Gables, a humungous property of disproportional levels, that was packed to the rafters with decades of family belongings.

It was a colossal task and not for the faint hearted but it was equally one that was neither my responsibility nor one that I had any motivation towards. So, in between supporting Emmeline's needs, afterschool activities, parents' evening, cooking, cleaning, shopping, trips to Hornsea, birthday celebrations, school runs, dog walking and medical appointments, I was now inundated with numerous other responsibilities.

On a daily basis, I was having to go over and sort through, drawers, cupboards and shelves packed with stuff, but the worst were the three bedrooms full of Emmeline's clothes. There were eight double wardrobes with one having 26 boxes of shoes stacked in it. It was a mind bending, soul destroying, back breaking project that I really was in no fit state myself to contend with.

But who else was there? Every single room I entered gave a cacophony of deafening alarm bells that ricocheted from one side of my brain to the other. I felt suffocated, drowning in a situation that wasn't mine to deal with. I make no wonder I ended up feeling so poorly, exhausted and plagued with severe migraines.

On top of this, Emmeline's property needed to be maintained, so I had to sort out her insurance, have her alarm serviced, the gardener to organise, a plumber to source for a leak from the upstairs toilet along with house viewings to monitor.

My head was spinning yet I still had to feature in bank appointments, getting her hair done, pad deliveries, managing her finances, ordering/collecting her numerous prescriptions, getting her ears syringed and then I had to have a minor procedure myself.

As the month of September drew to an end, I noticed that Emmeline was becoming more withdrawn. She did not stimulate conversation and appeared to be transfixed by the little people in the tv. Then Emmeline told me that she had seen Kelly and Ruby driving up and down the street, so the one place she did feel secure was no longer her safe haven, all because the investigation would have revealed her location.

She then started to become paranoid that my brother may try to gain access to Grey Gables, so her state of mind began to plummet again. This time I had to contend with poo smearing. It was literally all over the toilet seat, on the taps, the towels everywhere, not just once but over and over again. She became disorientated with garbled speech, unable to find the correct words she wanted to use, repeating the same things in quick succession, or not making any sense at all.

Inevitably, this was frustrating not only for herself but also for me and the boys, who had no idea what on earth was going on. Joe asked me one day if she needed her batteries changing because she sounded much like his remote-controlled car when they were coming to their expiry.

I really was at the end of my tether. It seemed to me that no matter what I did or how hard I tried to support her, it was persistently undone at every opportunity. It came to a head when she started banging about in the early hours of the morning at 04.45; coming upstairs opening our doors turning the lights on and waking us up to make sure we were all still there. The house suddenly felt cramped, and we were plummeted into crisis, unable to escape the extreme behaviours that dementia can produce.

'Emmeline, we really cannot go on like this. I feel close to a breakdown, and I am concerned for the welfare of the boys' mental health and well-being,' I told her.

'You want me to leave, don't you?' She said.

'No, but we need to do something quickly, otherwise I am not going to be in a fit state to look after you, never mind the boys, and my fear is you are going to end up spiralling so far out of control that I fear I won't be able to get you back,' I said.

'I can't go back there, Lois, I just can't,' she said getting emotional.

'What about if we do what you suggested and renovate Grey Gables,' I said.

'Really?' She asked.

'I have to tell you it is the last thing I want to do; I am exhausted and at breaking point so NO, I don't want to do this but neither of our houses are selling. If I don't do something before it's too late, I dread to think what the outcome will be,' I told her feeling beyond all hope.

'Do you really think we could get it done and move back?' She asked.

'At this point, I don't feel that I have any other choice. I am being backed into a corner,' I told her.

'You can take whatever it costs out of my bank,' she said.

'Not being funny, Emmeline, but it is your property that has been neglected all these years, so yes, it will have to be at a cost to you. However, the way I am looking at it is what Matthew, the dementia Nurse said, if you were to go into a home it would cost about £45k per year; if we get it done below that you have broken even after the first year.'

'Equally, it's in your best interests to remain in your own environment for as long as possible to access what is familiar to you so, as Rob, your financial advisor, said no one can argue it is not money well spent. But I have to make it clear, I really do not want to take this on,' I emphatically stressed.

'How long do you think it would take?' She asked totally ignoring my feelings.

'If I was going to do it I would endeavour to get everyone in by Christmas as I wouldn't want it to drag on any longer but that will be me breaking my back to get it done. Are you sure this is the road you want to take?' I asked.

'Yes please,' was her quick and simple answer, just two words that would cause another 2 months of immense stress and pressure on my shoulders whilst she simply waited in the wings for the curtain call to say it was all done for her.

I had spent approximately 3 weeks at this point sifting through the boxes of her life at Grey Gables, done over twenty-five runs to either the tip or charity shops taking over hundred binbags and forty boxes of belongings weighing down my car. I didn't have the energy for anything else, but I honestly could not see anything else giving and we couldn't carry on, so if I had to invest in another 2 months of back breaking labour for our long-time goals rather than her go into a home, then that's what I would have to do.

There was little choice so when I collected the boys from school just before their October half term week, I asked if we could have a family meeting. The boys sat to the left of Emmeline next to each other on the settee, Joe with his legs barely touching the floor but Jack upright, alert and awaiting to hear what was going to be delivered. I got the pouffe and placed it in front of them not really wanting to have this conversation.

'I have been talking to grandma about our current situation with regards our living conditions, and for all intents and purposes, it just doesn't seem to be working,' I ventured.

'Yes, it is difficult for all of us,' Jack said.

'It is, love,' I continued. 'The house suddenly feels cramped and being here is causing Emmeline much stress which is why she is so unsettled. Plus, I don't like how both of you are reverting back to being alone in your rooms, it's not good for you,' I told them.

Jack looked at Emmeline gave a half smile as if to say, 'I know it's not your fault,' then reached out and gave her hand a reassuring squeeze.

'The thing is, I want to put something to you that is a bit off the wall, but I cannot think of any other alternative at the moment, and we need to change things and quick,' I said.

'What, Mummy?' They both asked in unison looking afraid of what I may be suggesting.

'How would you feel if we packed up and went to live at Grey Gables with Emmeline there,' I said letting the cat out of the bag.

Immediately Jack teared up. 'No, Mummy, please. I don't want to go there. I don't like it,' he pleaded.

'What is making you feel so upset, Jack?' I asked.

'It's too big and it is scary. I really don't want to, please,' he said almost hysterical. 'And sorry, Grandma, but everything is so old.'

'Jack,' I reassured him, 'it won't be immediately and for a start, I will have to fully renovate the place because at the moment we couldn't even make a meal in that kitchen LITERALLY, so everything will have to be updated first.'

'It is not just that, it's really dark,' he admitted.

'I promise you that I will change those things for you, but I do need everyone to be on board with it for me to go ahead,' I said, as he went quiet.

'What do you think, Joe?' I asked.

'Sounds great. Can I have the back bedroom?' He said which surprised me because it was never a room that was in use and this one had contained most of the things I had to go through.

'All I am asking, Jack, is for you to be on board so we can press ahead, and I will try and get you in by Christmas,' I told him.

'So, we wouldn't have Christmas at home?' Jack sounded even more defeated.

'We will have it in our "new" home,' I said trying to sound hopeful.

'You're going to do it anyway, aren't you?' He asked.

'I just don't have another option. We have tried to sell both our houses and had no luck. We have tried with grandma living here but you can see the impact it's having, not just on her but on us too, so we need to explore another avenue until we find one that works for all of us,' I tried to reason.

'What if that plan doesn't work either?' Jack played devil's advocate.

'All I am asking is that we all give it a go. I will spend the next 2 months renovating it to bring it up to today's standard, then I will concentrate in redefining the areas to ensure we utilise the space that best meets all our needs,' I said.

'But what if we are not happy there,' Jack asked.

'We are not happy here, love, so it cannot be any worse,' I began. 'How about you agree to give it a go and I agree that if by the end of the academic year any one person is unhappy, then it goes on the market?' I then addressed Emmeline. 'Are you happy with that?'

'That sounds fair to me,' she agreed.

'Joe?' I asked.

'Yes, I am up for it. It will be great, I get to have a big bedroom,' he said easily pleased.

'Jack?' I asked.

'It's not fair. I feel like I am the only one who doesn't want to do it but everyone else does, so I don't have a choice!' He said getting upset again.

'Jack, if we do the renovation and it doesn't work we can put it up for sale and Emmeline will get her investment back and we can get somewhere else. The disrepair that it is currently in means she is losing a huge sum of money off the asking price. This way it is a win, win choice for all of us as it gets us out of our current situation and moving to Grey Gables will either work for all of us or it will be a stepping-stone to finding our forever home.'

'OK,' he said, 'but only if we have another meeting in July to decide if we stay or not.'

'Perfect,' I said then opened my arms for a group hug. 'Thank you, love.'

By the end of October, I was literally buckling at the knees, so welcomed our break to Hornsea for the half-term week then I could recoup and gain some control of the runaway train that had become my life. At this point, I had been able to liaise with B&Q, Homebase Wickes and Ikea getting both designs, costings and installation times for kitchens and bathrooms. I had also retained a decorator in situ and organised quotes for the three new bay windows with stone sills that occupied the main rooms downstairs.

Things were beginning to take shape so whilst we had some breathing space, I took the opportunity to discuss the costings with Emmeline so she could decide whether or not she wanted to proceed now we had a better idea of what we were dealing with. There was no doubt in her mind; it was money well spent if she got to go back to Grey Gables with us in tow, allowing us to also alleviate the stress and pressures we were all under at the same time.

So that was it; on our return I would now have a stressful 2-month property development project on my hands. Wow, the many hats that I was having to wear seemed to be constantly expanding.

The first job was to remove a multitude of furniture that I could manage on my own like chairs, side tables, boxes and then Emmeline's neighbour, Dick, took an interest in the project and came to my aid to assist with everything else. There are three main lounges which run in a row downstairs and the first to be tackled was one with a piano in it. This was cleared out first minus the piano so that the decorator could begin simultaneously with the window being installed.

I wanted to start here as it was going to be a downstairs bedroom for Emmeline. Whilst the contractors did their work, I was busy with Dick clearing out the next two rooms and bringing down everything that had been in Emmeline's bedroom upstairs to the middle room. Once Andrew had replaced that window, he moved to the adjoining room whilst Graham from 'Out of Hours' Decorators concentrated on the third room.

I was trying to use not just reputable tradesmen but people I had already had personal experience with from the past so could vouch for their work. For instance, I had known Andrew as a child, and he had installed the windows that Kelly and Ruby had accused me of making Emmeline pay for. Graham had not only done lots of decorating for myself, Leanne and Mia, he was married to Hazel who I worked with at Home-Start.

I then had the carpets supplied by Mick Peace from the Carpet Mill, East Ardsley who had already furnished two houses for me. All three gentlemen were flexible and adaptable to my changing needs and scheduled their worked in conjunction with each other, helping me wherever they could. Once the carpet had been fitted into Emmeline's room, Dick and I then focused on installing her furniture as an exact replica of the room above so that it didn't confuse her, and I bought little trinkets to make it homely and welcoming.

I concentrated my energies and the financial input upon the downstairs communal areas as these were where Emmeline would get the most benefits.

The beauty about knowing people in the trade is that they also know many others whom they can confidently recommend. Graham was a mind of information whose passion was ignited in my goal to get Emmeline home. He not only signposted me to the right trades people, but he enthusiastically promoted our joint goal to encourage their input to meet our timelines.

He was a great motivator not only to the people he knew but to myself too for when I was tiring; his continued presence gave me added strength. One of my Godsends was Shaun Coates, Hazel's son-in-law, who came to give a quote to install the kitchen as the major suppliers were grossly overpriced. He was amazing not only did he know an electrician, but Neil's wife, Yvonne, was a kitchen designer.

Yvonne arrived at 12 noon to see what was required and within 7 hours, I had a 3D printed out image meeting our exact needs with costings and timeframes included. She met with Emmeline and I to finalise everything and for Emmeline to give her the go ahead. All of them worked cohesively together during the last week of November, and the first week of December to rewire the kitchen, plaster it, measure, build and install the units, lights, dishwasher, and cooker.

During the project, every door that we knocked on seemed to open up to the next door that we needed yet up to press nothing had gone right for us. Despite my misgivings of such a large project and my exhaustion, God was confirming to me this was where we needed to be. Inevitably along the way, there were delays, like when the plaster hadn't dried sufficiently for the kitchen to go in, or when the boiler wasn't working, or I decided to pull off all the polystyrene tiles of the ceiling of the 30 foot upstairs landing, creating a bigger job for Graham.

At one point, I had fourteen tradespeople in at the same time: two plumbers, a tiler, two window fitters, a decorator, two kitchen fitters, two electricians, two guys fitting granite surfaces in the kitchen and two carpet fitters. Then there was little old me managing all these areas, along with moving furniture, sewing curtains, painting, scraping paper off the walls, removing old tiles, breaking the old kitchen up, pulling carpets up, taking rubbish to the tip, running for supplies, making teas and coffees, and supplying them all with breakfast sandwiches just to keep them working.

As if that wasn't enough, I then decided it would be a good idea to upgrade the old brick-built fireplace that Emmeline had tripped over and fractured her foot on the year before, and organised for a log burner to be installed. My thought process had been that if the boiler of 20 plus years packed up, at least we had another source of heat, especially as all the gas fires had been capped because they had never been serviced and were even older than the boiler.

I was working some very long hours to get this done for my family, often until 10 pm including weekends preparing areas for the next day, each night falling into bed beyond broken but then getting back to it first thing the next morning. I was in the thick of it and contributing to all the work, my hands crippled with glossing and other work. One day the plumber told me I was an 'excellent project manager as anything he needed clearing or doing was ready for them so they could get straight on with their part the next day.'

It made their work easier and less time consuming, my purpose to save Emmeline as much money as I could. Another day there was only me and the tiler working, he joked that he would have to come with a bag of breadcrumbs just so he would be able to find his way back out again.

That day, one minute I was in the toilet next door to him painting, then I was in one of the lounges sewing and hanging curtains, stripping settees to wash covers, then he found me painting the wall lights in Emmeline's room and lastly in the downstairs bathroom furiously removing the tiles in the shower. The following week, he arrived with a bunch of flowers and some chocolates and told me he had been so impressed with my extensive skills set and work ethic that he had been talking about me to his wife, Glo.

He said, 'I told her I am working at this great big place where this young woman is like a tornado, Glo. She's up and down ladders, sewing, and doing a whole host of jobs just so she can get her mum home. I was getting the lads a bottle for Christmas, and I wanted to get you these,' he told me.

I was absolutely thrilled to bits. He didn't know me, had only been to the house once the week before but could see the effort and massive work I had ahead of me. It was very heart-warming and a source of inspiration in my down days to spur me to keep going.

On Sunday, 11 December, Graham was painting for me when his wife, Hazel, came over to lend a hand wanting to support me. She ended up shampooing an upstairs carpet that I decided would be a chill out zone for the boys then she used Graham's van to move some of the children's things over. Everything upstairs that I could do, I did with no real expense apart from the bathroom upgrade; it had been a 1980s burgundy coloured suite so it had to be replaced.

I cleaned everything up, stripped walls and painted, updated the light fittings and wardrobe handles at my own expense, so I couldn't be accused of taking anything from Emmeline that she wouldn't ultimately benefit from herself.

During the second week of December, the upstairs bathroom was finished, the log fire installed and the hall, stairs, landing and downstairs carpets fitted. Whilst this was going on, Laura's husband, Alan, and her brother, David, hired a van and began with the removal of the heavy furniture from Netherton Brow. The boys thought it was ace.

They were on their last week of the winter term, and it was 10 days before Christmas, so with the exception of Emmeline, we didn't mind sleeping on the floor. On the 19th, the electrician was finishing off with the last of the light fittings. On the 20th, the granite worksurfaces were being fitted, and on the 21st, was the vinyl for Emmeline's downstairs bathroom, the laundry and the kitchen.

When the granite went on, I couldn't watch I had to hide upstairs I was so stressed it would either crack or wouldn't look right, so when it had been done Graham came up to coax me to have a look reassuring me it was brilliant. That night when everyone left, I walked around this transformed property that had taken me just 7 weeks to renovate with a mixture of amazement at its beauty, excitement because my family would finally see it tomorrow and sadness my dad wasn't here to enjoy it.

I was running on the fumes of burn out but kept going enough to do a full grocery shop to fill the cupboards, freezer and fridge and to put up the Christmas tree and arrange presents underneath it. It truly was the most magnificent sight and an awe-inspiring achievement by my band of multiskilled trades people. I didn't know it yet, but Emmeline would later want another three rooms upgraded, and in the end, I would personally invest over 500 hours!

The next day, I was nervous and trembling with excitement. My family knew I had been working hard to make a home for them, but they had no real conception of the lengths I had gone to. At around 4 pm, everything was finished so I telephoned them. Jack picked up the phone.

'Hello, darling,' I said.

'Hi, Mummy, where are you?' Jack enquired.

'I am just leaving Grey Gables,' I began. 'What are you doing?'

'We are just playing on the Nintendo Wii with grandma. She is so funny on Mario cart she keeps crashing,' he laughed.

'Can you do me a favour?' I asked.

'Yes, what is it?' He said.

'Can you help grandma on with her shoes and coat, then get yours and Joe's and meet me at the door, ready?' I said.

'Yes, Mummy, why? Where are we going?' He wondered.

'You are moving now,' I informed him.

'Moving? What do you mean?' He asked puzzled.

'Jack, I told you I would get you in by Christmas. Grey Gables is finished so all you have to do is get your shoes and coats on and be ready to go when I come over. It's done.'

'Really, Mummy, is that *all* we have to do?' He asked.

'Yes, darling, so hurry up, I am on my way,' I said and ended the call.

I had so many positive emotions racing around within me, probably a result of the adrenalin from weeks of slogging it out finally coming to an end. I could barely believe the time had come to showcase all my hard work to my family whose love and belief in me had kept me going. So, I gave thanks to God for making the impossible, possible!

I made my way to them and took a moment to give myself a virtual pat on the back too. I had taken on a project even a harden builder would be proud of and I had done it well. It was amazing and for a fraction of the cost too; thanks to some amazing people and their years of experience and knowledge.

As I pulled up outside the house that was no longer going to be called my "home", I saw three eager faces confused at this sudden request to "be ready to go". One minute they were happily in the warmth of the house the next stood here not quite sure what was happening. When we arrived at Grey Gables, it was a fight to see who could get out of the car first and a race to the door.

'First of all, guys, I am going to go in, but I want you to wait here until I call you as I am going to film your immediate reactions when you see each room whilst we go through the house.' I went inside and placed myself on the little step of the laundry opposite the door to get a full view of each of them, then told them to come in.

Their reactions were priceless. Jack was stunned to find a new kitchen; he thought the old one would have still been in place and that I would have just cleaned it up. Joe loved the island, the light up corner, walk in pantry style cupboard and chose his bar stool immediately. Jack found Poppy's integrated food bowls under the island whilst Emmeline was simply overwhelmed by it all.

Next, I went into the middle room with its log burning stove crackling away and the corner settee facing us, then it was Emmeline's bedroom. She burst in to tears and hugged me weeping with joy to find I had followed her care plan and she would no longer have to go upstairs. The downstairs bathroom with its new suite, the smooth plastered freshly painted light grey walls that accentuated the large, smooth tiles was just for Emmeline.

The boy's bedroom was set out with single beds donned in new Marvel bedding with curtains and matching canvases on the wall. There were toy boxes at its foot and a teddy on each bed with new pyjamas awaiting their owners. After showing them the change to Emmeline's old bedroom that I would now occupy (so I could hear her below me), we visited the upstairs bathroom and then I revealed the chill out zone.

This was a child's paradise of consoles and games, their Trofast units with a tv on top, a desk, corner settee to relax on and more Marvel Canvas's upon the wall. What I had wanted to create was a space where the boys would be able to escape the effects of dementia and lose themselves in what interested them. A safe place where they could socialise with their friends without impacting Emmeline and without her impacting them.

I decided if they were not having a bedroom each then they could share both spaces to ensure they were no longer subjected to the isolation of the past 6 months.

Everyone was thrilled to bits, especially when they realised the fridge was stocked, the Christmas tree was up and this was now our new home for real. All we had to do was forget about everything that had gone before and enjoy our new life in an environment that would cater for all our needs in a space that we could all function in. That was until Ruby was seen climbing over next doors wall at 1 am hoping to avoid our cameras only 2 days later!

Chapter 24
Emmeline
Making New Memories

I was absolutely thrilled to bits when Lois said she would renovate Grey Gables. I knew it was a massive project, one I couldn't have contended with, but I had every faith in Lois, and she didn't disappoint. Over the month of October, she made enquiries and connections with several different trades people along with getting ideas of costings and covered all the groundwork of running around prior to my involvement.

I then enjoyed the most exciting parts of viewing everything she had shortlisted before being able to choose our final products like the kitchen cabinets, tiles, bathroom suites. I wasn't able to retain all the information, but I was kept abreast of the costings and before anything was decided, I was included each time and then able to give the go ahead or query anything I was uncertain of.

That is one of the things with dementia; you have to simplify the decision-making process, narrow things down helping me to understand thus continuing to have a say in the matters that concern me. This is what Lois had off to a fine art, not only because she knew me so well but also due to the extensive studying she had undertaken in order to provide a person-centred approach for me. These were very exciting days indeed and it not only kept my mind occupied, but it also eradicated my concerns regarding Kelly and Ruby.

By the time we had reached the school's October half-term, Lois had gathered together all the information I required to make the decision to either press ahead with the project or pull the plug. To be honest, I wouldn't have cared if it had cost me every penny I had. If Lois and the boys were willing to look after me and live at Grey Gables with me, it was the easiest decision for me to make.

And my attitude was that if I spent everything that I had, good; it meant there was nothing left for either of Kelly or Ruby to get their hands on.

When we returned from Hornsea, the boys went back to school, and Lois cracked on with the renovation project. I was continually kept up to date at the end of each day with what she had been able to achieve or the pitfalls she had found herself in. I could tell she was being stretched to capacity mentally with juggling all the various jobs that required her attention, not to mention the various tradespeople she had to retain and manage.

But equally I could see that she had a vision and when Lois was in this mindset, nothing would divert her from it until she had fulfilled it. She was the same every time she undertook any form of study, like the supervisory management course she took that was targeted at two grades above hers. We were invited to Dudley college for her to receive her certificate at their awards night because Lois had come first nationally attaining eight out of nine distinctions.

It was a very proud moment for me as she wasn't even bothered about going but I had managed to encourage her to go, and I went along with her. They kept her achievements right until the end of the ceremony then gave her a wonderful build up speech, and on walking up to the podium she received a standing ovation. I know she must have been shrinking inside despite her strong elegant walk to the front as she hates being in the limelight, and because Lois seems to work hard to achieve and then just moves on to the next challenge.

She likes to please and doesn't do praise very well. Maybe because of the way she was continually mocked and put down by the others growing up. Nowadays, she doesn't look to anyone else to confirm her abilities or praise her accomplishments as she measures herself by her own yardstick and rightly so.

From what Lois was communicating throughout November, the house was beginning to take shape. I hadn't wanted to see it in its infant stages, worried I may have felt my heartstrings wrenched. Having lived at Lois's now for 6 months, I had been able to detach to some extent but seeing it as a building site would probably have tortured me.

Therefore, I elected to wait for the day of the unveiling to achieve the most powerful affect. Most of the work was achieved in the first 2 weeks of December which was when the plumbers installed the bathrooms and when the kitchen was fitted. I knew we were nearing the end of the project when Lois arranged for the majority of the furniture to be transported across to Grey Gables.

My bedroom was left intact along with the tv and a chair in the living room so I could still sit and watch it, so really I was barely inconvenienced at all. It was Jack and Joe that didn't have beds, and then Lois was coming home after spending long, tiring days of physical labour to also have to sleep on the floor.

It was Wednesday, 21 December, as I was sat watching the boys on their Wii thingy that Lois rang and spoke to Jack. Then I was hustled into my coat and shoes awaiting her arrival. I can honestly say that even though I had been kept fully informed of the daily progressions, I had no idea the transformation would have been quite so dramatic.

I was completely speechless when we entered the kitchen that all I could do was sit on what Lois told me was the "shoe box" as the boys investigated all there was to see. All I could do was look on, was this really my old home? I couldn't help being overwhelmed. It was simply smashing and I was flabbergasted she had achieved such a high-end finish and completely redesigned it.

As we proceeded throughout the house, it was equally has stunning and magnificent but the most overwhelming for me was my downstairs bedroom. A couple of years prior to this, Lois had attended a course with Jack where Becki, who had advocated on my behalf with the investigator, had assisted me to make a "Living Will" which was a kind of advanced care plan.

I had put into this that I wanted Lois and the boys to look after me in my own home and for the piano room to be made into a downstairs bedroom so that it was easy access for carers, but should I become bed ridden it ensured I was still part of the action. You see when my husband became ill and bed ridden himself, he had remained upstairs and I felt he had become isolated. I did not want to make the same mistake again.

Lois had not only changed its usage, but it was an exact replica of the bedroom I had used upstairs, and she was going to be above me in my old room so I had the security of knowing she would hear me if I needed her. On the wall above the bed was a string of hearts and hanging over one of the bedposts was a little angel carved out of wood with the words *May there always be a guardian angel at your side.*

Along the mantelpiece and on top of the piano were photographs that had been in my bedroom at Netherton Brow of Jeff, myself, our wedding and a whole host of others. There was also a miniature plaque hanging from one of the wall lights that had a heart in its centre with the words *Don't try to understand me, just Love ME*; a reminder of what I had said to Lois as we sat in the waiting room about to receive my diagnosis.

The 1970s multicoloured swirly style carpet had been replaced with a new plain one which was evident throughout the downstairs, a must for dementia sufferers. We tend to see patterns differently, busy designs can appear 3 dimensional to us, so flowered carpets on a dark background may look like lilies on water or dark doormats can be mistaken as holes which we may try to step over for fearing of falling into them.

Lois had taken all this information and so much more into consideration so the house was "textbook dementia friendly" as the clinician from Fieldhead hospital later termed it. I was not just overwhelmed by the hard work and dedication by Lois but the depth of the love she had for me to take on this project just to get me home.

There was nothing at all I could ever do to repay Lois for all that she had done for me over the years, but I did hope that she would take time to bask in her achievements for once, instead of putting it to one side to begin the next challenge.

We had a wonderful first Christmas at Grey Gables, not only in the comfort of its surroundings but also in the knowledge that we had the space in which to grow together as a family. In January, Becki Dodds came to see us, as having supported us through the difficulties of the past year had heard we were now settled at Grey Gables. Having seen it in its old form, she was astounded at the transformation like everyone else who came to visit.

That was another perk about being back here. We started to have lots of visitors not only the boys' friends, but Lois' friends came too, and she had lots of them. The house was suddenly no longer just bricks and mortar for me anymore, it was now a home again that was brimming with the love and the lives of everyone who came across its threshold.

I was home and I was happy, especially as just prior to Christmas I was given notification that the allegations made regarding Lois' conduct had been concluded. Obviously as expected it was determined that there was nothing for Lois to answer to. However, its further findings were interesting. I was advised to remove Ruby as a "secondary" attorney as she was not deemed a suitable candidate. No shit Sherlock, I thought.

Over the next couple of months, there were a few incidents of them trying to unsettle us but as Lois advised, we simply ignored their existence and after much persuasion, she took me to seek a solicitor so I could remove Ruby once and for all. Despite the Office of Public Guardian Officer stating my wishes that they now leave me alone and not make any further contact, they still tried it on. So left with no other alternative; I had to ask the police to give them an official warning, enough was enough.

Of course, Kelly got straight on to Facebook to use it as a platform to not only ridicule the need for the police warning, making out her only offence was to send her mum a card but to also whip up support from a multitude of followers not knowing her real crimes. Even her daughter jumped on board ridiculing our faith, 'and they call themselves Christians' or the derogatory blame that was placed on "the carer", as though that was all that Lois was.

Ruby's response was that she couldn't care less if she ever saw me again, yet a year or so later, she was manipulating a neighbour with additional needs to monitor our every movement and getting him to send photographs of our visitors. The main objective of her newfound attention was Sarah, the friend who had got married against Ruby's wishes whose wedding she had ruined.

She had now teamed up with her brother whom she had previously declared she would 'get the bastard' yet having put him away in prison, she was now assisting him to try to get contact with Sarah's children. There seems to be a pattern here about using government bodies who are supposed to protect the innocent to bully them further, as if Sarah and her family hadn't already suffered enough.

She then went on to use Social Services to ensure Shaun was removed from the home he shared with Sarah, Danny and Elena, and charged with some serious offences. Unfortunately, we got caught up in the crossfire, but it just demonstrate yet more of Ruby's interference in other people's lives to bring as much devastation as possible.

For me, never again would they be welcome at my home. A home that hopefully Lois will remain in long after I am gone to live out her days in the comfort she so lovingly created for me, with Jack, Joe and her new partner, Daniel.

Part 3: Moving Forward

We ran the race, we did it all and as the cord began to fall, I felt your hand so tight in mine and knew together we would be fine.

Chapter 25
Daniel's Story

When I first met Lois, I was bowled over. There was something about her and I just couldn't take my eyes off her. I don't mean that in a corny kind of way that she was so stunningly beautiful, and it was love at first sight but there was something about her; she had an inner beauty that mesmerised me. Each time she was around, I had to mentally focus on looking away so that I didn't come across as a creep but soon found my eyes diverting back in her direction.

Over the next 6 months, I watched as she interacted with the people she was with and noticed where some people just sit with one or another, she moved around and gave everyone her time. She would walk around the pub collecting beer glasses when the staff didn't have the time, where she would chat and make everyone feel really special. I longed for the day she might notice me or come to my table but sadly that only occurred once when she knelt at my side talking to the person I was with.

Her presence alone was electric, and I had all on not to reach out and touch her hand. This may sound weird but that is the effect she has not just on me but all the people around her. She has a way of seeking out the needy and those who are invisible to others and making them feel alive again.

I now have the pleasure of reigniting that feeling every time I am in her company and today I watch her in a different way, in the knowledge that she is *with* me and how very proud of her I am. She still walks around the pub collecting glasses involving everyone, being the first to get up with her silly dad dancing routines or coaxing complete strangers to join in who once up cannot sit back down.

When she is in the building you can guarantee that everyone is going to have a good night, but when she isn't there or I go out without her, I feel lost and there is a sense of emptiness.

On the occasion we met properly for the first time, it was the night of the first lockdown, just my luck. I had tried to get her attention by getting up and collecting glasses at the same time or when she was going to the bar I had tried to instigate an accidentally on purpose introduction, but nothing had come of it. This was quite strange as she noticed every other person but for some reason she seemed to have totally zoned me out.

Anyway, she had been sat at the bottom end of the pub with a large group of friends and apparently, wasn't supposed to be out this night but as it was the last night before lockdown, one of her friends had dragged her out. I have thanked them ever since because that night she finally spoke to me. I was that nervous and shocked my response wasn't quite what I had hoped. She had just stood next to me at the bar and ordered her drink when she turned to me and smiled.

'Hiya, you ok? I am Lois,' she said.

'I think we all know who you are,' I blurted out, what an idiot.

'Wow, rude,' she said.

'Sorry can I try that again. Hiya, I am Daniel, pleased to meet you,' I said.

She smiled and said, 'Pleased to meet you too, Daniel,' then collected her drinks and returned to her friends.

I was elated she had finally seen me and spoken but equally as gutted that it was as quick as that, and she was gone again. I knew I couldn't leave it at that, because it had created a deeper yearning to be in her presence all the more, and my opportunity came when she gathered everyone in the pub together for a group photograph. It was one of those defining moments in time where the people you are banded together with are all experiencing something big, and you just want to capture it.

Some will say that the celebrating the silver jubilee waving flags with the whole street partying was theirs, but for me it was the night the country went into lockdown, and we captured it in a photograph. Lois was like that she wanted everyone to be included and there I was a part of it with her. I didn't know it at the time but the young guy who had just started behind the bar was Jack, her son, and he was stood next to me with his arm around my shoulder.

I guess I sound a bit like a stalker but honestly there was no harmful intention I had just fallen head over heels in love with this beautiful creature and I found her and all that she was captivating. I was not the only one. Everybody who comes in to contact with her are the same. It's like touching the coat tails of Jesus as he goes past because you know you will be healed.

She has a compassion and empathy that reaches depths for the lost, hurt and fallen that few could match together with a sense of humour that is interchangeable, quick, and hilarious all at the same time. She has the power to make me incessantly angry, then reduces me to tears with belly aching laughter at some crazy shit she has said. She is all of these things, but she can also be impatient, angry, frustrated, hurt, and upset.

When she is hurt, it is a deep, penetrating anguish that cuts her to the core, not necessarily manifested from today's experience but connected to her past. She is generally a strong independent person, and this is the side that most other people see of her, but I am blessed to see all the other facets of this beautiful diamond.

She once said to me surely if you had a diamond you would polish it so that every facet shone brightly, not just the ones that brought you pleasure; you wouldn't throw a blanket over it as this would dim the ones that need to shine. I guess we all have a past, and some parts are not so pretty, but if we try to hide these parts and only shine in some, the overall diamond doesn't reach its full potential brightness.

In the same way, I have found that Lois is greatly affected by other people's negativity and if she absorbs too much, she will regularly need her space and time to flush it away. I have to say, I still find this a difficult situation to manage as I always fear it will impact our relationship and she might not come back to me. You see my wife passed away when we were young, so I fear loss and would never want to lose Lois.

She explained it to me as like having a sponge full of dirty water and needing to wring it out, rinse it with warm water and to keep wringing it out until it feels clean. She seems to take other people's darkness away, leaving them with her positivity and light, which is ok as long as she has the time to reassess, realign and replenish her energies. She is at her best when we are in the open expanse of nature walking Poppy and Joe's dog, Luna, where we can chat privately and leave it all to be carried away by the wind.

Once the photograph had been taken, I stayed to drink with the others who were trying to coax Lois into having a party afterwards, but she wouldn't be bullied; though did suggest the next night to have it in the bar manager's honour to thank her for her services all these years. As the night came to an end and everyone went their own ways, she stayed back to wait for Jack to finish his shift and gave details of the party to the manager in her honour.

'Don't forget you are welcome to come too, Daniel,' she said to me.

'What?' I said trying to sound nonchalant but actually jumping for joy inside.

'Tomorrow, the party they were badgering me to have. You are more than welcome to come,' she told me as Jack came from behind the bar.

'I don't know where you live,' I said.

'It's only round the corner,' Lois said not being very specific.

'Where?' I was trying not to sound too eager.

'We are going down now, why don't you have a walk with us and grab a coffee?' Jack said.

I looked to Lois for confirmation this was ok, as neither Jack nor Lois particularly knew me, not to mention this was beyond my wildest dreams. 'Yeah, you may as well, then at least you will know where to come tomorrow,' she replied.

We walked down and chatted easily as though we were old friends, and I liked the relaxed, comfortable tone between Lois and Jack. That night, we had a cuppa and then I walked home thrilled at the unexpected turn of events in my life. I went to bed that night with a smile on my face contented and relaxed for the first time in ages.

The next day, I found Lois on Facebook and messaged to say *thank you* for the night before, and to my surprise, she messaged straight back reminding me about the party and reiterating that I was welcome to go. I did go and would say it was amazing not only being at her home but being around her friends and the way she navigated her way around them. I was engrossed and wanted more.

It was quite a while before I saw Lois again and this was a chance meeting in town where we shared a brief conversation, and then the next time was around 2 months after the night of the party. I was in a bit of a state, the isolation of lockdown was taking its toll on me. I had lost my job, my house was up for sale and I didn't even have the escape of my local to go to for adult conversation so was going out walking 4 to 5 times a day.

Lois immediately tuned in, she listened and could tell I was on the edge so invited me to an outside get together where her pensioner friends came to her garden to exercise their dogs. We sat out observing the mandatory 2 metre distance, and for the first time, I felt human again with a little hope of normality creeping back into my world. From that moment on throughout lockdown, Lois kept me under her wing, checking in on me, including me and giving me a reason to keep going.

I wasn't the only one she was supporting; there were the pensioners whose dogs she started taking on long walks, not to mention the get togethers in the garden. There was an elderly lady whose shopping she did and when we were out she would randomly pay for people's groceries just to bring a smile to their faces.

Her random acts of kindness are what she does best, whether it is the ambulance drivers who manage to stop for lunch that she pays for and leaves before they know what has gone on or for the homeless. She is more than aware of those less fortunate, and she goes above and beyond to make a difference. This is the person that I love so much and that I am lucky enough to be loved by, not because I can offer her great riches or because she needs anything from me, it is because she wants to be with me for me.

That makes a massive difference when you are seen by the person you are with and they love you with all of their capacity. Lois does not do anything by halves. She is an all or nothing kind of person so when she gives she gives abundantly. When she loves it is with her whole heart and when she sees you, you will never be unseen again.

In the July of 2020, it was Jack's 18 birthday and the pubs had just opened so we were allowed to mix again, and Lois was able to celebrate his birthday. This was the day I made it clear to Lois how I felt about her. The truth was I absolutely adored everything about her, and although, I probably didn't stand a chance with her, I couldn't be in her company for another minute without telling her.

About 4 days later, she told me that she couldn't promise me anything, but she was happy to see where it went, then we shared our very first kiss.

That night, I walked her home and in true Lois style, she got Poppy and Luna and walked me back to my home. She is a strong independent woman—a quality I love about her, but I have also found that this strength can also hinder her and become her weakness too. If she has set herself a task, she will often run herself into the ground to complete it rather than it taking her any longer than she wants it to.

She won't take a break to unwind or replenish her energies, she will just keep going determined to finish the race. I think this is manifested from the vulnerabilities of her past where if she showed any form of weakness, her siblings saw a chink in the armour and exploited it. She speaks quite candidly of the past as though it is a story that has happened to someone else.

I think that this is her automatic, self-protective default mode that she goes into. It devastates me to know that she has been so vilified by her siblings and that the household in which she grew up was so aggressive and harmful. It is a million miles away from my own experience whose family is extensive and has always been a hive of interaction through family holidays and celebrations surrounded by much love, support and genuine affection.

Some of the things Lois has shared have been nothing less than shocking. Her earliest memories of being convinced by Kelly and Ruby that she was adopted after being found behind the bins. Or that Ruby had got stuck down the plughole and couldn't get out, even placing a handful of hair in the sink to which poor Lois would be hysterical, fearing Ruby would drown in the drains.

Even from an early age, she liked to help her mum and was well liked so they termed her "skivvy" being the kind of mean girls that no one likes at school. For Lois, she couldn't escape it and inevitably as time went on, she became hard on the outside being forced to stand up for herself, but she never lost her inner love though she does find it hard to trust.

This is definitely the result of being ridiculed, put down and bullied as a child by the very people who should have looked out for her, nurtured her and taken time to actually get to know her and love her for who she was, not the image they had made up in their own minds. I know about the allegations she went through and the restoration of Grey Gables which is truly magnificent, but this too had a massive impact upon her.

She now lives in fear of anything happening to Emmeline, not just because she is her mum, although this is enough in its own right, but because of the threats made by Ruby and Kelly to attack her when she will be at her most vulnerable. For me, I couldn't think of anything worse to be grieving a parent yet looking over your back to see where the knives are coming from.

Equally, Grey Gables is the home she shares with Jack and Joe, so her long-term security is also in jeopardy. This has resulted in an unsettledness of not knowing what the future holds for her or her children, especially with Emmeline being 90 years old. Whatever happens it is my intention to be the tower of strength she will need and so richly deserves, not to mention the mountain they will have to climb to get to either Lois, Jack or Joe.

Chapter 26
Betty's Story (Part 1)

When Daniel started going out with Lois, I was thrilled to bits as he had previously been in a long-term relationship and his former partner had been controlling, creating an obstacle in our relationship. Lois was more down to earth, inclusive, welcoming of both his children and our extended family. I remember meeting Jack and Joe and being blown away at their maturity, kindness and acceptance of others.

It was evident from the start that they shared a tight bond, both with each other and with their mum, and I was struck by their absolute trust and faith in her. Both of them naturally gravitated towards whoever or whatever their mum had first positively identified as authentic and purposeful. This was not in a "mini me" follow my leader sense but in the fact that they had complete confidence in her instincts so, where she was relaxed and blossoming that was the most edifying place for them to absorb themselves.

The boys were so different. Jack was self-assured; he tended to watch and analyse before offering anything of himself. Joe was straight in there, talkative, unable to hold anything back. The first time Jack and Joe met Leah, my granddaughter, was when we were going out for a meal for my birthday in September 2020, and she was exceptionally nervous.

The meal was a great success; the boys just chatted and had great banter both with each other and between Lois and Daniel, yet remained respectful including Leah too. Afterwards she just said, 'They seem really lovely, Grandma.'

To which I replied with the truth, 'They are a really lovely family, Leah.' You see, she too had been nervous about her dad having another relationship and if truth be known, probably hoped for time on their own together.

During the past 18 months, we have developed into a close-knit, blended family where I really do see them as my grandsons and Lois as a daughter-in-law, even though she swears she will never marry Daniel. I have thoroughly enjoyed spending time together whether that has been going for a walk, shopping, meals out or celebrating special occasions with each other.

Like all of our birthdays have taken place at Grey Gables. When we arrive we are welcomed and treated to not just a present and a card but lots of presents that much love, time and money has been invested in. They all have a great sense of humour and when it was Leah's birthday, Joe bought her a pair of earrings but instead of just wrapping it up he put several layers on. Or when it was Christmas, and I was given a box, but when I opened it there were about 12 presents inside.

Last year, they tried to make me believe they had bought me a slow cooker; I didn't let on how disappointed I was and when I got the item out of the box, it was actually a handbag I had been wanting. Jack also got Lois a pack of 24 bottles of Budweiser and wrapped up each individual bottle. The first year Lois bought me a bald barbie doll because I have alopecia. I wasn't offended because I know it is all in good fun and without malicious intent.

They have also nicknamed me Big Bird due to my height, so for Mother's Day I got a cup with the Sesame Street character of the same name on it. We have a good laugh together and it has been a real pleasure getting to know them individually, along with as a family.

However, there has always been one member missing and that was Emmeline. I know it broke all their hearts being unable to see her during the first lockdown but for all the care homes it has been one continuous lockdown. Lois had originally thought it would only be for a couple of weeks, but the sustained separation had a massive affect upon her, especially when there were planned visits and the home would ring to say it was cancelled.

She had quite a breakdown when that happened in August 2020 as it was her late father's birthday too, so this was another event Emmeline would miss out on. The following month, she was absolutely devasted when she realised that they would not be able to see Emmeline for her birthday. It wasn't the same when Lois could only deliver presents to see the staff via video link, rip them open in front of Emmeline in quick succession.

Not only did she not have time to register what she had got but she was denied the pleasure of being able to open them for herself. There were times that Lois would go down with a bag full of pamper things to give Emmeline a treat, but when Emmeline came home, they were in her belongings unopened. She really tried in vain to keep the door of contact open and to remain positive but as we drew closer towards Christmas, she then realised that Emmeline would not be able to join us for that either.

It was heart wrenching here, I was being included in everything, yet Lois's own mother was locked up in a care home with no one to rescue her from the isolation or the torment of her family's separation.

I also couldn't understand why Lois had the care of her mum and the worry of her continued demise in just her hands; she had 2 brothers and 2 sisters after all. When my parents required care, they had lived with my younger brother, Adrian, at the time and although, he assumed the responsibility, we were always there as a family. Each one of my siblings did their bit and I would never have dreamed of abandoning them in their time of need, or worse still trying to put them in an early grave.

When Adrian needed a break, I would go and stay for a couple of weeks for him to go on holiday and get some respite. It made me appreciate just how hard his job of caring for them was, so naturally he had my full support. From the snippets I had caught from Daniel or Lois, it seemed Emmeline's other children hadn't even offered any support let alone bothered to visit, not even when she was alone in a care home.

Astoundingly, I heard they blamed Lois for not *allowing* them to see their mother. Not being funny but nothing and no one would have ever stopped me having access to my mother. The reality is, it's a poor excuse for simply abandoning Emmeline and to make it worse cutting off any form of support that Lois might need from the rest of the family, and through no fault of their own either.

I had a real infinity towards Lois, not only because of the love and close relationship she had with her mum but the fact she had taken on the responsibility of Emmeline's care where everyone else had failed. One of the things that is unmistakeable about Lois is her determination to achieve the things she has committed herself to, and the other is her independence. Daniel had always been in relationships with people who had needed him in some way, whether that was financially or emotionally, but Lois was a whole new ball game.

Lois neither needed nor wanted anything from Daniel, she just wanted him and that for me as his mother was priceless. Lois wouldn't allow Daniel to pay for her share of things and at times I think he struggled with that; after all he is a man and wanted to treat the woman he loved but she was fiercely independent.

Lois had never relied on anyone throughout her life, so she wasn't going to start now.

I guess looking back it was her way of protecting herself should the relationship not work out, then she wouldn't feel that she owed Daniel anything, so she was conducting herself according to her principles. It gave me the added assurance that Daniel was not going to be taken for a mug again unlike his previous partner who ran up thousands of pounds worth of debt and had left him to pay for it.

Lois and Daniel have not had it plain sailing. There have been some ups and downs, but I think that has a lot to do with Lois's inability to trust and the fact she has been on her own for such a long time. She is fiercely protective of her boys as they are of her, and she hasn't let anyone into their lives as far as a potential partner has been concerned.

They have a multitude of friends whom they all have good relationships with, but a partner in the mix is a completely different equation to implement. The boys have a great relationship with Daniel. Joe and he will go out for meals or even a drink to the pub. Joe may only have just gone 15 but for the past 8 months he has had a glass collecting job in their local.

He is a very mature boy and in tune with both his emotions and the environment around him. He is also straight to the point, so if he thinks you are talking bullshit he will call you out, especially Daniel where his phrase is 'So, is that how you're playing it, Daniel?' He has a great sense of humour, and when he first met Leah, I was pleased to see him taking her under his wing despite him being a few years younger.

He would message her regularly just to check in, and on one occasion, he called up with a bacon butty for her when she was feeling a bit vulnerable just to demonstrate his support.

Jack first appears to be more reserved but in reality he is a very strong, independent young man who sees all but only comments if he feels something needs saying. Daniel feels a strong connection with Jack too which I think is due to his self-assurance as he is unswervingly absolute in who he is and the world around him. He gives an opinion that is honest which Daniel knows he can trust, and I know if there was anyone Daniel would want to have on his side, it would be Jack.

Although, I am aware Lois has concerns about what will happen when her mum passes, not only due to the threats that have been made but also for their future, like what will happen to Grey Gables and where her and the boys will live, but I don't think she needs to feel so vulnerable anymore. Jack and Joe are no longer the little boys they once were.

Today they both stand at 6 feet tall, so with each of them at either side of Daniel and the three of them in front of Lois, they would provide quite a shield. I love all of them individually but together they are a formidable force which warms my heart in so many ways.

The depth of love that Daniel and Lois share for one another is palpable. If there was ever a term that could describe this couple it's that they have found their soulmates. I love them dearly and wish them all the very best and look forward to many more years of memory making together.

Chapter 27
Jack
My Hero

Growing up, I remember having such a fantastic relationship with the people around me. I loved it when mum had family parties as I got to hang out with all my cousins. They were the best times and I was always sad when the day came to an end.

The hero in my life was my grandad. He was so goofy convincing me of crazy stuff like he was my 11 year old grandad, but boy he could kick a football all the way up to the moon. I remember one day being in the super huge garden of Grey Gables, it was a hot day and grandad was showing off his football techniques. Grandma and mum were sat on a bench close to the lawn on the raised grassy area and grandad was taking a break.

Joe was busy with some little trolley he had found abandoned and rusting at the side of the shed and was furiously trying to get Poppy on to it, so he could give her a ride around the paths of the garden. Then I got a brilliant idea.

'Do you know what would look great here, Grandad,' I said pointing to the expanse of the tennis court sized lawn.

'No, lad, what?' He asked.

'A swimming pool!' I exclaimed.

'I think you're right, Jack. Quick get the key to my shed,' he said.

'Why, Grandad?' I queried.

'There are two shovels in there. If we make a start now we can have it done by tonight,' he teased.

'Really, Grandad?' I asked excitedly.

'No, Jack. Grandad is joking. You would need a digger and several weeks for a project like that,' mum said dampening my joy.

'Not to mention a whole lot of water,' chimed in grandma as grandad sloped off.

'What do we need a "whole lot of water" for, Grandma?' Joe asked, who had returned after losing interest in chasing the elusive Poppy.

'I thought we could dig a swimming pool, but grandad was laughing at me,' I said sullenly.

'Or we could just have a water fight,' said grandad sprinkling us all with cold water from the hose pipe, creating a shriek of delight from Joe and I as we scattered, much to the annoyance of grandma and mum.

My grandad was always fun. I loved his company and have many fond memories of him whilst I followed him around the garden at Grey Gables, digging the flower beds, pulling up weeds, planting flowers and always chatting. One time we had arranged to meet Auntie Ruby there with her two children before going to Little Monsters, a play gym in Ossett.

We had arrived early and found grandad power washing the side patio, so I went over to take a look, amazed at how clean the machine was making the slabs. When he saw me taking such an interest, he said, 'Look at this, Jack,' and wrote my name on the path with the machine much to my delight. When Auntie Ruby finally turned up, she was in yet another bad mood and then ended up having a go at mum because grandad had written my name on the path and not her children's.

'No one should have the highest honour,' she had screeched.

It was bizarre to say the least, but needless to say she stormed off in a mood and didn't end up coming to Little Monsters with us, which was a shame because her two children then ended up missing out. I liked my cousins very much but secretly hoped they could live with us, especially Jake. One day we were at grandma's, and she was shouting and screaming at him; told him she 'hated him and wished someone would just come and take him away.'

She wasn't a very nice person at all, and over the years it became apparent to me that both grandma and mum were happy to give her a wide berth. She always seemed to blow up over nothing and the atmosphere was uneasy whenever she was around. I know she didn't like me either because she was always cold towards me, blamed me for making it up when she had attacked grandma at Grey Gables and accused me of being an 'evil little shit.'

I was never sure if it was me as a person she didn't like or the fact that I was mum's son. Either way, I never did anything to warrant her nastiness and was always very pleasant to her.

When grandad became ill, I never really thought of it as serious or that he would die and I wouldn't get to see him ever again. I always thought he would get better and be the strong man I knew so well. We had just got back from Tunisia and were in high spirits, especially as we ended up getting an extra week there! Grandad was going into hospital the next day and I guess looking back, mum and grandma played it down for mine and Joe's benefit.

We were sheltered from all the hospital appointments and what I later learnt was chemotherapy treatment, but no matter how poorly he was he always wanted to see Joe and me. I remember coming home from school one day and he had left a message on our answer phone asking mum if she had fallen out with him because we hadn't been over for a whole day! We visited him almost every single day and when he went in to Dove Cote in Horbury, we would go after school and at the weekend.

I never tired of visiting him, but I didn't like leaving him there, so was thrilled when it was finally time for him to come home. We all knew the jobs he had wanted to get done but he had been too weak to achieve them whilst he was ill, so mum did them all for him as a surprise. She had arranged for two new carpets to be fitted along with lino for the kitchen, laundry, she even decorated the bedroom and had given them our new suite just so he was comfortable.

Inevitably, he was overwhelmed and not just at being able to finally come home. Mum, Joe and I were there eagerly awaiting his return. I loved the bond mum had with both her parents and I loved the bond Joe and I had, not only with each other, but with mum and our grandparents too; it gave me a great sense of security. Unfortunately, that all changed when he suddenly passed away.

I was absolutely heart-broken; my grandad, my hero had gone forever. I tried so hard to be brave as mum supported grandma and helped her with the funeral arrangements, so I looked after Joe and did my best to comfort him, often swallowing down my own grief. It was hard being a child in a grown-up situation that you couldn't escape.

To witness my mum trying to cope with her own grief yet being attacked by Kelly and her family demanding she should sing at the funeral. I could barely talk, my grief was so overwhelming that I couldn't imagine why your first thought would be to want to sing. It wasn't a karaoke bar, it was my beloved grandad's funeral!

Before the funeral I wanted to see my grandad one last time. I know mum didn't think I was old enough, but it was so very important to me. You see I hadn't had the chance to say goodbye. Mum waited until the day before to give everyone else the chance to pay their respects first and to allow me the time to think my decision through. We booked a slot, mum explaining my age and intention so I could attend in privacy.

I sat in the car for a few minutes with mum, trying to steal myself as she explained the procedure, the layout of the room, what I should expect to see and the reassurance I could back out at any minute. I was just about to open the car door when Kelly suddenly appeared at mum's window basically screeching, I had no idea what she was on about but the stress she induced in me (I was 9 years old) meant I could no longer go in.

We returned to grandma at Grey Gables, who was livid at Kelly's lack of insight, care or compassion, especially as mum was later told she had rung the chapel of rest to find out when we were going but instead of avoiding the time she had purposely sat in wait. If that wasn't bad enough, she then rang the house to induce more stress, accusing mum of wanting to be the last person to see grandad; another ridiculous accusation.

In the end, Joe decided he wanted to come. I think he just wanted to stand in the gap for me, even though he was only 4 at the time, bless him. Once we were sure it was safe to return, the four of us went together and mum ensured that the last person to see grandad was grandma, and rightly so.

The next day was the funeral, a very sombre affair where both Joe and I were dressed as miniature grandads in a suit, tie, and waistcoats with flat caps upon our heads. Despite my inner grief, I felt so proud to resemble the man I loved, and I remember as we got out of the funeral car mum saying, 'Hold your heads-up high boys and remember all eyes will be on you, so do your grandad proud!'

As we steadied ourselves to enter the church, Joe and I at either side of my mum. I suddenly realised grandma was stood all alone, so I thought I will do you proud grandad, and I marched forward, linked her arm and said, 'I've got you, Grandma.' She smiled, squeezed my arm then patted my hand with her free hand and nodded, in appreciation she wasn't alone. We then held our heads up and walked down the aisle of a packed church for all to see we were going to do my grandad proud.

I do not remember much, only that my grandma squeezed my hand so tightly throughout the service I thought I would lose all feeling in it, but I didn't mind one bit, and then it was time for my mum to read a poem that she had written for my grandad. It is a very personal piece, but I wanted to share it with you as it means so much to me and it is a part of my story. He was my grandad, I loved him dearly and he will always be my hero.

Trucks a rattling, dark long nights,
Roping and sheeting, the cold wind bites,
You did your best, you worked all day,
A heavy burden for such small pay.
Out in the wagon all alone,
Well in those days there weren't mobile phones!
Tensions rising, wagons need loads,
Drivers stuck on busy roads.
Robing Peter, just to pay Paul
Banging your head against the wall.
Rising costs, legislations imposed
How much longer can we keep afloat?
Then it was home for a bite to eat,
Gravy, two veg and a piece of meat.
Got to scrub off all that dirt
Find yourself another clean shirt.
Up and out to entertain and sing
For now, it's time for Johnny King.
You never stopped you worked so hard
Without recognition, toiling in that yard.
Your love didn't end, it just kept on flowing,
To provide for a family that kept on growing.
We needed a bigger house for our table,
So you moved us across town to Grey Gables
When you retired you didn't stop?
You cooked and cleaned and went to the shop.
Chatting to many along the town,
Always a smile, never a frown.
You'd deliver a joke with a dry sense of humour,

You brought such joy to those around you!
You encouraged, uplifted when others were down,
You'd guide and direct us and turn things around.
You taught compassion, gave insight no end,
A dad, a grandad, loyal husband and friend.
To Jack, a hero, a man he could trust,
With Joe you would chuckle and cut off his crusts.
Today I am sat here so full of pride,
With heartfelt sorrow that's difficult to hide.
I love and I miss you more than words can say,
You touched us all in so many ways.
I gave my heart and soul to you,
And in return you gave yours too.
But now there's no searching for your glasses,
No flat cap, or hospital dashes.
No seaside trips, just for a paddle,
Oh, by the way 'you were right about that saddle.'
No more talking until it's dark,
Or a McDonalds ice-cream in the park.
You've left behind a whole lot of love,
But I know you will still send it, far from above.
There is one thing for certain, there is no mistake, Jeff,
To have you back, I'd give my last breath!

The crematorium and the wake were filled with much tension created by my aunties and uncles, who I would have expected could have at least presented a united front on such a difficult day. At no point at all did I witness either of them show my grandma any ounce of kindness or demonstrate the love and respect she deserved, instead they grimaced in her direction, moaned about everything, and made us all feel uncomfortable.

Even when mum was paying tribute to her dad, they stared cold heartedly at her. No words of support afterwards or congratulations at the well written poem. Grandma was not only heartbroken at losing grandad, but she was intentionally given the cold shoulder by each of them throughout the day.

I remember Joe excitedly being picked up by Kelly's younger daughter, Haley, but as soon as her mother saw her interacting with him she was rebuked, and Joe sent away like he had done something wrong. That was the first day I recognised a massive divide had been created where grandma, Joe, mum and I were on one wide and everyone else was on another.

To this day, it has never been repaired because from the day of the funeral, they never came to see grandma again but have tried to make her life a living hell.

Chapter 28
Joe
Cillit Bang

My earliest memories are of loving life whether that was school, going on holiday, being at church, my childminders or visiting my grandparents. I loved arriving at nursery where I would race into the cloakroom to find my best buddy and shout 'Jakey Matie,' and in return I would be greeted with 'Joey Maloney.' We absolutely loved each other and had developed a very close bond from the moment we had met at our childminders.

I would often pick up silly sayings that I'd deliver and then both of us would spend the day seeing how many times we could introduce it. My favourite was, "Cillit Bang" when we had done something really good, I was only 4 at the time. Unlike most kids who keep their dummies and nappies on until they are way too old, I was independent of such things from my second birthday and instead of a "comfort" blanket or teddy, I carried a wooden spoon everywhere.

I enjoyed church where I would sing to my heart's content. My favourite song was *oh happy day when Jesus washed my sins away*, and I would get up, dance and sing at the top of my voice. Much to the amusement of those around me.

At church, we had a lovely friend called Wendy who often took me out supposedly to give mum a break but in reality, she loved my company because I amused her and had good conversational skills. Wendy came on our first holiday together to Spain. I was only 7 months old, and mum needed the help as she still had mobility issues.

Whilst she was pregnant with me, she had Pubic Symphysis Dysfunction which resulted in her having a c-section at 34 weeks, followed by 15 months of physiotherapy. The following year, Wendy came to Tunisia with us, where I ended up with Chicken Pox and was nearly refused the pleasure of boarding the flight home. I remember when I was 3, we went to Tunisia again with Wendy and we travelled by quad bikes out in the country.

It was awesome for a little boy to have a mum who had such a free spirit. That was the year that we had an extra week there due to the effects of the Icelandic ash, however on our return, grandad was going into hospital.

My grandad had always seemed like this mountain of a man. So strong, able and the only male focal point in my life, so to think he was ill really hit me, however he was soon back home. Little did I know just how ill he was, but for me life just carried on as normal in the uninhibited, freedom of exploration and excitement of all that was new.

I began taking swimming lessons soon after our return from Tunisia, so proud that my grandad was sat up in the gallery watching my every move. Each week, I would put extra effort into every stroke, climbing quickly up the ranks until after only a few months, I was able to do six lengths without stopping. I loved the rush it gave me and the praise from both my private tutor, Amy, and my mum, but especially my grandad, who cheered me on each week and made me feel like I had won the Olympic gold.

When grandad was at Dove Cote, I didn't mind being at the home and never pestered to go home or ran round being a nuisance. I was just happy to be in his presence as he always made me feel so special. He would often chuckle and shake his head when he looked at me and I would throw back a cheeky grin, my dimples showing and the blond locks of my hair slipping into my face.

I loved it when he came home because him and grandma started getting meals on wheels, so I used to watch for them being delivered and hover round hoping to get some like a dog begging at the table. Of course, I thought I was being subtle, but grandad would chuckle, make me a sandwich, cut off the crusts and let me sit with him whilst they ate. He knew I was waiting until it was time for him to have his pudding, so he would tease me and pretend to save it for later.

Then change his mind and share it with me. I loved my grandad and he loved that I was a funny, cheeky little imp who enjoyed making the adults in my life laugh. My teacher called me smiler because I was always happy the joy welling up from deep within me. I loved being at school and I loved it when my mum came into the nursery as a volunteer once a week, or when her and grandma were on the side lines cheering me on in school plays or at sports days.

Life was great. I loved it and I loved everyone and everything around me. That was until the day grandad suddenly passed away. On that day, everything around me changed and I changed forever!

It was hard for me to put it into words at the time but inside I was literally broken. It felt like my world had collapsed around me and I was beneath its rubble. I have to say that 11 years on, I have never got over the loss of my beloved grandad.

Maybe a massive part of that was because of my sudden vulnerability becoming a sign of weakness to the school ground bullies, who despite mum's force at challenging this, it never really stopped until I changed schools 4 years later. Jack and I had always been very close. We were the best of buddies and whilst the funeral arrangements were taking place, we went away for the weekend camping.

Mum's friends were astounded at the 9-year-old Jack who made sure my needs were attended to first before himself, whether that was to supervise me in the shower, assist me to dress or get me something to eat. This is how he has always been and yet I threw it back in his face, shouting and carrying on due to my grief, not realising that he was having to swallow down his own.

I wish now that I could have drawn closer to Jack so we could have supported each other, not him just looking out for me but I was too young to understand at the time. He did continue to be the best brother ever and I am glad to say that although, I never understood his humour, I not only get it now, but I have managed to develop my own.

Chapter 29
Daniel's Story (Part 2)

Three months after beginning our relationship, I was accompanying Lois to the Care Home where I was to meet Emmeline for the first time. I had heard so much about her and desperately wanted to meet her, so when Lois invited me I was thrilled and jumped at the chance. We were sat outside on a cold but sunny October day; Lois at the office window and myself to the side awaiting my introduction.

When the staff brought Emmeline through, Lois's face lit up and I was struck by the instant love that radiated through that window to Emmeline. I had taken down a bunch of flowers and some chocolates so when Lois told Emmeline about me, the staff presented her with the flowers as I appeared, so she knew who had bought them for her.

She was sat in a wheelchair, looked a lot older than I had anticipated and seemed very frail as she was handed her gifts but when she turned to see me, her smile was extraordinary her whole face lit up. We sat and chatted for a while although, I wasn't sure how much she would retain as I knew she had dementia, though was very talkative.

I didn't see Emmeline again until Christmas, although we tried on several times to have video links but she didn't seem to understand the concept of 'live' chat and thought the staff were playing her a video to watch. I know this upset Lois as she could feel her mother slipping further away with no real control of being able to stop it or help her in anyway. Then with Christmas Day approaching, she became distraught at the prospect of what "could be" her last, that Emmeline wasn't able to spend it with us.

Like Lois, I wanted to get Emmeline home. I could see a decline in the short time I had seen her so for Lois, she felt she was fighting a losing battle. One day we sat down and had a candid conversation about the feasibility of Emmeline coming back to Grey Gables. The thing was after she had fallen and broken her femur, Social Services felt her needs were too great for Lois to manage alone at home, but now she had my mum, myself, willing friends and an extended family who were willing to achieve this.

It was the beginning of December when Lois first approached Social Services, but it had to be transferred from the Wakefield borough to Kirklees where Emmeline's home was located, which took a month. It wasn't until Christmas Eve that Lois was able to have a face-to-face meeting behind a screen at the home, but this brought challenges as she was now profoundly deaf.

Into the New Year, Lois was visiting Emmeline three times a week but neither Jack, Joe nor I could go as it had to be the same person throughout. Lois battled with Social Services filling in a multitude of paperwork and urging them forward, but their time frame had been given a 7 week period, so the social worker didn't start her part until the week before. I found this as frustrating as Lois, as I was desperate for her to fulfil her wish to get her mum home and I wanted to get to know Emmeline for myself.

On the 18 March 2021, unbeknown to me, Lois had arranged to collect Emmeline with Jack and brought her home to celebrate my birthday with us. It was the best surprise I could have wished for, so I rushed out to buy her a bunch of flowers and to get her a card to welcome her home.

It was lovely to see this beautiful lady in the clutches of her family and the rapport they all shared, particularly Jack who spent the whole afternoon sat next to her on the settee, his arm wrapped around her. All of a sudden our blended family felt whole, where Emmeline was the heart and soul that had been missing.

It took a few weeks to implement a routine that worked in everyone's favour. There were carers coming in on a morning to shower and dress Emmeline, and then again on an evening to get her washed and ready for bed. Our focal point had changed so instead of having the freedom to do as we pleased, we suddenly had to work around Emmeline's needs and rightly so. Lois and I jointly assisted each other to meet her basic needs of eating and drinking, although Lois takes full responsibility of her toileting needs.

We have days out, whether it is a run over to Hornsea where she can retain her friendships, visiting areas of interest or whether it is to maintain the relationship Emmeline still has with two of her granddaughters and their families. I love spending my time in Emmeline's company. She is a kind-hearted, beautiful lady who is a joy to be around with a laugh that is infectious. She has no malice in her at all and it beggars' belief why someone would want to treat her in the way her other children have treated her.

I find it heart wrenching that this poor lady has been subject to such horrendous behaviour, then when you throw in the mix that she is also a dementia sufferer too, there is only one word, heartless. Hopefully, they will reap what they have sown because after 2 ½ years of being in her company, I can quite categorically state there is nothing that she could have done to warrant such disgusting behaviour.

Over the last year, we have struggled at times to manage Emmeline's failing health with emergency doctors attending her but have also enjoyed the highs of taking her on holiday, seeing her laugh, enjoying life and having one too many Malibus. But if you cannot do that at 90 when can you do it.

We have celebrated her 90 birthday, where she got her first pair of Doc Marten shoes, and she was the centre of attention at my daughter's 18, where to everyone's amusement, she systematically took off all the brownies from the cake then swiped her licked finger across the cream. She is a character and a half who just by being herself has given me a greater insight into Lois and her roots, to which I will always be grateful.

Three years ago, the woman of my dreams was out of my reach and to her I wasn't even a face in the crowd. Now I have so much more than I could have ever dreamed of. Jack has secured a job as joiner, Joe is doing well at school, Leah is turning out to be a fine young woman, my mum and Emmeline have been the very best of friends and I have carved out a successful career.

It has been an absolute pleasure of getting to know Emmeline, who like her daughter is a wonderful woman, who smiles with her eyes and allows you to see through into her soul. To some Lois may not be perfect but she is perfect for me, and somehow like our families I have become perfect for her.

Chapter 30
Betty's Story (Part 2)

On the 18 March 2021, I was on my way to Grey Gables to take some presents over for Daniel's birthday. They hadn't planned to have a party or anything, Lois had just included me so I could see Daniel open his presents. When I got there, I could hear a lot of excited chatter coming from the middle room but when I opened the door, I got the most wonderful surprise. There sat on the settee was Emmeline, snuggled into Jack's loving arms.

I felt so overcome with emotion as I had prayed for this day for the past 6 months but never in my wildest dreams had I thought for a minute it would be granted. Previously, I had only had the pleasure of saying 'Hi' to Emmeline via video link if I had happened to be at Grey Gables when Lois was speaking to her, and she obviously had no idea who I was. I know for Lois it was a yearning that both Daniel and I meet her mum because she was such an important person in her life and the only family member she could share with us.

I think that Lois knew in her heart of hearts that Daniel was the man for her, so it became increasingly urgent to her that we should meet properly because Emmeline seemed to be getting lost to dementia. As Lois's life was taking shape and she was enjoying this new relationship, she didn't want Emmeline to be left behind, she wanted her to be a part of it too.

And she desperately wanted Daniel and I to get to know her but periodically it felt at times like we wouldn't even get the chance to meet her face to face, let alone being able to hold her hand or build a relationship up with her. Yet here she was, sat on the settee back at Grey Gables, revelling in having her family all around her.

The thing that struck me first about Emmeline was her smile. It literally lit up the room and then it was her piercing blue eyes. I could see that Jack adored her and she was enthralled by him, captivated by his presence. She looked up at him with such devotion, all her faith and trust instinctively rested upon him safe once more in his arms.

Surprisingly, Joe was more reserved; he seemed to hold back and not engage as easily but maybe he was just letting Jack have his moment. The boys were like that with each other, instinctively giving the other space to engage and have their turn in whatever the situation was, like opening Christmas gifts. They would take turns without rushing themselves or each other.

Lois has the most staying power, she can still be opening her Christmas presents in the summer, not because she doesn't care about them, but she likes to savour them and do them in her timeframe not someone else's.

As I inched closer towards the table in the centre of the room, a reminder of the large gathering we had enjoyed at Christmas, Lois stepped forward to get her mum's attention.

'Emmeline,' she said, 'this is Betty that I have been telling you about, Daniel's mum.'

'Hello, Betty,' she said to me and looked back to Lois for confirmation she had got it right.

'Hello, Emmeline,' I said holding back the tears of absolute joy that were trying to push their way through. 'It is such a pleasure to finally meet you.'

Emmeline looked up at me and said, 'Aww that's lovely and it's a pleasure to meet you too.'

It was amazing to not only be in the presence of this lovely lady but to watch the interaction of her family around her, and to witness the abundance of love they had for one another. She may have been in a care home and got lost there throughout the past year of the covid and lockdown, but now she was here in the bosom of her family once more.

Over the next few days, there were challenges for them as Lois attempted to implement a routine for Emmeline and themselves, adamant that she would do this alone. For Lois, this was her mum and we had to step back initially to give them the space to reform, reconnect and regain some of all that had been stolen. Over time, she gently incorporated Daniel's presence, not wanting to overwhelm Emmeline, but she needn't have worried.

She accepted him as part of the furniture, and he was soon attending to her every need with Lois. They both stepped into their new roles with confidence and became a tag team supporting each other, and finding the time for each other when I would go over and sit with Emmeline.

One of the things that has probably surprised me the most has been Emmeline's humour. Yes, she may have dementia and she may sometimes forget what she is saying but she has me howling. Like one day, when we had some chocolates as we snuggled on a settee apiece under our nana blankets watching telly.

'We won't tell them we have got chocolates, Emmeline,' I said referring to Daniel and Lois.

'No, we won't. They are only for us, aren't they?' She says just before Lois comes into the room.

'What are you doing eating all my chocolates?' Lois said jokingly.

'She gave them to me,' Emmeline says as quick as a flash pointing at me and totally throwing me under the bus, so much for solidarity.

I really do love being in Emmeline's company, so I soon committed to sitting with her every Saturday evening so Daniel and Lois could go out together on their own. You see they were taking her out everywhere they went, and she certainly loved sitting outside the George pub in Ossett, watching the world go by. On one occasion, they told me about her raucous laughter.

'Have you seen what that woman over there is wearing?' She suddenly declared cackling at the top of her voice.

'You can't say that, Emmeline,' Lois urged her.

'I can, I just did,' she said.

'But you might offend her,' she explained.

'Well, she is offending me with what she is wearing,' Emmeline said and continued to laugh, much to Daniel and Lois's embarrassment. Then Nadine, the landlady, came to collect the glasses from the table and Emmeline spied her out of her eye corner. 'What does she want?'

'I am just coming to see if there are any empty glasses, Emmeline,' Nadine informed her.

'Well, you can't have them,' she retorted.

'So, you don't want yours refilling then?' Nadine played devil's advocate.

'Yes, we want another one, don't we?' She turned to ask Daniel and Lois.

'Yes,' Daniel said. 'We will have another round please, Nadine.'

'Does that mean I can have your glasses then, Emmeline?' Nadine asked.

'Ok you can have it if you're going to refill it,' Emmeline said holding it out and handing her it.

I get a lot of satisfaction being with Emmeline as it reminds me of the times I spent taking care of my own parents, and she is so pleasant and thankful of all that you do for her. She hasn't got a bad bone in her body, and I feel privileged that she is happy for me to assist her. I am the only person other than the carers who Lois trusts to toilet Emmeline and to maintain her dignity, which has brought Lois and I closer. I know that Emmeline enjoys my company too because when it is time for me to leave, she is disappointed.

'Right, Emmeline, I have to go now,' I tell her.

'OHH, you don't have to,' she tells me.

'I do, love, I have to go home now,' I say.

'Well, can't you stay here? I am sure we will have a bed you can have,' she reasons.

'I am sorry, but I have to go back to my home now, but I will come back again soon,' I say.

'Alright as long as you do,' she will say.

I am truly thankful for the opportunity of getting to know Emmeline, and of all the memories I now hold of her and will always treasure, like being able to sit on the beach under a parasol watching Joe and Daniel splashing about like kids in the sea. Or going out for meals each night; we were in Skegness with Daniel, Jack, Lois, Joe, my brother, Adrian, his partner, Dale, myself and Emmeline.

Then there was the time we had a walk around Sandal castle and stopped off at the little café for drinks; the walks in the park or shopping at McArthur Glen and eating our lunches at the picnic tables outside in the sun. She has brought a new light into all our lives. I can honestly say I love Emmeline with all my heart, and it is such an honour that she calls me 'my friend.'

Chapter 31
Jack
I've Got My Shoes On?

I am not quite sure when I became aware that grandma had dementia, but I do remember the incident when she was supposed to be meeting us at the Pizza Hut and got lost. There were times that I noticed she didn't seem to know how to react, like when Joe fell off his bike and was screaming he had hurt his leg, but she just stared at him. I think she knew she was supposed to do something, but her brain couldn't connect with what that was.

I think her seemingly lack of emotion, love nor care towards him hurt him more than the fall itself. Then there was the time she came to stay with us over the Christmas period as she always did until New Year's Eve. Joe was washing the dishes and I was drying them. Grandma walked into the kitchen and as she came past us, she suddenly pulled back her arm and took a full force swipe at Joe, slapping him really hard.

We were both very shocked, but he didn't say anything he just wept silently, his little lip quivering and his shoulders jogging up and down. He wasn't going to say anything but I felt it was important, so I had a word with mum so he could receive the comfort he required. She then helped him to address the situation with grandma, which was hard for him, but he did need to speak out to set firm boundaries for himself and make sure he could stand up for himself in a positive way in the future.

'Grandma, I didn't like it when you came into the kitchen and you slapped me for no reason. It really hurt my feelings and it was wrong of you to do that,' he bravely ventured.

'I never did,' she said adamantly.

'You did, Grandma. Joe was washing up and you walked behind him and slapped him really hard,' I said softly to support Joe.

'Look, Grandma, I still have your handprint here,' Joe said showing her his arm.

Poor grandma looked distraught, not only the fact that she had committed such an act but just as equally because she couldn't remember anything about it, and then she began to sob. 'I am so sorry, love, I didn't know I wouldn't ever want to hurt you like that. Please forgive me?'

It was from that moment I noticed how Joe would pull away from his grandma and as time went on, he became more distant and not as eager to be around her nor did I think he was quite as loving. It wasn't his fault, he had just had an horrendous experience where he now knew his grandma could be unpredictable, so naturally he took a step back in self-preservation.

At the time it did make me cross because I knew she couldn't help it, so I decided to ask mum if there were any courses I could do to learn more about dementia. She found a Dementia Awareness course that the Alzheimer's Society was running in Pontefract (March 2015) facilitated by a lady called Becki Dodds; it was on a Saturday morning from 09.30 and it was for 4 weeks.

During the first week, we learned about the different forms of dementia and the importance of putting things in place for grandma so she could make decisions about her care in advance. The second week was all about grandma's entitlement to benefits which was Attendance Allowance for her and Carer's Allowance for mum. We also learnt that if you are an individual living alone and have a diagnosis of dementia, you are exempt from Council Tax.

Equally if you leave your home to look after someone as their carer, you get a 50% reduction, and if the property you left is unoccupied, that is totally exempt.

This wasn't really of any interest to me and after a week of school, it was heavy and deep, but I still paid attention because I knew it would help mum and grandma. The third week tackled the area of the brain which did get my creative juices flowing because I wanted to understand why grandma was behaving so differently. This was the real reason I wanted to learn so I could help Joe to understand that it wasn't grandma's fault.

It was the plaque that was forming in pockets in her brain that didn't connect the receptor. Hence, she knew she needed to do something in the case of him crying but nothing connected to let her know the appropriate action she needed to take. I wanted to help him understand that although, it was her physically in front of us that we could see, and she was still the same on the inside, it was like a wire coming loose and the electrical current wasn't passing through efficiently.

It was very hard to hear that this was a progressive disease, which meant not only wouldn't grandma get better but that it would probably get a lot worse. I was devastated. I had already lost my grandad, so I wasn't ready to lose my grandma too! The last week was all about being an advocate for the individual, understanding the power of attorney role and being signposted to the other agencies that could help.

We also took in a sample of a Care Plan to show Becki that we had created with grandma on our usual Sunday lunch gathering, just to get some pointers and advice on how to best protect her. We had to make a few changes, like its flexibility. Grandma had stated she never wanted to go into a care home, but Becki said it may be the only solution for palliative care or if we are unable to implement a care package at home, or mum was not able to give the level of care she required.

It was very informative, and Becki became a huge source of help and much support over the years. She would also nominate mum to do several talks, both for Alzheimer's Society and Carers Wakefield where she was asked by the big boss to represent them in front of the Quality Commissioning Group of Wakefield. One day, I even came home to find grandma and mum had been filmed to appear on Calendar news as part of the People's Choice Awards, with mum being interviewed on her role as a carer.

It has never been an issue for me that my grandma has dementia. I know some people see it as a slur or that it has some old-fashioned stigma attached to it but then they have probably never taken the time to understand that the person is still present. My grandma has it really hard because she not only has a disease attacking her brain causing the plaques (Alzheimer's) but it is also not as oxygenated as it should be (Vascular), so she is at risk of T.I.A.'s.

However, she still has the same award winning, beautiful smile that lights up when she sees me. She still has love pouring out of her heart and thankfully she still recognises who I am, even if she cannot always find the right name. Maybe that is why her condition is now known as an "invisible" illness because it is not a broken arm that you instantly recognise. Therefore, if you didn't know her, you may think she was absolutely fine and not realise she actually has a severe mental impairment.

I think we have done well as a family to help her mask her condition. We have used humour a lot like when she got her cup that said, 'I smile because I have absolutely no idea what is going on.' She found it funny and had us all in stitches. The problem is she has lived with dementia now for several years, so it has become a self-confessed prophecy.

There have only been a couple of occasions during this time where it has really affected me personally. The first was the summer of 2016, when grandma was going to be with us for the full summer and Glen our next-door neighbour told mum of the information about the Public Guardian stuff. It was beyond disappointing to have to forfeit our summer holidays, not only to come home but then grandma ended up in hospital with the stress of it all and became really withdrawn.

The other major time was the following summer when mum sold our caravan because it was more than clear grandma wouldn't be able to come again. We had hoped that we would restore our ability to have a full summer together but after having a week in respite, grandma was in no fit state to go anywhere. She wasn't making any sense believing that the people she was staying with were going to be coming home with us and living in our kitchen cupboards.

So we spent 3 weeks back at home to resettle her before trying to have a week in Hornsea together. It was a week from hell for all of us. We found used pads rolled up in socks, hidden in her case and in her wardrobe amongst her clean clothes. She wet the bed almost every night, so mum spent each morning at the laundrette then the rest of the day drying and replacing her bedding.

Everyone's stress levels were high as she began walking around partially dressed, and then we found her in the middle of the night fishing her poo out of the toilet bowl and putting on top of the cistern because she had forgotten how to flush it away. I was overwhelmed and it wasn't a nice experience having to rationalise what was going on to try to protect Joe from such a horrible situation. In the end, we had to pack up and go because she then started walking around weeing along the carpet.

I know that this was an outward response to her inward anxiety and because she couldn't verbalise her feelings, so it was displayed through these unexpected behaviour patterns. I am surprised mum didn't swing for Shelli's wife, Karen, when they turned up unexpectedly. She stated to mum that she 'Didn't think grandma was as bad as mum thought.'

There have been lots of highs and some pretty deep lows throughout our journey together, like the last time she came over to Hornsea with us. I had started the season a little sad that friends had sold up or moved to other sites. I never wanted to leave so made mum promise we never would but by the end of the summer, I vowed never to go back. The stress of being surrounded by the effects of dementia too difficult to deal with.

Then, not long afterwards. mum sat us down one day after school to declare that she thought it would be better for all of us to move over to Grey Gables. I was absolutely devastated. I didn't want to leave the only home I had ever known nor the quiet environment with its park and lovely walks to live in a massive house that was dark, full of old furniture, smelt and seemed eerie and foreboding.

I had already changed to a school in the area, and although, I enjoyed staying periodically with grandma, the last thing I wanted was to be there full time, with no chance of ever returning home. I loved my grandma with all my heart, but this felt like a sacrifice too far. I was also not impressed that no one else seemed to be taking my feelings in to consideration, all Joe could see was that he would have a bigger bedroom.

I was scared of the dark and could not think of a worse place to live. The prospect filled me with dread and unlike the rest who were counting the days down I was hoping the time would never come. However, when mum rang to say she was collecting us, I was intrigued to see what she had been doing for the past 2 months.

It had seemed to me that she was constantly painting because that was the only answer she gave each day when I asked what she had been doing. I don't know quite what I expected, maybe that she had just painted the house, so it was brighter or that she had got rid of the old furniture and replaced it with ours, I don't know.

When we arrived, we were all excited beyond measure to see the fruits of her labour, intrigued we were being allowed into the world she had lived for the past 2 months. When we entered the kitchen, I was literally blown away. Gone were the old units and in their place the most magnificent site, I couldn't believe it.

Both Joe and I explored every nook and cranny seeing what new delights we could find. It was so well thought out and designed to meet all our needs. I particularly liked Poppy's bowls under the island so grandma wouldn't keep knocking them over like she did at our house, and the shoe box that doubled up as a seat for grandma to steady herself when she put her shoes on.

It was beyond my wildest dreams and a far better design than I had ever seen. Mum had also moved the cooker and put an island in place to use as an obstacle to ensure grandma's continued safety, and had it made so that grandma's seat was positioned for her to see out of the window. Joe chose the seat at the opposite end which meant mine was in the middle but there wasn't one for mum. I was a bit upset for her because she always thinks of everyone else but never puts herself first.

I understood when she explained she had purposefully done it this way to ensure we all stayed at this side of the kitchen whilst she was able to cook and keep everyone else safe. The tour of the house was a gift that kept on giving. It was absolutely stunning and I was so proud that my mum had done all this just for us. I couldn't say I had a favourite part, like the kitchen, the bathrooms were a massive transformation, but I loved the fact Joe and I were in a room together and that Joe had also got what he wanted, the back bedroom.

The chill out zone was a treat and a half and when grandma saw her room, I cried overcome with joy but sad that I had ever doubted mum would pull it off. From that moment on, I never looked back and was so proud to be living at Grey Gables. I have enjoyed many years of being able to have my friends over in our own private space along with filling the house with love and laughter once more. It was not only the right decision as it opened up all our lives and access to the local community, but it was the best decision in the long run for grandma.

During the next few months, there were some teething problems, not about settling into Grey Gables, that was easy. The moment we arrived we were sold on the idea. It was because Ruby and Kelly started preying on grandma again which had an effect on her mental health. I was beginning to do my GCSE's and grandma was becoming disorientated, confused and would then leave the bathroom before pulling her pants up.

I was having to deal with issues that were impacting my stress levels prior to school on a daily basis which is why mum implemented some care for grandma on a morning. It enabled me to get myself off whilst the carer was tending to her needs; washing, toileting and dressing her, so she was safe. I could get off to school and mum could tend to Joe.

For the next two of years, we were able to manage her condition quite successfully at home despite having to involve the police on a couple of occasions to warn Kelly and Ruby regarding their continued inappropriate behaviour. One of the occasions, they were involving our neighbours where our movements were being monitored, either via their cameras or him taking photographs of Sarah and her husband visiting.

It was weird behaviour on all their parts, not to mention invasive of our privacy. All we wanted to do was live peaceful lives in the privacy of our own home, but they just could not leave us alone. Then she went for a week's respite, and she fell fracturing her femur.

She then ended up in hospital for 6 weeks and Social Services wouldn't let her return home. She then got stuck in there during covid and we weren't allowed to see her. Much to our despair her condition worsened, and she was no longer living a happy life. Mum fought for 3 months to get her out and finally after her second vaccination, she was allowed home 18 March 2021.

Thankfully, everything we lost during that time has been restored. All our birthday celebrations, anniversaries, special occasions, Christmas, New Year, Valentines, Mother's Day, Easter; absolutely everything! We even took grandma away for a holiday to Skegness; a place mum used to go as a child with her parents. She spent time at the beach under a parasol, went out every evening for drinks and a meal, and enjoyed day trips out, she even went on a pedalo!

So, I am proud to say that her life is full and enriched again. She is an important part of our family and I love here dearly.

Today my relationship with Emmeline is wonderful. She is happy and giggly whenever she is around me. They say that a smile is infectious and hers is for me as much as mine is for her. Each time I come in, I always go into her lounge to say hello with the habitual 'Boo,' when she jumps out of her skin and laughs at me.

She sings to me and dances as I lead her from the dining room to her lounge and has a cackle of a laugh every time she sees me, and believe me that can be several times throughout a meal if she looks down, forgets that I am there then sees me again for the first time. She is very funny though, especially being partially deaf.

'You're having goujons for tea,' I tell her as I take her to the table.

'What?' She asks puzzled.

'You're having goujons for tea,' I repeat.

'I've got my shoes on?' She asks.

Or there will be times when she looks a little vacant as though she has left the room briefly but then realises I am talking to her and checks back in, so I ask her, 'Are you back?'

She just responds with a 'yes, I think so.'

I particularly enjoy praying with her if she is going to bed before me, as I think it is important that as she closes her eyes, she knows that she is loved and cared about whilst she drifts off to sleep. For myself, if ever anything happened to her during the night, I know I have covered her in prayer. When I finish she will say, 'Aww that's lovely,' then cackle. I then tell her I love her, and she always says, with determination, 'and I love you.' Before we say 'Goodnight, God Bless' to each other.

In general, she tends to call me by my grandad's, brother's name, but it doesn't bother me because I know it is me that she sees and has such love for. I am lucky because I have had a lifetime of memory making events with her, so my childhood has been equally enriching for me and I am still here to tell her all about them now she has long forgotten. Grandma has always been involved in my life and in later times, my life has been even more enhanced with Emmeline, the lady who we love and appreciate for who she is now.

Chapter 32
Joe
Guilt

I was perhaps only just reaching the summit of peace regarding my grandfather's death when grandma received the diagnosis of dementia and then I seemed to instantly become unbalanced all over again. I know now it was symptomatic of the panic I subconsciously felt about losing another major figure in my life, however this manifested through some erratic behaviour on my part.

Here was the person who made up our fourth wheel and I felt that to lose her would disconnect all that we represented and inwardly I imploded through fear that my mum might be the next. I didn't understand the concept that it was her brain making her behave the way she was, after all it had been her hand that had slapped me that first Christmas.

Jack tried in vain to support me to gain some understanding but even though he'd been on a course so that he was talking to me in simple terms rather than adult terminology I couldn't grasp it. It was grandma in front of me and as far as I was concerned, she had chosen not to comfort me when I fell off my bike or when I woke from a nightmare, so she was the one I was angry at.

As a result, my relationship with her began to fall apart and I was not able to have a conversation with her without shouting at her. I found it hard to be left alone without crying, overwhelmed by the depths of the grief I had reached losing grandad, coupled with what I perceived as the loss of grandma too. Unlike Jack who seemed to take it all in his stride, the simple act of forgetting my name seemed to enrage me.

The anger I felt from all three scenarios of grandad's death, the bullying and the demise from dementia was unparallel to anything I had felt before. I would shout full of rage then be bowled over with the enormity of the overwhelming power of guilt.

I did not understand dementia. How could I grown adults find it difficult to comprehend and manage so how could I, a young child? For me looking back now, it is hard to recognise how mercilessly I demonstrated my pain. This was the person that had loved me and yet I could not return that favour the way that had been so natural at one time.

I had all these memories of her spending time daily in my presence, going on holidays with me, going on the big ship at Alton Towers, she had watch me grow so I couldn't rationalise why I wasn't important enough to her to treasure those memories of me as I did of her. I was in pain, unable to grasp my reality that I was losing her too. I hated myself.

I knew my behaviour was wrong, but I was powerless to supress the anger of being persistently bullied at school, so it came out at an equally vulnerable person. She represented me in some ways; unable to fight back, unable to stand up for herself so the guilt and hatred of myself ran like a hamster caught in its wheel.

Jack would scold me and try to help me to understand but I wasn't interested, too caught up in my own misery of a mixture of loss and grief. Mum would be my safe place but even the roadrunner getting splattered in the cartoons caused me such grief as it represented death and loss. It wasn't until I was 8 years old, I finally got a place in a different school and could then have grief counselling.

It helped but then I was devastated when the sessions were over, and I wouldn't see my counsellor again. It became a bit of a pattern whereby I made connections quickly like a DJ at a wedding but at the end of the night, I was upset at "never seeing my friend again".

It wasn't until I started at this new school that I met other children whose vulnerabilities stood out to me and so I became a champion to protect them, to give them a voice and to assist them in the difficulties they felt in a mainstream school. I became all about inclusion and speaking up for the lost as I found my voice and channelled my energies through a more positive direction.

It gave me insight and inspiration to begin to understand what I was being taught about my grandma's illness that she didn't have control over the things that were happening to her. A little like the impulsive behaviours and involuntary ticks of the children with additional needs. My grandma exhibited this behaviour but in a different format and neither were wrong nor the individual's fault.

Finally, I understand, although it had taken many years; my development was stunted when I lost my grandad. I was so young and at the time my emotional growth was occurring, but the event of this trauma hampered me, throwing me off course of my natural progression. It has been a dramatic psychological roller coaster for me where I have had all the support possible, but I have had to also find my own way through.

Although, I never want to ever go through anything like this again it has given me a wealth of experience, and as a great man taught me 'Nothing is ever wasted if you can find the time to find the lesson and to learn from your mistakes.' Thank you grandad for being my inspiration, and if I manage to be half the man you were, I will know I have done you proud.

Chapter 33
Jack
On Reflection

Today, I look back at all that my life has been thus far, and I am so grateful for everything. I have had a wonderful childhood having been blessed with phenomenal grandparents who in turn created my mum, who has been a major influencer and inspiration. She has walked in front of me when I have been scared, been at my side when I have been unsure and gently nudged me in the right direction when I couldn't find the right path.

I never knew the hurts and pain she has suffered along the way because she has been an expert in camouflage, protecting Joe and I from any unwanted harm or bad influence. I love her company and trust her guiding light because she has an insight and experience that I have yet to develop. Even my friends will ask me to get mum's thoughts on a situation because she delivers a rounded, well thought out perspective.

If she is unhappy with someone, I would find it very difficult to be right with that person because if she is hurt then I feel hurt too. That is where Joe and I differ so much he would just be fine with everyone his attitude 'They haven't done anything wrong to me, so I take on board what you're saying but I have no reason to be difficult.' He is right of course and with any other person I am the same, but not when it comes to mum.

I think I am so fiercely protective because I know how badly she has been treated by her siblings and to be honest, so have we. They have chosen to not only ostracise grandma and mum, but Joe and I too. We have been cut off from our cousins because of their parent's inability to act in a grown-up fashion which I find utterly outrageous now looking back.

Neither of us did anything wrong so why we were suddenly unworthy to receive childhood Christmas or birthday gifts is beyond me, other than it displays the level of contempt they have for mum and grandma. And knowing now more about who they are as people having lived through the issues of the allegations, them persisting with their mind games once we came to live at Grey Gables and monitoring our movements via next door, I am glad they have not been present in our lives.

Mum has always been firm but fair. She is honest, open and transparent in everything she does and continues to delve into her creative ingenuity like writing this book.

She read me some of her story the other day, the part where she sat us down after school to discuss the idea of coming to live at Grey Gables. I remember being terrified of what it was she was going to say or what she had found out and was I going to get into trouble. You see it was the first time I remember her asking for a "family meeting", so I knew it was something big.

Since then, it has become a customary format to have a family meeting when we are making important decisions that affect us all, like when she had decided she wanted to start seeing Daniel. For me, I was thrilled to bits she had finally found someone who loved her beyond measure and whom she seemed to equally like. Since Joe's birth, it had just been the three of us, which became four when grandma came to live with us.

Mum has never ventured into a relationship because she wanted to give her time to us without the angst, discord, or distraction that some relationships can cause. I am thankful for her dedication because it has meant that we have had continuity in our guidance, direction and stability which has given me great insight in how to parent myself.

Daniel is a great asset to our family in so many ways and generally speaking, he is a good all-round bloke who is kind, generous, thoughtful and reliable even if he gets some really important stuff wrong. Like at Christmas, I had just landed myself my dream job as a joiner after 3 years at college and I wanted to get something really special for my mum. You see, she always goes to the end of the earth to make every occasion special for everyone else and no one has ever done that for her.

(Apart from when her friend, Niki, threw her a surprise birthday party at her own home.) So, I wanted to be that one person for her. I wanted to get her something lovely that she would treasure as much as I cherish her and sent for a Pandora bracelet with charms personal to her. I showed Daniel who never thought to remind me that it was a replica of her nomination's bracelet, nor did he reveal that she had already told him she hated Pandora and having got three bracelets the year before, she had recently said she didn't want another.

No, Daniel said nothing and even bought into my idea by purchasing two charms himself and reassured I wanted Joe to be included, so got him to buy one too. I was devasted when mum burst into tears, she loved my thought, concept, and generosity but because she hates wasting money, she couldn't bear to think what it had cost me and knew it wasn't something she would wear. If only Daniel had shared what he knew, I could have taken her out for lunch and used it as a guide to find out if she wanted my gift or not before the day and then returned it and got something else.

As it was we were all really upset, and it continued to linger in the air throughout the day. I know it wasn't a mean thing he did, but it was a really important moment for me too not just being able to afford to buy her something so unique but wanting to make it special just for her. When I spoke to him afterwards, he had thought I knew something he didn't so rather than burst my bubble he said nothing. However, he has learnt that it's far better to give his opinion than say nothing.

The thing is, I couldn't be angry as we are all still learning our quirks, foibles and positive attributes and how to merge these together to enhance our experiences as a blended family. I am of the mindset that grudges do more harm to the individual then the person your angry at, and like a poster I once read, it is like drinking poison yourself and expecting the other person to die.

It is lovely to see my mum happy and witness her growth in this area as an individual, where she is part of a team rather than her taking the weight of the world on her shoulders. I do sometimes take the mickey out of her and her "high school" relationship with Daniel because she can be quick to want space to deal with issues rather than facing them with Daniel's support. But I guess that is probably due to her being on her own for much of her adult life and having to fend for herself and to protect us.

I will always be thankful to Daniel for the love, care and dedication he has shown my grandma, and I am sure if it hadn't been for his support we may not have been able to get her home when we did. You can tell he genuinely loves her, and he looks after her needs whether it is pushing the wheelchair, making her food, shopping, assisting her to the table, putting on her coat, shoes or socks.

He is also the first to include her in everything they do together, whether it's a walk in the park, going to the pub, shopping or the cinema. My grandma is right there with them living life to the full and enjoying their relationship too.

If covid has taught me anything it is that family relationships are important. They ground you and give you the foundations that you need to have a fulfilling life. My family is here at Grey Gables they are my life and all I will ever need.

Chapter 34
Joe
A Tower of Strength

I am so proud of my mum. She has been all things to me; my teacher, my comforter, the person who has picked me up when I am down, put me back on my feet when I have fallen and given me the inner strength of titanium. She is such a force to be reckoned with, whether that is giving my teachers a piece of her mind, standing in court to represent a friend or fighting the injustice of false allegations.

She faces the trauma's and struggles of life face on with the gusto of the north wind bellowing its way through. She will take anything on whether it is standing up in front of two hundred people to give a talk, do a bungy jump or liaise with a team of surgeons like she did on behalf of grandad. Both Jack and I have such admiration for our mum who we both tower over much to her despair.

There are a couple of personal things I would like to share with you that encapsulate her. One is a poem she wrote during our separation from Emmeline when she was in the home during covid and the other is a copy of her notes for one of her talks she gave.

The poem depicts my grandma sat at the other side of the glass, desperate to be out in the fresh air enjoying the garden, and was published in Ashworth Grange, Care Home's newsletter in the March edition 2021.

Isolation

I look at the window but what do I see?
There is a reflection of little old me.
I yearn to be there, on the outside,
I held it back, but I could have cried!

Time goes by, be it fast or slow?
The days roll in to one, so I just don't know.
I want to feel the cool winter breeze,
My nose agitated with a spring sneeze.
I want to feel the sun on my face,
But all I can do is look out and gaze.
I see the snowdrops pushing through,
And the clear sky, of baby blue.
The birds are singing, though I can't hear,
And again, my eyes begin to tear.
I see the trees so stark and bare,
And the bench, where I used to love sitting there.
The ground is hard though the sun does shine,
One day soon, the garden, will again be mine.
As I ponder the thought and sit for a while,
I notice my reflection has begun to smile,
So, I nod in agreement as I close my eyes.
Now I am my reflection, enjoying butterflies.
My mind is a flood like an open well,
Of thoughts, sounds and feelings and beautiful smells.
And then, an idea begins to take shape,
And the sadness I felt slowly dissipates.
Now the next time we meet I will use the same tool,
And imagine my reflection is me sat there with you.
I wish I could touch and hold you tight,
But for now, I will be patient until it's alright.
This isolation, makes life simply rotten,
Just know that I am here and haven't forgotten.

In her talks, she would always begin by showing photographs of my grandma at various times throughout her life so that the audience could visualise who she was speaking about, and ensure they saw her as a person first then she would begin…

This is my mum. I wanted to begin by introducing you to her so you could see her for herself and learn something of her life before I share my story as this is about her. She is not an NHS number, a DOB, an address, or a NI number. They may be used to identify her, but they do not define who she is as a person and nor should dementia. Mum should first and foremost be recognised for the unique human being that she is with thoughts, feelings, achievements and a past which have brought her to the place she is today.

She was married in 1955, had five children by 1967; raised 55k during the 70s for ARC due to her son's diagnosis of Rheumatoid Arthritis; she was the director of a haulage company for 35 years; an accountant all her life and in later life, a volunteer at Pinderfields. She wore many hats; she kept her finger on the pulse and juggled everything effortlessly.

She is a strong independent woman, a respected person in her community, was a much-loved wife, is a cherished mother and grandmother. She was the glue that kept everything together and the heartbeat that just kept on giving. My mum is still all of those things, and they are still all in her...only now she has a diagnosis of Vascular Dementia with Alzheimer's, so these things are hidden.

My Story

A number of years ago when I was a Prison Officer and Drugs Dog Handler, I sat down to formulate a 5–10 year career plan depicting a rise through the ranks to a Governor 5 level. I can safely say that nowhere on that plan had I envisaged becoming a Carer. But there again, being a carer is not something that you necessarily plan; it's more like a curve ball that's thrown into the mix of life spinning you totally off course. It is no longer about your dreams or hopes for the future but an unconditional love that puts everything else into perspective.

For me, it all began in April 2010. My friend, Wendy, had accompanied me on a holiday to Tunisia with my young sons, aged 7 and 3 at the time. You see I had been a single parent for several years and I was now ready to embark upon a life, able to get out and about more exploring the world, its cultures, cities all as an educational tool for the boys.

I had great hopes and dreams and this trip was merely the gateway to all that the world had to offer us, it felt exciting and free. However, on our return I was informed dad had stomach cancer and was going in for surgery the next day. Inevitably, we were at his bedside through that surgery and others that followed, along with all the treatments he went through.

I became his confidant and full time Carer as his weight plummeted and he became bedridden. Nothing was too much trouble. We even had Christmas dinner in his bedroom that I'd cooked at home and had taken over to eat with him, just so he wouldn't miss out. Yet despite his illness, he shared his concerns regarding mum that he thought she had dementia, due to some very strange behavioural patterns she was displaying.

He then went into Dove Cote for a 6-week convalescence period and the staff there also voiced concerns upon mum's mental health and inability to retain information, so much so they wouldn't discharge him to her care. So, I arranged a doctor's appointment, and she was referred to the memory clinic where she had a full psychological assessment and a brain scan. This was in August 2011, a week later my dad sadly passed away, and so we then became the rock that mum needed.

However, when we went back to see the consultant, they didn't give us a diagnosis and basically passed it off as normal, degenerate changes associated with ageing, mum was 80.

Instinctively, I knew there was more to it than that so started to keep a diary of the changes she was experiencing, namely: not paying her bills even when she received red letters (as I said earlier mum was an accountant); she was saying random things that didn't correspond with our conversations; not being able to find shops that she had used for years; appearing vacant, not following conversations or joining in; finding it hard to process simple requests and suddenly stopping the car unsure where she was...to name but a few.

The next time we went to the memory clinic, I produced my list, and a community mental health nurse was sent out to do further tests. This was very frustrating as when mum persistently got questions wrong, she was coerced until she found the correct answers and then marked a lot higher than her abilities had demonstrated. It took 2 years of going back and forth, providing continuous diary proof and further psychological tests, this time conducted at home and in the community before we finally saw an actual consultant.

Inevitably, mum was terrified upon what the tests would show so before being called in and with tears in her eyes, she made me promise that 'whatever happens you'll just love me.' When I asked the consultant if mum needed a second brain scan to compare the changes with the first, he said that it was unnecessary as it was quite clear from the first brain scan (2011) mum had Vascular Dementia with Alzheimer's.

I was shocked at why it had taken them 2 years to formally diagnose, yet at the time it had been passed it off as mild degenerate changes due to age. Some people may receive a dementia diagnosis with horror but for me, it was relief as it now opened the doorway to specific research. I wanted to understand what I was dealing with to ensure I could provide the best care possible to enrich mums' life and assist her to maintain some control.

I spent several hours viewing seminars with Teepa Snow to comprehend the effects of the disease visually, mentally, physically etc from mum's perspective.

Now, it was one thing being a carer for dad and his physical needs, but it created a whole new dimension to care for an individual with a diagnosis of dementia. Over the years, I have had to constantly adapt to her changing needs along with looking for new skills to adopt, to help her feel safe and secure.

In the earlier stages, I introduced mum to several shops, like the cafe owned by her new neighbours, the pharmacist who I went to school with, the bank where special measures were put in place to ensure her vulnerabilities wouldn't compromise her, the newsagents where my dad's cousin worked, along with establishing the safest route and places to cross the road. I then did this route with her nearly every day until it was engrained and mum's second nature to ensure she was not only safe when alone but to enable her continued independence.

Whenever anyone at these businesses thought mum was not quite herself, I would get a call and I knew exactly where to find her along the route, so I could accidently on purpose bump into her and we would go for a cuppa.

I have found that being mum's carer has focused my heart and mind on that one person's needs to encourage them to maintain their skills without imparting your own opinions and without inadvertently taking over. I've stood back, bit my tongue and swallowed the words that sound critical in favour of uplifting kindness all to promote her wellbeing and to give her a sense of safety and security.

Unfortunately, though not everyone has the privilege of a family member willing to devote their life to caring for them. Therefore, some individuals slip through the net and are cast into a life of loneliness through isolation, unable to maintain valuable human connections. For similar reasons, we Carers also experience isolation as our role dominates our lives.

It alienates us from our loved ones, de-values our role from other professions, along with robbing us of the person we used to be. It's easy to become withdrawn and to slip into depression as you "exist" in a parallel world where it seems other people can choose the kind of life they want to "live".

At times, things have got so bad it's not been uncommon for me to feel isolated in a room full of people or like when I went to the first Creativity Group with Carers Wakefield, I ended up having a panic attack. I was that isolated I couldn't cope in a small room with a group of people I didn't know, me the former Prison Officer who could cope with hardened criminals and murderers! Crisis comes in all forms but due to my pride, the belief I had to "just get on with it", along with not knowing what support was available, I was left feeling a wreck.

So, where do carers access the support they require? And how do you know what is available or what would best suit their needs? When you are so used to blocking off your own thoughts and feelings by putting others first it becomes impossible to identify your own needs and nigh on impossible to realign a healthy balance to establish equilibrium. On the one hand, I had the clinical diagnosis but what about the care?

I am a single parent with two young children and a full time Carer of an elderly parent with dementia. I was suddenly alone in the world with such huge responsibilities that I found debilitating to the point of not wanting to get up on a morning and of not wanting to open the door because I didn't know what I would find behind it; at times it's been utterly soul destroying!

Eventually, I remembered that when we'd received the diagnosis, we had been seen two ladies from the Alzheimer's Society, so I made contacted with them. Initially, I attended a 4-week course on a Saturday morning which my 12 year old son also completed, to enable him to gain some understanding of the disease too. It was priceless and a deluge to accessing other information and support appropriate to meet our needs.

Despite her young age, the facilitator, Becki Dodds was highly educated and experienced in Dementia that when she moved to Carers Wakefield, she became my support worker. She continues to equip me with the skills required to maintain my caring role. She was a source of reassurance bringing calm and normality in times of distress.

She would research things then signpost me to appropriate services along with being that one person to just listen. In August 2016, at a moment's notice, she sat with my mum to advocate on her behalf because I couldn't be present. Becki is one of several workers at Carers Wakefield who don't just work so they can live, but they love their work so much and execute it with such dedication so that we carers can feel we have lives again too.

The staff are well trained, educated and equipped to meet all our needs. During times of anxiousness, depression or isolation, they made me feel safe, supported and able to carry on. Through Carers Wakefield, I have been able to normalise my feelings by establishing contacts with other carers, along with developing better support networks enabling my continued role, otherwise mum would have had to have gone into a care home.

An example of this was when I was invited to attend the "Looking After Me" course delivered by a life coach through funding secured by Carers Wakefield. This equipped me with the skills to re-connect with who I used to be. It encouraged me to revisit what my hopes and dreams had been prior to my role as a carer, as it gently nudged me to push the perimeters of my comfort zones whilst challenging me to recall my positive achievements and helped to redefine who I was at the time along with who I wanted to be in the future.

Above all, it encouraged me to adopt a positive mental attitude and to capture the negative thoughts before they were allowed to fester and take root. It gave me an allotted time each week for myself with the headspace to unravel the complexities of my own feelings in a safe, non-judgemental environment. It became a platform to learn new techniques on how to best look after myself so that I could give my best to the person I was caring for, my mum.

Fundamentally, it gave me hope, not only in the present but a hope for a better future. Having the opportunity to listen to others is what helped to normalise my feelings, thus shining a great big floodlight at the end of a very deep, dark tunnel.

Over the years, I have shared many tears of both joy and sadness and I am sad to say anger at my enforced role and the disease that ravishes the person I once knew. Most of the time, I feel I am carrying the weight of the world on my shoulders because although she is my mum and it's a privilege, she allows me into her world to look after her, it's also a huge responsibility.

I am my mum's access to the outside world and assist her to maintain any form of life connecting with it. When people tell you they are an individual's carer, they clearly won't break down the work entailed, so please don't brush it off. Give them your time they are multi-skilled people who work a 24-hour job, come rain or shine. They have no leisurely weekends, no days off or holidays and you may be the only adult they have spoken to that week.

In April 2016, mum's dementia took a nosedive and I had to install CCTV at her home to try to make her feel safe and in control but after only a week, she wasn't coping and started hallucinating. 2 months later, she came to live with us. In the first few days', mum slept soundly and soon she was like her normal self and decided she was never going home again.

However, after a few months of mum living at my home, we were all becoming isolated again. Our lives were morphing into one existence as everything was being dominated by her care needs, not to mention her not having access to her local community. I quickly fell into running on autopilot as the responsibility became a long list of chores, swamping me, thus diluting my time with the children, resulting in them escaping into their rooms and becoming isolated.

Afraid of the effects of our unhealthy lifestyle, seeing mum was slipping away again, we collectively made the difficult decision to renovate mum's old house. I could see that once redefined it would provide us all with the space required to allow us to grow independently and as a family, along with re-establishing her roots. I moved everyone in 7 weeks later, 3 days before Christmas.

Since then, it has progressed to the point she shuffles along muttering to herself, forgets to wear pants or incontinence pads, so either wets herself or the pad ends up travelling down her trouser leg. She will start a task but not finish it, so there will be a trail of items that she has put down because she cannot remember what she was doing. She cannot retain information, so is unable to process requests or operate the tv.

We have found she cannot do the simplest of tasks without supervision, even using the toilet and therefore, requires 24-hour care so cannot be left alone. We are also no longer able to take her to our holiday home as the trauma exacerbates her condition but equally a short stay in respite in the summer of 2017 magnified it beyond measure. So, in a catch 22 of we were, unable to take her but also cannot leave her behind, so heartbreakingly we had no option but to pursue its sale.

What has continually worried me is knowing that dementia is a progressive disease and as the years go by, having already stolen so much from us as a family how much more we are destined to lose. Mum always said that the two things she couldn't abide were thieves and liars, as you don't know where you are with either of them. Well, Dementia is a thief that steals the person, their thoughts and memories right before your eyes.

But let's not forget it also steals the life and independence of their carers' and their children too. What's worse is, there is nothing you can do about it. It lies to you, making you believe you have it under control and then there's a sudden, unexpected decline, so quick you feel your trying to grab running water through a sieve.

It's heart breaking, destructive and is reactive without provocation. No matter what support you put in place, the measures you take or the plans you make they are all futile. This disease affects each individual differently. It is unpredictable so there is no education that can prepare you and nothing that can protect you against it.

Life is difficult. We don't always choose the path we walk, but we can help make each other's path that little bit easier by ensuring that provisions are widely available, for things like the "Looking After Me" course, Creative Carers and Therapeutic sessions, especially if it enables our carers to maintain their own health whilst continuing to care for the most vulnerable members of our society.

Following my attendance on the "Looking After Me" course, I also completed a Level 4 Working with Parents with Complex Needs, First Aid, Food Hygiene and Safety and a 24-week course in the Principles of Dementia to equip me to look after my family. 3 months after the course, I was approached to volunteer at a new Dementia Cafe where I could put in to practise shared skills.

It was here that I have been able to support other carers along their path, by providing support, advice and signposting them to the appropriate services applicable to them. Sometimes the most important skill is to just listen, as we are not looking for a solution to a problem but simply want to share with someone how we feel.

It has been an honour to share their most precious thoughts and for me to be able to help normalise their emotions through my own valuable experience. If it wasn't for the support and courses made accessible to me, I wouldn't have developed the confidence, experience or knowledge to be able to give this back.

In July, I was asked to do a talk for the Clinical Commissioning Group in Wakefield; in May another to healthcare professionals; in March I was honoured to take part in the People's Choice project being filmed by ITV's Calendar and last year, did a talk during an afternoon tea with the Mayor of Wakefield. Being a Carer may change our lives, but they do not have to cease altogether, we just have to redefine them to still be ourselves.

Now I am reconnecting with my love for painting through my attendance on the Creative Sessions run by Carers Wakefield. Despite the panic attack, I continue to attend these sessions to use the time to completely shut off and immerse myself in my art as a therapy. I have also chosen to claw back my sense of self by creating a painting studio at home so I can escape mentally whenever I require it, without it imposing upon my looking after mum.

Seven years on, I am still a single parent, but the boys are now aged 15 and 10, so the weight of the complexities of my role as a carer along with their developmental needs can become overwhelming, especially as I continue to struggle to meet my own needs too. Trying to juggle everything to keep things running smoothly and to be all that you can be for everyone else, I am sure you will all agree is exhausting! But I had a great teacher in my mum who seemed to do this effortlessly when I was a child.

As I said at the beginning, my mum is a human being with thoughts, feelings and a past. It is essential to see all suffers and carers as individuals who deserve a whole package of care because alone we struggle beyond measure, and without support it would devour us all much more quickly.

I don't want to feel under pressure to always get it right at the expense of enjoying this precious time with mum or at the expense of my children's childhood. You can help by seeing us as individuals too, understanding the complexities and demands of our role, 'and sometimes it does just get a bit much which can be overpowering..

The key is: **Carers Also Require Effective Respite Services** *to escape, to re-establish a balance of "me time" with responsibilities and to gain vital support.*

This was a talk mum did 4 years ago in front of the Mayor of Wakefield to publicise the "Looking After Me" course delivered by Carers Wakefield, and to highlight their work and the essential support they give. She has always been the most selfless person putting others first and doing her best to assist others wherever possible.

She has raised both Jack and I from birth singlehandedly, always putting us first and ensuring we had the best childhood full of laughter, love and security. I shudder to think of the added stresses I have put her through, but there is no doubt in my mind she would go through it all again because her love is unconditional. My proudest moments have been to see her always cheering me on and knowing that I have her continued support throughout my life. I know I will be able to overcome anything.

I hope you have enjoyed reading of our experiences both individually and as a family. It has not been easy and hopefully, you will see dementia doesn't just affect the individual it affects everyone around them. It is a little like witnessing a car accident. We have all seen the same crash, but we have viewed it from slightly different angles.

So, though we have lived the same experiences, our feelings, struggles and our accounts may differ because we are individuals of different ages, abilities and strengths. There is one thing that we will all agree on and that is without the love and support for each other, we couldn't have got through it.

I am glad that mum now has Daniel too because it is time for her to take rest and hopefully, begin to regain the pleasures that life has in store for them both. So, I will finish with the toast that we as a family always raise our glasses to:

'To those we love, to those who we wish were here but cannot be, and to those that love us, cheers!'

Chapter 35
Emmeline
Last Thoughts

I cannot believe I am 90 years old and still going strong, especially as my parents only reached their early 60s. I have had a long and interesting life and achieved many things, but the most outstanding person who has shared it with me has to be Lois, and then there are her two boys. I can never repay the dedication, love, support nor protection that she has afforded me, especially in times where I was totally out of my depth, but she will remind me that I first taught her.

So, who knows maybe I did get the whole parenting job right regardless of whatever the rest of my children may say. It is true their behaviour has hurt and upset me to the point it has often sickened me; the level to which they have plummeted but of that I have had no control. They are their own people who have made some bad choices and decisions, but they were theirs to make and despite the hurt they have caused others, I have never stopped loving them.

When I was first diagnosed with dementia, I was terrified I would end up alone and forgotten but that has not been my journey; for Lois has promoted my abilities, empowered me and assisted me to maintain my independence throughout, and of that I will be eternally grateful. In the early days, I knew I was forgetting things, so Lois bought me a little book to write my thoughts in to help me.

I found it hard when people in town would chat to me, obviously recognising me, but I had no idea who they were so would make an excuse I was in a rush. This became a pattern that I would try to laugh off but obviously it didn't always work, as soon I couldn't disguise the vacancy upon my face. I hated the parts of dementia that took away my skills, even in the easy tasks of putting on the tv or making a cuppa.

It made me feel stupid because I should easily have been able to achieve these. The worst parts were probably me telling Lois to keep me present and in the moment so I wouldn't get lost, because that just made her feel like she was being unkind having to keep watch then telling me what I was doing wrong. She was right to raise the issue and put a stop to it as it would soon sound like criticism, and potentially I could feel like I was never doing anything right.

So, take heed dementia sufferers definitely do not need reminding what they are doing wrong, so if you are in this position remember this practise won't help your relationship.

We have had a great time and using humour to overcome the silly things have been a huge benefit. Lois is quite cheeky and even now as I am walking through to the toilet, she will jig about at the side of me singing 'Hey, fatty bum bum,' and regularly calls me 'fat lass' much to the amusement of the carers. My point is if you cannot laugh and have fun, life becomes too serious.

Lois once said that 'My mum may have dementia, but it is not the only thing that defines her,' and she was right. I am Emmeline. I have thoughts, feelings, and an opinion to give, so allow me to express them and allow your individual to share theirs with you and your bond will be as strong as Lois's and mine.

It's true dementia is a cruel disease, but it didn't rob Lois, Jack or Joe of me. It taught them to love me in a different way because they removed the fear element and took the time to educate themselves. Dementia has had an effect on my brain, but it has not had an effect on my quality of life. In fact it has probably enhanced it because without it, I may not have had the pleasure of spending my later life with Lois and the boys.

Chapter 36
Lois's Story

When I look back over my life like everyone else, there are some things I would have done differently and yet others I would still do in a heartbeat, like caring for my elderly parents. For the past 12 years, my life has been devoted to firstly my father and later my mother whilst also juggling the needs of my young sons and homelife. These years have not been easy and at times heart wrenching and soul destroying, but mainly exhausting.

However, they have also stretched me to reach my full potential as a human being and taught my boys some excellent skills for their life, not to mention compassion, kindness and loyalty. It has been an immense privilege and honour for not just one parent to choose me to care for their needs but both of them, and in this role I can honestly say I have done my very best.

My mother continuously said, 'When anything happens, love, you will have nothing to reproach yourself for.' I don't think it will be that easy for me though. You see I am a perfectionist, but I am only human so will have got things wrong, and it will be these things I will have the hardest time forgetting.

I know in my heart of hearts that I have got at least 95% right, so I will rest in Daniel's loving arms and let him remind me of this when I am beating myself up. His yardstick along with Jack's and Joe's are the only ones by which I will measure my performance, as no one else was here to witness the hardships that I have had to endure so have no right to judge or comment. It has been an emotional turmoil, at times trying to deal with some horrific behavioural traits but inside, Emmeline was always there and she never left me.

I am not sure if I let you in to my secret of why I call her Emmeline and not mum? The one thing throughout her illness that bothered me was that she may not remember me, and although that would have absolutely killed me, there was one thing that would have been worse for her. And that was someone she did not know calling her mum. It would have caused such turmoil for her and confused her beyond reason.

So, around 2014 whilst she was still able to understand, I began slipping in her name when I was referring to her or getting her attention and continued until it was natural to her. You see a dementia sufferer may forget who you are, but you will always know them, and I have seen too many carers destroyed at this prospect, so it was my way to not be hurt and not to confuse Emmeline.

I am glad to say it worked, both for me the boys and Emmeline, who actually never did forget who I was but maybe that is because I have been the one giving her constant care. She does mistake my role sometimes, like when we had to dash to A&E once with a suspected T.I.A, the doctor asked who I was to test her capacity, and she said, 'My mother.'

Incredulously he said, 'Your mother?' Emmeline looked at me nudging her head sideways towards him as if to say, "is this fella an idiot?" Then repeated her initial answer in an exaggeratedly slow manner so he could understand.

'Y…E…S T…H…I…S I…S M…Y M…O…T…H…E…R.'

In reality, all she was communicating is this is the person who looks after me, and the person who generally provides for all your needs when you are unable to is your mother. She will sometimes say that Jack is her brother despite never having had a brother, but again she sees my role taking care of everyone as head of the household of which she is included.

So, it is hardly surprising really, and actually it is quite a clever interpretation which shows her brain is still functioning highly. Unfortunately, some people will deduce that they have no idea what they are on about or take umbrage at this inference, but I feel that is dismissive and devalues the individual's perspective on life. It doesn't take a lot to interpret their view especially if you build a good bond and relationship with that person, but it does take effort, understanding and plenty of patience.

I have given many talks to both professionals, carers and the general public, along with personally supporting many others in their roles as a carer, and one thing that seems to arise more and more is anger that their lives have been taken over. It is a very difficult emotion to manage as it seems to creep up and before long it can turn in to contempt for the cared for person.

There is no mistaking that being a carer is an exhausting role that can be enforced in some way rather than done by choice, so is there any wonder carers feel angry or overwhelmed. After all, you may not have chosen this for your life, but it now totally dominates everything you do or in many ways all the things you can no longer do. Obviously, anger in its extreme is never acceptable if it has manifested into physical, mental or emotional abuse.

However, in its everyday, anger has a place. It is how you express it that matters the most. So whether that is standing at your gate and shouting or hitting a pillow or through some form of art therapy would be a more positive approach. The worst thing is when people then start beating themselves up because they have retaliated by being a bit sharp in a situation, or because they are irritated because their cared for person doesn't seem to appreciate anything they do.

You are only human. You were not a perfect person before you became a carer, so why do you expect to have become perfect now? It's OK to feel down, it's OK to feel like you are out of your depth and it's OK to think I have had enough or that you cannot do anymore. Take a breath, take a break if possible; have some respite but don't give up you have got this, and you are doing the best job you can possibly do.

It doesn't have to be perfect, you're not perfect and neither is your cared for person.

Being a carer is a very demanding role that few will undertake willingly. Just do what you can and when it's pressing down on you, do not be afraid to ask for help. There are so many organisations at your fingertips on the internet that can assist in a variety of ways, whether it is a sitting service, a day centre, the carers association, benefits, etc.

The key is to assess where your strengths lie and to focus on those elements, but we cannot be everything to that person as it takes a multidisciplinary team to care for an individual. The onus is not just on you but that is how carers think and to seek help somehow equates to the fact we must be failing. In reality, our role should be in providing not only a good quality of care but the best quality of life.

When I was struggling with some of mum's behaviours, I sought out a day care centre because she was displaying behaviours that suggested she was frustrated wanting to occupy herself but unable to quench this desire. I had different terms for some of her behaviours like "pinballing", where she would excessively repeat the same pattern over and over again.

I was studying Spanish but couldn't concentrate in the same room where she needed the tv on really loud, so because she was alone she kept getting up, walking through to the kitchen opening a drawer, closing it and going back again. This was happening in quick succession.

Then she extended it going into the laundry, out through the back door where she would take a piece of clothing off the line, walk around to the side of the house, peg it on that line then come back in and sit down. Within minutes, she did it again and carried on until every item of clothing had been moved.

This pinballing was an attempt to occupy herself whilst she felt anxious at my not being in the same room. At this stage of her dementia, she was unable to tell me how she felt but unlike you or I who can pick up a book or sit and watch tv to relax, she couldn't. So, I realised she needed more in her life and arranged for her to access a daycentre where she thrived, enjoying some arts and crafts activities, dancing, singing, a meal and they picked her up in their minibus.

It was ideal for her because it was independent of us and all about her. She started going just once a week to begin with, which soon became twice as it was having such a positive impact on her. She was more settled and actually slept better too because she was occupied and enjoying a new element of her life with new stimulations and friends.

She then started getting up each morning asking if she was going to the centre that day, so enjoying to the degree she was she started to go every day. We can never know in advance what help we might require, so it is advisable to keep an open mind and just tap into what there is available, test it and try it. Some will work others may not but at least you have tried.

I often think how awful it would have been if I had taken the attitude her care was only my responsibility as she would have missed out on having her life enriched meeting lots of other people.

The aim of the carer should be not to burn out, because if anything happens to you and you cannot go on looking after your individual, where would that leave them? Despite our best intentions, we are not invincible so let's give them the best of us not the worst of us because we have been a martyr doing it alone. Seriously that does not help anyone, empower your individual to live the life they would wish to live so that you can also live the life you are yearning to live without letting time pass you by.

The moral is, we can still have a full, varied and interesting life whilst being a carer and continue to build a strong loving relationship with our individual despite the adversities of life, if we choose to.

At the point we are today, Emmeline is at the later stages of her dementia. She enjoys nothing more than sitting in front of the tv escaping into the film world of imagination. My routine is to get her up at approximately 09.15 to assist her to the table for a morning cuppa, her breakfast and tablets.

The carer comes to shower her every morning around 10.15, and washes her hair Monday, Wednesday and Friday each week. Afterwards, I will blow dry and style her hair and bring in the huge oval mirror from her room to show her the results, and she will say, 'That's beautiful, love.' I will take her to the toilet every two hours throughout the day, not only to use the facilities but for mobility reasons too.

She will generally have a sandwich, a banana, yogurt or crisps for lunch and a meal or soup at teatime. I initiate her bedtime at 10 pm because Jack, now aged 19, works as a joiner in Bradford and has to be up at 6 am, whereas Joe, now aged 15, is studying his GCSE's. So, we close the house down from 10 pm respecting each other's needs and schedules, otherwise Emmeline would sit there all night and then her brain would drain its battery and she would not function the next day.

I assist her to bed, she has a tablet, removes her slippers, glasses and teeth and then we pray. Each night, I thank God for this beautiful lady. I tell her I love her and wish her a 'Goodnight, God Bless,' and in return she says the exact same back to me. Another fixed routine so I would always know the last words we had spoken were "I love you", should she leave me to be with my father.

Being a carer is not an easy job but as I lay down each night, I muse over the day's events and sometimes my mind may wonder into the cavity of "what if's" until I capture it and put a stop to it. The only focus of importance are the two fine young men who sleep in rooms near me and the lives they will live, having experienced a multitude of experiences during their young lives.

I rest in the knowledge that whatever has happened along the way, I have "just loved" her as she asked me to do and that I have done my very best, not only as a carer and as a mother but also as a daughter, to *both* my parents. I have run this race with absolute determination and true grit to the absolute end, and do you know what? I did a bloody good job and of this, I will always remain exceptionally proud!

As the music fades to the spotlight of the soloist, I show my face, I raise my bow for all to dance, to bring life and joy to the souls of the lost and yearning.